LOST AT SEA

ALSO BY JOHN HARRIS

Lost at Sea

True Stories of Disaster

John Harris

GUILD PUBLISHING
LONDON · NEW YORK · SYDNEY · TORONTO

This edition published 1990 by
Guild Publishing
by arrangement with Methuen London Ltd.

CN 4169

Printed and bound in West Germany
by Mohndruck, Gütersloh

CONTENTS

ILLUSTRATIONS

14c HMS *Captain* in dry dock.
15a HMS *Victoria* rammed by HMS *Camperdown*.
15b *Victoria* plunges to the bottom.
16a *K22*, formerly *K13*.
16b *M1*, formerly *K18*.

The photographs in this book are reproduced by kind permission of the following: BBC Hulton Picture Library: 1a, 1c, 2a, 2b, 4a, 4b, 5a, 5b, 6a, 6b, 11c, 12c, 15a; Peter Newark's Historical Pictures: 1b, 3b, 8b, 9a, 10b, 11a, 11b, 12a, 12b, 14c; Mary Rose Trust: 3a, 9b; Illustrated London News Picture Library: 7a, 7b, 10c, 14a, 14b, 16b; Royal Geographical Society: 8a, 8c; Royal Naval Museum, Portsmouth: 10a, 15b, 16a; Contemporary Films, London: 13a; Orkney Library (Photographic Archive): 13b.

ACKNOWLEDGEMENTS

Among others, my thanks are due to naval friends for information, and to the library staff of the *Portsmouth News* for allowing me to see their files on numerous occasions. I am also grateful to the Department of Printed Books at the Imperial War Museum and the National Maritime Museum, and for the fact that I live within reach of the Portsmouth Naval Dockyard, where three of the great ships mentioned in this book are on view.

INTRODUCTION

On 21 October 1988, in calm weather, the 6306-ton Greek cruise liner, *Jupiter*, with nearly 500 British schoolchildren on board, came into collision with a roll-on-roll-off car-carrying freighter, *Adige*, just outside the port of Piraeus, Greece, and sank in a matter of forty minutes. In February 1986 the roll-on-roll-off ferry, *Herald of Free Enterprise*, capsized and sank in just forty-five seconds in the harbour of Zeebrugge, Belgium, with the loss of almost 200 lives.

Both disasters appear to have been the result of negligence, and passengers who had been happily looking forward to their journey were a few minutes later either fighting for their lives or dead.

When steam power began to be used at sea there was a great rush to cash in on the transatlantic trade, and by the 1840s ships powered by steam were regularly crossing the Atlantic. Many were hell ships but not all. *President* was not much more than a year old when she disappeared. Launched in 1839, she was a paddle vessel also rigged for sail, with a tall smoke stack just forward of the paddle wheels. She was a handsome ship with a rakish bow and, because steamships were still a novelty, a huge crowd turned out to watch her leave New York on 11 March 1841, for Liverpool. They were the last people ever to see her because she never made port.

However, her captain had a good reputation, and even when stiff gales blew up no one worried. When on 1 April there had been no news, *The Times* announced that she had been delayed by storms. She had been expected to reach Liverpool in sixteen days, but there followed the sad sequence of her being reported first 'late', then

1

'overdue' and finally 'posted missing'. It was thought at first that she had been delayed by some minor trouble with her machinery, a not uncommon problem with early steam vessels, but she carried enough canvas to bring her to port. There were the usual rumours, among them that she had put into Madeira and was undergoing repairs, and opinions were expressed by experienced seamen that she *must* be safe. But no trace of her was ever found.

Titanic, another great vessel that was considered unsinkable, disappeared in 1912 in less than three hours – which, considering her size, wasn't very long. Again and again ships have vanished incredibly quickly and, while shipbuilders and naval architects endeavour to take every possible eventuality into consideration, each new sinking produces something they haven't allowed for. It was claimed that *Titanic* would be able to withstand having any two of her sixteen watertight compartments flooded, even with all her first four gone. But the designers hadn't allowed for the monstrous iceberg which ripped her open so that the first five were flooded.

When loss of life is considered, *Titanic* is the ship that springs instantly to the mind, with 1503 dead. After her comes *Lusitania*, with 1198 dead, holed through enemy action in 1915 and sunk in forty-five minutes. During the last war the losses were legion. 'First blood to the Germans,' was the comment of the radio operator of the ship I was in, during the first hours of hostilities. 'They've sunk *Athenia*.' There were plenty of others. *Lancastria*, evacuating troops and refugees from St Nazaire, was sunk in June 1940 and over 3000 people lost their lives.

When Germany's own Dunkirk took place from East Prussia in the last months of the Second World War, around 7000 went down in *Wilhelm Gustloff*, nearly five times as many as died in *Titanic*. With two other over-laden liners, *General von Steuben* and *Goya*, lost in the same operation, the total casualty list numbered an unbelievable 18,000. But these and the great naval disasters – *Hood*, for instance, with 1423 men lost in a matter of seconds, and her contemporaries at Jutland in 1916 – were the result of enemy action. It is the loss of hundreds of lives in a single incident in peacetime that makes people realise the voracity and ruthlessness of the sea.

After *Titanic*, which did not have enough life-saving equipment for all her passengers, the authorities insisted that every ship that went to sea had to have sufficient boats. But this didn't allow for a ship listing as she sank, so that the boats along one side became useless. It didn't allow for human frailty and panic, or for the fact that when a lifeboat is lowered the people still on deck see only a great gap and a deep drop to the water. During the war, when the lifeboats of the ship I was in were lowered, I was one of those ordered to stay behind until they were in the water and then jump to the falls and climb down. It was daunting enough looking down at the surface of the sea below. What would it have been like in darkness with the ship listing and the falls hanging away from the ship's side?

The sea requires explanation, and the following chapters cover some of those aspects which most concern the people who make their living from ships and on the ocean, but which most puzzle those who live deep inland. Obviously not all instances have been touched on because there are too many, but some of the more famous ones have been examined and placed in their proper perspective.

First and foremost, I have looked at some of the sudden and unexpected disasters that can beset a ship, and followed this with that most important of questions – survival. Treasure is included because treasure has always been associated with the sea, and there have been several much-publicised searches for it. That event all ships' captains dreaded – mutiny – was known to be infectious, and is here shown starting in England and spreading across a whole continent before, generations later, returning to its place of origin. Finally, I have covered that period of the Royal Navy when, with new techniques of gunnery and new building materials as wood gave way to iron, the fleet went through a phase of unhandiness and uncertainty because unqualified men had too much influence on the production of new ships.

To landsmen there is always an element of mystery in the sea, and an element of danger, because things that are easily understandable on dry land just don't make sense when they happen on water.

When the pleasure steamer *Princess Alice* left London Bridge for an excursion to Gravesend and Sheerness on 3 September 1878, she was one of the largest and best known of the vessels owned by the London Steam Packet Company. As it was a fine warm day, she was crowded with excursionists, most of them women and children determined to enjoy themselves, all gaily decked out in their best and covered with lace and ribbons and clutching parasols and picnics. Returning in the evening, her passengers were replete with food, drink and sunshine, and music was coming from more than one spot on the crowded deck.

It was the days before Rules of the Road had been formulated for the assistance of masters of ships, and it was the habit for traffic to hug that side of the stream which favoured them with the tide, and *Princess Alice* was rounding a sharp left-hand bend near Woolwich when she was faced with the collier *Bywell Castle*, bound for Newcastle in ballast. *Bywell Castle*'s stem almost cut the excursion ship in half. As water rushed in, she broke in two and sank in a matter of minutes. Little could be done to save lives, and though nearby watermen lay on their oars and other vessels hurried to the scene, swamped in the voluminous clothes of the period, the people in the water had little chance. Around 640 men, women and children were drowned almost within sight of their disembarkation pier.

Even when the Rules of the Road came into force, navigation on the busy swiftly-flowing current of the Thames always remained hazardous; and in the early hours of 20 August 1989, the ninety-ton pleasure cruiser *Marchioness*, a veteran of Dunkirk, with over a hundred young people aboard enjoying themselves at a waterborne party, was run down and rammed amidships under Southwark Bridge by the 1475-ton sand dredger *Bowbelle*, with a large loss of life. It was a clear night and both vessels were going in the same direction.

It takes some understanding, but so did the *Princess Alice–Bywell Castle* collision. The coroner's court investigating this accident felt that the ships should have stopped in time. Certainly they should, and to many people reading the report it probably seemed an easy thing to do. But ships don't have brakes and can only be stopped by going astern, a manoeuvre which is accomplished by putting the engines into reverse. Unfortunately, the effect of reversing the engines does not take effect immediately. A ship moving at a good speed requires a distance several times its own length before it starts to slow down, and considerably more before it stops. The difficulty in understanding is indicated by the fact that when the 81,235-ton *Queen Mary* cut the 4290-ton cruiser, *Curaçao* in two in 1942, it was seven years before the responsibility was finally decided in court. It laid the blame on the liner, but as one merchant captain observed, 'Those on the bridge of *Queen Mary* will perhaps find some consolation in the thought that it has taken the efforts of the best legal brains engaged in . . . Admiralty Law just about as many weeks as they had in seconds to decide . . . the correct action to be taken.'

At sea, tide and current have to be considered – sometimes even the wind, because in a wind a ship can move sideways. It is the awareness of these things that makes sailors so different, and venturing on the ocean such a perilous business to landsmen.

'Men who like the sea life are not fit for the land,' it has been said, and the reason why is perhaps expressed in two more quotations: 'Seamen are nearest to death and furthest from God' and 'The Church and yard are full of seamen's graves and few have any names'. An eighteenth-century seaman, Samuel Kelly, explained why. 'Seamen are neither reckoned among the living nor the dead,' he said, 'their whole lives being spent in jeopardy. No sooner is one peril over but another comes rolling in like the waves of a full grown sea.'

Throughout history the ship has predominated as man's most versatile form of transport, and the sea, with its danger, has always gripped his imagination and aroused in him wonder, curiosity, fear, awe and exaltation. I was born and brought up about as far from the sea as you can get in England, but throughout my youth I never failed to be fascinated by it and always had an itch to become a sailor. I managed it at the age of twenty.

I was under no romantic illusions, however, and I was dead right. The forecastle was an iron prison as inviting as the inside of a tank. The men who inhabited it, with one or two exceptions,

5

were old shellbacks who spent their time between ships drunk. One of them I had met in a pub boastfully waving a bank roll representing his wages for a voyage which had lasted around two years. The next day, his head bandaged, he had to sign on the same ship as I did because someone had caught him down a dark alley and rolled him for his money.

Times have changed, of course, and these days life at sea is more comfortable. Before the Second World War, though, times were hard. None-too-scrupulous shipowners took advantage of the Depression and wages were kept low. Ships were withdrawn from trade and laid up in Cornish creeks, and men demoted themselves to get a job. Masters went to sea as mates, mates as bosuns, bosuns as able seamen. Conditions were poor. Food was appalling and quarters were cramped and uncomfortable. Even when the owners weren't cheeseparing, there were sometimes crafty masters or pursers, even just bad cooks. I helped make lighthouses out of the rubbery bread that was issued and placed them on the ventilators outside the captain's cabin to remind him of the cook's lack of skill. It was over the food that the cook ended up in a tremendous fight with the fifth mate in Port Said, one with a carving knife, the other with a two-foot wrench – in which half the crew were involved in the attempt to separate them.

With changing times and changing ships, men have changed, too. Sailors are no longer outcasts. Modern ships have every gadget imaginable to make the work quicker and easier and the life safer, and seamen are more technical. But there is still no answer to seamanship, and the men who work ships still have to get out on the decks in the wind.

An entire volume could be compiled of accounts of drownings, storms, founderings, wrecks and collisions. By its very nature, man's contact with the sea is a constant contest in which the truces are unpredictable and usually short-lived. And though ships and men have changed, the sea hasn't, and the moment a vessel casts off from land, living and working become the same thing. There is no question of simply going home at the end of the day, free to relax. Even passengers in a luxury liner are aware of this difference, and the resemblance to a hotel ashore is really only superficial because at sea life is geared to the ceaseless demands of the weather and its potential for sudden violence. Whether made of wood or iron and steel, ships behave in exactly the same manner when circumstances dictate, and, with every imaginable aid to seamanship, navigation and safety available, ships still collide, disappear, founder or run ashore in bad weather.

To be in a ship caught in a gale is quite an experience. Nothing stays in one place; the ship is full of terrifying noise and movement; clothing hangs at impossible angles; shelves and cupboards shed their contents to decks which are already aswill with debris, lost food and vomit; and being flung into the sea in darkness is a heart-stopping ordeal. It once happened to me, and the picture of a huge black wave lifting between me and the vessel from which I had so suddenly departed is with me still.

There is a feeling that the size of a ship makes for safety. Usually it does, but certainly not always, and there is a saying among seafaring men: 'Worse things happen in the big ships.' One of the biggest was *Titanic*, and look what happened to her.

J.H.

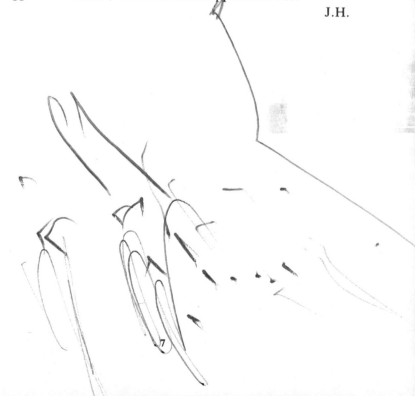

CHAPTER 1

Like a hog in a ditch

Royal George

Toll for the Brave!
The Brave who are no more,
All sunk beneath the wave
Fast by their native shore . . .

Toll for the Brave!
Brave Kempenfeldt is gone;
His last sea-fight is fought;
His work of glory done . . .

There were eight more verses to William Cowper's turgid ballad on the sinking of HMS *Royal George* in 1782, and they were to bore every schoolboy in England between the wars. Set to the music of Handel's *March*, they became a favourite standby at Victorian musical evenings. Eight or nine hundred lives were lost in the sinking – it was never ascertained exactly how many – and with them went sixty-four-year-old Rear Admiral of the Blue Richard Kempenfeldt, often called 'the brains of the Navy'.

Royal George was a 100-gun ship, and during her lifetime she had worn the flags of seven admirals, among them Boscawen, Anson and Hawke. Originally her name was to have been *Royal Anne*, but she took ten years in building and Anne, the sovereign after whom she was named, died in 1714. There was already a *Royal George*, but she was an old ship and, since it was considered more fitting that a new ship should carry the name of the reigning monarch, the original *Royal George* took the name of *Royal Anne* and the new ship, when she was completed in 1756, was christened *Royal George*.

She was the first man-o'-war to exceed 2000 tons, by modern standards nearer 4000 tons. She had the tallest masts and squarest canvas of any British-built ship in the Navy; 5760 loads of timber had gone into her building – roughly 3840 trees, each weighing a ton. It was small wonder that Collingwood, Nelson's deputy at Trafalgar, always carried a pocketful of acorns which he scattered whenever he was home – so that there would never be a shortage of oak for the fleet.

There were only two other comparable ships, Nelson's *Victory* and *Britannia*. They were all huge vessels because they had been built to be flagships and, in addition to their officers, had to house an admiral and his staff and be virtually unconquerable, because in battle they would inevitably be at the heart of an enemy's fire. They were designed so that their lower gun ports would ride about five feet from the water, and it was always a risk to open them in a heavy sea to allow a full broadside to be delivered.

Though twenty-six years old when she sank, *Royal George* had spent half her life laid up and during her ten years with the fleet had spent nearly five in port. During her lifetime the enemy was always the French and her job was to watch the coast of Brittany, the Channel approaches and the Scillies, and in these storm-bound areas things were regularly in need of repair from the ravages of the weather. In addition, there was always the problem of freeing the ship of barnacles, and to do this, whenever conditions permitted, the ship was heeled to expose a few planks below the waterline to allow them to be cleaned. Ships were heeled on a beach or alongside a hulk, and captains were always interested in how well a ship could be tilted when afloat.

Royal George was with Hawke when he caught the French at Quiberon Bay but, with the end of the Seven Years War, she was laid up until a new alarm gave her another refit. The American War of Independence brought her to life again and, present when

Rodney beat the Spanish at Cape St Vincent, she was sent home with the prizes. By 1782 she was the oldest first rate still in service and was beginning to feel her age. Rear Admiral Kempenfeldt joined her on 7 April.

Richard Kempenfeldt was a tall man of sixty-four. He was born at Westminster in 1718, the son of a Swedish mercenary who became lieutenant governor of Jersey. The son, Richard, first saw service under Vernon during the War of Jenkins' Ear, and it was during the Seven Years War that he began to think of naval signalling. He saw his admiral's attempt to halt the build-up of enemy forces frustrated in an indecisive battle in 1758 by what were known as the Fighting Instructions, a set of rules drawn up in Charles II's day and virtually unchanged since, by which sea fights were supposed to be conducted. They allowed no initiative and any admiral who dared to fight a battle in any other way but by laying his fleet, ship by ship, alongside the enemy and banging away, was in danger of court martial.

Admirals, Kempenfeldt decided, needed room for initiative, and he set himself to devise the signal code which made his name. Its possession enabled Admiral Howe in 1782 to baffle the French and Spanish fleets at Gibraltar, and after the Battle of the Nile, Nelson acknowledged his indebtedness to the code. In 1780 Kempenfeldt was promoted Rear Admiral of the Blue, his flag captain in *Royal George* being Martin Waghorn, who had been born and bred in the service.

In August *Royal George* reached Spithead to join Lord Howe's fleet, due to sail in a few days' time for the relief of Gibraltar. Provisioning had been almost completed by 28 August, and in the meantime a carnival atmosphere, with sailors' wives and children aboard, was allowed.

Cowper's ballad invests *Royal George*'s end with a glory it did not deserve, because she wasn't struggling against the enemy or battling with storms. She sank in a matter of seconds in a flat calm as she rode at anchor, disappearing at twenty minutes past nine on the morning of 29 August. The time is known to the minute, because six flagships with their admirals were assembled there, and with them were over thirty ships of the line, many frigates and over 200 merchantmen.

There were about 300 women aboard – among them 'the most depraved characters' – and about sixty children. There were also hucksters, eager to cash pay notes at a discount or display their wares, and they were all aboard because the ship was due to sail and no captain dared allow his men ashore in case they disappeared inland beyond the reach of the Navy.

The ship was held by two anchors from the head. The wind was from the north-west but was so slight that the ship hadn't a stitch of canvas on. As the people aboard danced and skylarked, they found nothing odd in the slope of the deck because they were seamen and seamen's wives, aware that at times repairs had to be undertaken which involved heeling the ship, and an inlet pipe which fed a cistern by which water was drawn for washing decks was being repaired. Normally the ship would have been careened on a receding tide, which would have left her stranded; heeled against a jetty or hulk; or drydocked. But none of these things was possible because the ship was due to sail shortly, and it had been decided to use the weight of the guns. With the guns on the larboard – or port – side run out as far as they would go and the lower-deck guns on the starboard side eased as near as possible to midships, the ship could be caused to tilt.

With her ensign hoisted and Kempenfeldt's blue flag at the mizzen mast, the heel began about 8 a.m., the water almost to the portholes of the lower gun deck on the larboard side. But as the work started, three vital warrant officers, William Harrison, the gunner, Richard Searle, the master, and Richard Talbot, the boatswain – all of whom should have been on board – were in Portsmouth, despite a signal that not a man was to be permitted ashore. By 9 a.m., the dockyard 'plumbers' had been working on the pipe for about an hour. The ship's company had finished their breakfast and a sloop run by three brothers, delivering rum, was lashed to the starboard side of the ship and hands were piped to get the rum out of her and stow it in the hold.

Although water kept dashing in at the ports with every wave, no one worried and mice, disturbed by the water, were hunted by the men in a great game. At about 9 a.m., with the additional quantity of rum on board and the sea water, which had rushed in through the ports, bringing those of the lower gun deck almost level with the sea, the ship's carpenter became worried and went to the quarterdeck to ask the officer of the watch, Lieutenant Monins Hollingbery, to order the righting of the ship. Hollingbery, a martinent known as 'Jib and Foresail Jack', answered the carpenter with a brusque 'No' and disappeared below. Kempenfeldt was in his cabin and his barber, who had been shaving him, had just left. After a while the carpenter made another attempt to persuade Hollingbery to give the order to right the ship and once again Hollingbery gave him the short answer. 'Damme, sir,' he snapped, 'if you can manage the ship better than I can you had better take command.'

The weather was calm, the sea as 'smooth as a duckpond' with tiny wavelets, but the rum, with the weight of the men employed to get it inboard, was causing the ship to heel still more so that every ripple came in at her midships ports. Soon she had so great a weight of water in her hold that she gradually and imperceptibly began to settle, and water began to pour into the lower ports.

Richard Searle, the master, who had been visiting his wife in Portsmouth, had asked a boatman to row him back to the ship, and as they neared the *Royal George*, he suddenly yelled: 'She will sink! Give way!' Turning his head, the boatman saw that the ship was in danger and, with the towering masts leaning dangerously over him, began to back his oars. 'Give way, man!' Searle yelled. 'Give way!' A few strokes enabled the frightened boatman to reach the ship and Searle was able to spring aboard. As the boatman hurriedly backed off, Searle hurried to the captain on the quarterdeck to add his own warning to that of the carpenter.

James Ingram, a seaman in the waist of the ship, had already sensed the danger and shortly afterwards Hollingbery ordered the drummer to beat 'Right ship'. Ingram ran to his station and by the time he reached it men were already coming down hatchways, tumbling over one another to get to their positions. Ingram's station was at a gun on the starboard side and he suggested to the gun captain that they should move their huge weapon back at once without waiting for the drum. When they tried, however, it ran back on them; then everything movable began to fall across the deck on to the yelling and screaming men, women and children.

As the water rushed in, Ingram pushed the gun captain out of the port and, following him, as he broke free saw that the port was full of the heads of people trying to get out. He seized hold of a woman and dragged her free, but then all the heads dropped back because, with the ship so far over, it was like trying to get 'out of the top of a chimney'. Soon after, the air between the decks blew out like a puff of wind and removed Ingram's hat.

The ship now lay with her masts flat on the water, and continued like that for several minutes. Many men and women scrambled on to her bottom, but as the air which had been supporting her was forced out she sank beneath them. As she filled she swung upright once more and settled almost perpendicular, the cap of the bowsprit and part of the flagstaff just above water. A Southsea woman, writing a letter in her window, looked up to see the ship lying between the shore and the Isle of Wight. Finishing her sentence, she looked up again and realised to her amazement that the great vessel had gone.

Boats heading for the rescue were driven away by the whirlpool swell the sinking had caused. Ingram was drawn down, but as the ship touched bottom he was blown to the surface and appeared in the middle of the contents of a barrel of tar so that his arms and head were covered with it. About eight or ten yards away, the main topsail halyard block was above water, which at that point was about thirteen fathoms or nearly eighty feet deep, with the tide rising. As he reached the block and clung there, he could see the fore, main and mizzen tops sticking out of the water, as were part of the bowsprit and part of the ensign staff with the ensign still attached. In going down, the *Royal George* had taken down the rum lighter with her, drowning two of the three brothers who ran her.

The admiral's baker was in the shrouds of the mizzen mast, and soon Ingram saw the woman he had rescued floating past. The baker caught her and hung her over one of the ratlines of the mizzen shrouds, but a wave knocked her off. The boat of a nearby frigate dragged her aboard. The men clinging to the rigging were taken to *Victory*, and on board Ingram saw the woman he had saved being revived; he also saw women trying in vain to revive the ship's carpenter.

Deaths and survivals from sheer luck came in equal numbers. Searle, the master, who had just reached the ship on his return from shore, was lost with the ship. The gunner and the boatswain, still ashore, were safe. A midshipman who had just left the ship in a boat asked to be put back because he had forgotten his dirk. When he didn't return the boat was ordered away again and the midshipman was among those lost. Henry Bishop, a nineteen-year-old seaman, was carried up the hatchway from the lower deck by inrushing water, as was the plumber who was working on the inward end of the pipe, and both were saved. A marine sentry guarding a sailor in irons freed him from his shackles and both survived.

As the ship rolled over, Captain Waghorn asked a ship's boy aged twelve if he could swim. On being told 'No', Waghorn said, 'Then you must try,' and threw him overboard. As the boy hit the water a seaman jumping to safety landed on top of him and, being a good swimmer, took the boy to the main shrouds and pushed him to the topmast. A child so young he didn't know his own name hung on to one of the sheep which had been carried as meat on the hoof and had floated off.

Lieutenant Jeremiah Viguers had been detailed to go ashore to get the men's pay. He questioned the order, but fortunately for him Waghorn insisted. As the ship rolled over, Lieutenant Philip Durham, who was to reach the rank of admiral and win a knighthood, was on the quarterdeck. Because uniform coats with their bullion of gold lace were valuable, he decided he had better save the one he wore and, holding it in his arms, jumped into the sea. He found a floating hammock but was twice carried down by a panic-stricken marine whom he shook off by tearing loose his waistcoat, to which the marine clung. He finally reached safety, but the body of the marine was washed ashore a fortnight later, the waistcoat still twisted round his arm.

Many of the seamen had climbed into the rum sloop to save

their lives, but were lost as the sloop was overwhelmed. Of all the women and children on board only one woman and one child were saved, and for days afterwards bodies rose to the surface, the watermen stealing their money, watches and silver shoe buckles. Ten days after the disaster thirty-five bodies were buried in Kingston churchyard. More were buried at Ryde in the Isle of Wight. In the towns of Portsmouth, Gosport and Southsea almost everyone had lost some relative, friend or acquaintance. Every hour corpses came ashore along the beaches and every hour bells tolled as funeral processions wound through the streets. Since Spithead was on a fishing coast, for some time the sales of fish went down because to eat fish just then was considered cannibalism.

The court martial to discover the cause of the sinking assembled on board HMS *Warspite* in Portsmouth Harbour on 7 September 1782. It was a period when naval courts martial had sunk into disrepute. In the eighteenth century admirals were often Members of Parliament, some of them peers, and in the bitter political atmosphere of the time their outlook was often influenced by politics, so that courts martial often tried to produce the verdict that politiical exigencies demanded. The court enquiring into the loss of *Royal George*, however, was composed of distinguished sailors who did not have to be told what had happened because they had seen it with their own eyes, and for once politics did not come into it. They seemed determined that Waghorn, who had lost both his ship and his son, should not have to endure more suffering.

Nevertheless there *was* bias. Almost every sailor, whatever his rank, detested the Navy Board, and it seemed that with this court martial there was a chance, without harming the reputation of any of the dead or living, of hitting out at it. The Commissioners of the Navy, though under the control of the Lords of the Admiralty, held independent control over virtually everything that affected the fleet and the well-being of the sailor. Their interests covered everything from building, docking, repair and the outfitting of men-o'-war, and they were totally corrupt. If the officers sitting in judgement on Waghorn could prove that *Royal George* was not lost as a result of folly and carelessness or the wind and the weather, but through some defect or weakness in the ship herself, it would be an opportunity to hit out at the Navy Board – and with that judgement no sailor would ever argue.

A statement prepared by Waghorn was read. It indicated that the admiral himself had given permission for the ship to be heeled. There was no apparent danger and Waghorn ate breakfast without any inconvenience. As the ship settled he rushed to warn the admiral, but before he could open his door the ship went down.

George Aynon, a dockyard shipwright who had been working on the underwater pipe, said he had found the ship's planks sound, though some of her timbers were rotten. John Smart, a gunner's yeoman, said he jumped out of the starboard stern port because he had heard 'a great crack'. Asked: 'What crack did it appear to be?', he replied that it appeared to be 'a bodily crack' and that it came from below. When asked what he meant by a 'bodily crack', he said that the ship gave a great jerk or crack, then within a moment went down.

William Murray, a quarter gunner, said that before the sinking he had been apprehensive enough to walk backwards and forwards with his breakfast in his hand. He maintained that everything that was taken from the lighter alongside was allowed to remain on the larboard side. Before the ship rolled over, he saw that the water inside her was almost level with the water outside. Ten or fifteen minutes later the drum was beaten and the larboard ports, he then saw, were dark and under water.

The court's verdict was 'that the ship was not overheeled, and that the captain, officers and ship's company used every exertion to right the ship as soon as the alarm was given'. The court was also of the opinion 'from the short space of time between the alarm being given and the sinking of the ship, that some material part of her frame gave way, which can only be accounted for by the general state of the decay of her timbers'. The captain, officers and ship's company were acquitted of all blame. There it was in black and white. As one writer claimed, *Royal George*'s bottom had dropped out of her.

Soon after she sank several guns were raised, and the ship's bell was brought up and hung in the Dockyard Chapel until it was destroyed by Hitler's bombers. The ship herself lay smack in the fairway, a danger to shipping, and her masts remained out of the water until 1794, when they were run down in the night by a frigate and the Navy demanded the ship's removal. William Tracey, of Portsea, proposed a scheme using two ships or lighters lashed alongside with slings passed under the ship's bottom to lift her with the rising tide. The Navy Board were not keen to have the ship salvaged as it might prove that her bottom really had fallen out, but despite the difficulties put in his way Tracey managed to lift her and she was actually moved a little. But, thanks to the obstructive intervention of the Master of the Dockyard, his efforts came to nothing. It ruined him and he was reduced to beggary.

In 1839 Colonel C. W. Pasley, of the Royal Engineers, planted explosives to remove the danger to shipping, and among the dead fish that floated on the surface were found such relics as candles, inkstands, glasses, salt cellars, china, Durham's telescope, even butter – and finally the collar of a dog which had belonged to a man called Thomas Little who appeared to have escaped. The work went on until 1843.

The court-martial decision that the ship had sunk because a material part of her frame gave way saved the reputation of Waghorn. The court had made much of John Smart's story of a great crack, but no one else heard any crack, and perhaps Smart was encouraged to say what he did by subtle questioning. Yet, swung in Tracey's cradle, the *Royal George* was moved thirty or forty feet, something which could never have been done if she had been rotten. Cowper, who wrote his pedestrian verses soon after the event, clearly didn't believe she was rotten, and attributed the disaster to the heel.

Brigadier R. F. Johnson, a barrister-at-law, delved deeply into the sinking and, despite the court martial's findings, pointed out that, after being on her beam ends, the capsizing ship could not have resumed an upright position if the bottom had not retained the weight of the cargo and the water that rushed into her lower decks. He laid the blame firmly on Waghorn and his officers. Many of them were not performing their proper duties. The master, the gunner and the boatswain were ashore and the men on the quarterdeck were not paying attention. It was folly to leave the lower gun ports open and more folly to take in through them further heavy cargo. He claimed that the bottom of *Royal George* did not drop out, and it seems clear that the court never really thought it did because two years later Admiral Duncan, who sat with the court, sent Howe, who was then First Lord of the Admiralty, a detailed plan for raising the ship which he must have known, if she had fallen to pieces through sheer rottenness, would have been totally impossible.

Ironically, it was *Royal George* that led to the finding of Henry VIII's *Mary Rose*. Colonel Pasley's divers, trying to descend on to the wreck, got their bearings wrong and landed on *Mary Rose*. Alexander McKee, the author and diver who helped discover the position of *Mary Rose*, worked out where *Royal George* was by transferring old positions to modern charts, and landed on a mound of shingle where he found a thirty-two-pound cannon ball and a small pottery jar dating from about the time of the sinking of *Royal George*. Investigating further, he came across accounts by divers who had found *Mary Rose* long before Pasley's men arrived on the scene. Working on the wreck of *Royal George* in 1836, they had been asked by Gosport fishermen to help clear their nets from some obstruction and, diving to investigate, found *Mary Rose*.

Empress of Ireland

Capsizing is the swiftest and one of the most terrible forms of disaster at sea. To the children of *Jupiter* the horror of such a sinking is expressed in their own words.

'All the chairs were sliding down the floor and glasses were smashing about us'. 'Everyone was trying to hold on to anything they could as the ship listed.' 'The feelings of going down under cold water, swallowing oil, alone in the darkness . . . it's the stuff of nightmares.' 'I never thought a ship could sink so fast.'

'*I never thought a ship could sink so fast.*'

The children had been aboard *Jupiter* only a matter of hours and were listening to a lecture on what to do in an emergency. Had they been in their cabins asleep they might not have escaped.

When a ship sinks slowly and remains more or less upright there is always an opportunity to get boats away and avoid panic. But when a ship capsizes, it is sudden and shocking. The decks become vertical and what a minute or two before was upright becomes the deck. Stairs are no longer of any value because they lie parallel to the sea. Heavy objects are flung to one side, adding to the list. People are flung off their feet and find themselves in the water before they can do a thing to save themselves. People in their cabins are trapped because the doors which were once upright are now lying flat and cannot be opened.

Survival in such a disaster depends on sheer luck. Where you happen to be when tragedy strikes makes all the difference between life and death, and without doubt most of those who survived from Henry VIII's *Mary Rose* when she capsized would have been from the fighting tops.

The flagship of Henry's vice-admiral, Sir George Carew, *Mary Rose* sank off Portsmouth in 1545. Bound for action against an invading French armada, she went down probably without firing a shot. Watching from Southsea Castle, Henry could see the ship's gun ports open ready for the impending action and, as she came up to port of *Henri Grace à Dieu*, or *Great Harry*, she was seen to heel over. A heavy ship, she was never intended to heel like a racing yacht and as the heel continued she dipped her gun ports below the sea. The French claimed that her loss was due to their cannon, but their gunships were not within range and the truth was that she was mishandled by her crew.

As the heel continued, sailors and soldiers fell into the lee scuppers and with them went insufficiently secured guns. Her normal complement was 415 but there were probably 600 or even 700 on board – some sailors, some soldiers, many of whom would have been in armour and on deck, contributing to her tophamper. The landsmen, unused to the sea, were sent staggering to one side, adding to the uneven weight. Carew, his captain and hundreds of men went down with the ship, some trapped below, some thrown into the sea, some sucked down by the sinking vessel, others tangled in the rigging or anti-boarding netting, or stunned by falling spars or guns. The men in armour would have sunk like stones.

Capsizing, by its very nature, can bring death in a matter of minutes when everything seems safe. Even the Royal Family was once involved in a capsize. On 18 August 1875, the royal yacht *Albert*, carrying Queen Victoria and members of her family, rammed the schooner *Miseltoe*. Steam should always give way to sail and there was little excuse for the collision except that the officers of the royal yacht probably thought that they exercised a certain privilege, but as the yacht backed off *Miseltoe* capsized and sank with the loss of one life.

A ship under sail, caught by an unexpected violent squall, could not hope to remain upright. On Sunday, 24 March 1878 HMS *Eurydice*, a training frigate of 921 tons, was caught by such a squall off Dunnose Head, Isle of Wight. She was under plain sail, top gallants and royals set, and was sighted off the island in calm weather. When the storm, which lasted no more than half an hour, struck her she was flung on her side so abruptly that most of her complement of 368, mostly cadets, were caught below deck. There were only two survivors. Yet within fifteen minutes the squall had gone and the sun was sparkling on the water again.

When *President* was lost in 1841 it is possible that she struck an iceberg, always a danger in those days when ships took a more northerly route across the Atlantic, but the stiff gales that had blown up make it seem more likely that she had been caught with the wind and sea abeam and had capsized.

At the time Lloyds' rules for iron ships did not exist. Though rules had been formulated, many shipbuilders ignored them and the tremendous demand for ships for the emigrant trade led to a number of scandals. It was the loss of *Royal Charter*, an auxiliary sailing clipper of hybrid design, that brought matters to a head. After a voyage from Australia in 1859 she made a safe landfall on 24 October at Queenstown, Ireland, and after dropping some of her passengers was expected to dock at Liverpool on 25 October. Instead, she ran into a hurricane in which the small auxiliary engine designed to help her passage when there was no wind for the sails proved insufficient, and she ran aground on the Anglesea shore and broke in two, so that some 450 people perished only a few hours from a safe arrival. Though the Board of Trade enquiry found that no blame could be laid on either the ship or the crew, there were repercussions. Poor material had contributed to many disturbing failures in the early years of iron ships, and scandals about chain cable also came to light. The loss of *Royal Charter* made it clear that it was necessary to build according to the rules in order to obtain a full safety classification, as it ensured a standard for strength and the quality of the materials used, and the chain cable scandal led to the setting up of public proving establishments.

But no standards in the world are proof against top-heaviness, and perhaps the shortest voyage ever was that of *Daphne*, an iron steamer of around 640 tons built at Linthouse. On 3 July 1883 the ship was christened and, overcrowded with workmen, sent sliding down the way into the river Clyde. She was barely waterborne when she listed about ten degrees and eventually fell over. Within a minute or two she had completely capsized and foundered keel-uppermost.

Most capsizes result from collisions when the sharp bow of a ship ploughs into the vulnerable side of another. No matter how many safety precautions are taken in the building of ships, such an event reduces them all to nothing because it lays open a ship's side from deck to keel in such a way that the inrush of water cannot be halted. And there is no answer to this because until ships are built in a different shape, they will always be vulnerable when broadside-on to an oncoming vessel.

On a bitterly cold night in January 1895 the Norddeutscher Lloyd liner *Elbe*, on passage from Bremerhaven to New York, was rammed off Lowestoft by the small British coaster *Craithie*, on her way from Rotterdam to Aberdeen. *Craithie*, with a damaged bow, was able to put back into Rotterdam while *Elbe*, nearly ten times the tonnage, heeled and sank in half an hour, taking 340 people with her. It was an unpleasant reminder that a small ship can sink a much larger vessel without suffering serious injuries, a reminder that has often been repeated.

To enable ships to pass each other as they go about their

business, of course, there are the Rules of the Road. At night there is an arrangement of lights which enable ships to understand what other ships are doing. On each side of the bridge is a navigation light, green for starboard or right, red for port or left. From dead ahead both red and green are visible, indicating that the approaching ship is coming straight towards the onlooker. The minute the ship's course is altered to starboard, only the red is visible and the green vanishes. If the course is altered to port, the red vanishes and only green is visible.

In addition, a vessel under way carries two masthead lights, called range lights, the rearmost higher than the foremost. These are visible long before the coloured navigation lights become visible and, from dead ahead, they appear directly in line, one above the other. As the ship alters course the lights move apart, the after light always higher than the forward light, and they inform the onlooker of the angle at which the ship is approaching. Close together, they indicate that the ship is on an almost parallel course. Wide apart, she is presenting her side to the onlooker. It is a simple system and easy to understand, and enables a ship's captain to gauge at once the course of an oncoming ship and decide whether to hold his course or alter to avoid the stranger. All it requires is good visibility. In fog, however, when visibility is nil, it becomes valueless.

In 1909 the Italian liner *Florida* rammed White Star's *Republic*. They were groping their way through thick fog at the mouth of New York harbour and *Florida*, a much smaller ship, was filled with emigrants rendered homeless by the Messina earthquake, when her stem crashed into the port side of *Republic*. She was able to make port but *Republic* sank under tow.

The need for new maritime safety measures became a matter of grave concern after *Titanic* sank in 1912. Rules, known as Solas ('safety of life at sea'), set standards for sub-dividing a ship so that if water enters one section it does not spread to the rest of the vessel. Fire precautions, stability, life-saving apparatus and the carriage of dangerous goods are also covered by the rules. Yet ships still sink, because with every collision a new set of circumstances arise.

The first version of the safety rules, inspired by the British government after the *Titanic*, was not adopted immediately because of the outbreak of war in 1914. A revised version was internationally accepted in 1929, updated in 1948 after the Second World War and an entirely new convention was adopted in 1974. Ships continue to capsize.

Egypt, one of the largest ships in the P. and O. fleet, was rammed and sunk in the Bay of Biscay in 1922. She left the Thames with only forty-four passengers instead of the full 500, because in those days it was considered a social error to join a P. and O. ship in the Thames, the proper thing to do being to travel by train to Dover, cross the Channel, then travel across France to join the ship at Marseilles.

Fog was encountered off Ushant and, hearing the faint sound of a whistle, *Egypt* sounded the regulation long blast in reply. Almost immediately, however, the *Seine*, a small vessel with a bow strengthened for ice, crashed into her port side. Torrents of coal and water poured into the boiler room, starting a panic among the Lascar seamen that was never really controlled. *Egypt* took on a heavy list and foundered within twenty minutes.

The panic of the Lascars was unusual. Asian crews had had a magnificent record during the First World War and in complete contrast was the exemplary behaviour of the Lascar crew of the P. and O. *Shillong* in 1949, when she was struck by the Belgian tanker *Purfina Congo* in the Gulf of Suez. The *Shillong* fell over into an immediate list with imminent danger of capsize, but this time the Lascar crew behaved splendidly.

In July 1965 the Swedish ship *Stockholm* and the Italian liner *Andrea Doria* were approaching each other on roughly parallel courses some nineteen miles off the Nantucket light guarding the sea approaches to New York in patchy fog. The Nantucket light vessel is one of the most important focal points in the world's sea lanes, and at all hours of the day and night ships set their courses south of this outpost of the United States. She lies in an area of fog and her importance is shown by the fact that the liner *Olympic*, in May 1934, sought her so earnestly that she rammed and sank her.

The *Andrea Doria*, 29,083 tons, was one of the most graceful ships ever built but she sank, nevertheless, after a collision with the smaller, uglier *Stockholm*, which, like many ships working in the ice of northern waters, had a specially strengthened bow. *Andrea Doria* shrugged off the smaller ship in a shower of sparks and continued for nearly two miles, but a list developed and she foundered eleven hours after the collision. Though down by the bow, *Stockholm* showed no signs of undue strain.

Car ferries are particularly vulnerable to capsizing because they are high out of the water and have a shallow draught to allow them to come alongside quickly and easily. When they founder, because they are usually packed, the loss of life is high. Third World ferries are notorious for overloading and there have been many cases of enormous numbers being lost after a foundering. The Sulpicio Lines ferry *Doña Paz*, which collided with a tanker in December 1987, with a loss of 2000 lives, was followed in October 1988 by the 3000-ton ferry *Doña Marilyn*, with a loss of around 500.

The foundering of ferries nearer to home is more unusual but they happen, as the loss of *Herald of Free Enterprise* at Zeebrugge showed. Her loss was due to the major weakness of such vessels – her entrance doors – something which was clearly demonstrated as long ago as 1953 by the loss of *Princess Victoria*. That disaster came as a shock to the travelling public because she was a modern cross-Channel ferry. Certified to carry 1515 passengers, on her trip to Ireland on 31 January she carried only 125 and a crew of forty-nine. The weather forecast was for severe gales, and in fact it turned out to be one of the fiercest storms in living memory. The main novelty in *Princess Victoria*'s new-style lay-out was a large car deck loaded through stern doors so that cars could be driven aboard instead of, as had happened up to that time, being hoisted aboard. At about 9 a.m. the stern doors were forced apart by following seas; it was impossible to close them properly and a further succession of heavy seas burst them wide open. An attempt was made to get the women and children away but the ship took on a forty-five-degree list and in the end she capsized. There were forty-three survivors, not a single woman or child among them, because, true to the traditions of the sea, they had been the first to be put into a boat and it had capsized.

The enquiry drew attention to the inadequacy of car ferries in general with the vast undivided space of their car decks, and the lesson was driven home by the loss of *Skagerrak*, a Norwegian ferry, off South Norway in 1966, and of other car ferries, notably *Herald of Free Enterprise*, which was not even in the open sea but went ahead in Zeebrugge harbour before her bow doors were closed.

But of all the disasters caused by capsizing, perhaps the worst in the northern hemisphere – in terms of loss of life – was that of the Canadian Pacific liner, *Empress of Ireland*, sunk in a mere fourteen minutes on 28 May 1914. The loss of life was as large as that of *Titanic* but, because it occurred just before the First World War began, the casualties were lost in the appalling figures of the early days of that holocaust. The ship was virtually stopped at the time, the water was calm and she was not only within spitting distance of the shore, she was also 200 miles from the open sea inside the boundaries of Canada.

The St Lawrence entry to and exit from the New World had never had the glamour of the New York run because the passengers normally contained no great names from the business or entertainment world, or from London or New York society, and, in addition, during the winter months the St Lawrence was closed by ice. During those months passengers had to use the ice-free ports of Halifax, Nova Scotia, or St John, New Brunswick, and this meant a train journey of several hundred miles to the cities of Montreal or Quebec. With summer, the crack liners could steam all the way up the St Lawrence to these ports and captains were always eager to be the first to arrive. *Empress of Ireland* was on her first round trip of the summer.

Canadian Pacific, which had spanned Canada from coast to coast by rail, in 1904 entered the North Atlantic trade by ordering two large passenger liners, *Empress of Britain* and *Empress of Ireland*. They were the biggest Canadian Pacific had built and were designed and constructed to be 100A1 at Lloyds, the highest seal of approval possible. They were twin-screw ships of 14,000 tons with quadruple-expansion coal-burning engines and a designed speed of twenty knots; they made the crossing between Liverpool and Quebec in about six days. Of this only four days were spent in the North Atlantic, a point stressed by Canadian Pacific for nervous passengers. The other two were passed in the St Lawrence surrounded by land and well away from the noisy waters of the ocean.

Empress of Ireland could carry around 1550 passengers, though she never had the ostentation of the ships that sailed into New York. Nevertheless, she provided good solid comfort and had space and the elegance of the age. When *Titanic* foundered two years before, the shock disclosure had been made that she had lifeboat capacity for no more than one-third of her passengers. According to Canadian Pacific's publicity, *Empress of Ireland* carried so many lifeboats that they were piled up on the decks, and this was literally true. For around 1860 people, including crew, which was considerably more than her capacity, she had sixteen steel lifeboats, seven on each side of the boat deck, with a further two aft. They could hold 764 people altogether, and, after the *Titanic* disaster, Canadian Pacific had increased the height of the davits and placed under each steel boat a further collapsible boat. There were twenty of these, capable of holding 920 people. In addition, there were four other collapsible boats capable of carrying a further 176. She also carried 2200 life jackets of regulation pattern, including 150 designed specifically for children. She was considered to be as safe as care and thought and experience could make her. Despite this, the view remained that the best lifeboat was the ship herself and she was built to the 'two compartment' rule. In other words, she was expected to remain afloat with any two of her compartments flooded.

Her captain, Henry George Kendall, aged forty, was a tall handsome man who had been promoted ahead of many of his contemporaries. He had been at sea for twenty-five years and had taken command only four weeks earlier. He had grown up in Liverpool and had gone to sea first in a square-rigger. Joining CPR, he had steadily worked his way up the ladder and, by sheer luck, had become known on both sides of the Atlantic as the man who had recognised the fleeing Dr Crippen, who was bolting for the New World with his mistress after murdering his wife.

Crippen and the girl had taken passage in Kendall's ship, *Montrose*, and, recognising him from photographs, Kendall had communicated his suspicions by wireless to the authorities in England and, in a dramatic chase, Chief Inspector Dew of Scotland Yard, taking passage aboard a faster ship, was waiting at the St Lawrence riverside town of Rimouski to arrest Crippen and the girl. Kendall's skill as a seaman earned him high praise two years later when he took his ship to the aid of another which had hit an iceberg.

When *Empress of Ireland* sailed, she had on board a crew of 420. There were six watch-keeping officers but only thirty-six seamen; 130 men worked in the engine-room department, most of them firemen and trimmers, whose job it was to keep the boiler fires fed. The purser's department, which consisted of 240 men and women, existed solely to look after the passengers. She also carried two radio operators who, following the custom of the day, were not employed by CPR but by the Marconi Company. Wireless telegraphy was still in its infancy, but as recently as 21 May on her inbound journey the ship, encountering heavy ice floes, had radioed a warning which had prevented another *Titanic* disaster.

The passengers were a mixed bag, about half of them Canadians, mostly from Toronto. There were a few celebrities, chief among them Laurence Irving, son of the great Sir Henry Irving, who had dominated the British stage until his death in 1905. Laurence Irving was an actor-dramatist who had taken a company to Canada and was now returning with his wife while the rest of the company, because of problems with scenery and costumes, had been switched to the White Star liner, *Teutonic*. Only their juvenile lead, Harold Neville, and his actress wife were with them. There were also 170 members of the Salvation Army, including the sixty-year-old Commissioner for Canada, Newfoundland and Bermuda. Third-class passengers were for the most part immigrants who were returning to Europe to visit families or because they were disenchanted with the New World.

At 4.30 p.m. on Thursday 28 May the liner moved out into the stream to the music of the Canadian Salvation Army Band on the promenade deck. She had roughly 700 miles to go before she reached the open sea and even then there were still around 250 miles before she passed the last tip of the American continent, Cape Race of evil memory, near where *Titanic* had foundered.

Because they were anxious that commerce should flourish along the St Lawrence, the Canadians had spent millions of dollars on navigational aids like lighthouses, automatic light buoys and pilot stations. But although the river was free from shoals, with deep water right up to its banks, fierce gales could blow up with tremendous speed and accidents were far from infrequent, the victims mostly fishing vessels and other small craft. And when the warm spring air met the river water chilled by newly melted ice, the St Lawrence was notoriously susceptible to fog.

Even with radar, fog is an unnerving experience; without it a ship's captain was like a blind man crossing a street. In those days he could only indicate his presence and what he intended to do by using his siren, but fog has a habit of playing tricks with sound waves so that the sound of a siren can seem to come from quite the wrong direction. In fog, while it is safe for two ships to move slowly ahead when they know each other's courses, it is highly dangerous to alter course, and that is exactly what *Empress of Ireland* and the ship she met just after midnight did.

Approaching *Empress of Ireland* upstream was the Norwegian collier *Storstad*, carrying 11,000 tons of Nova Scotia coal. Because she was expected to meet pack-ice in her journeyings, she was built with her main frames running horizontally from stem to stern instead of being arranged in close-set rows from keel to deck. This made her enormously strong and, because the unyielding knife-edge of her stem reached down for twenty-five feet below the waterline, it also made her a lethal weapon to anything which crossed her bows. It was a dangerous construction. Raked overhanging stems which crumpled back to a reinforced bulkhead could lessen the force of a collision, but in 1914 construction rules made straight stems almost obligatory.

The *Storstad* carried thirty-six men, of whom only five were on deck, and the skipper, Thomas Andersen, was in bed with his wife, who was making the voyage with her husband. The ship was due to pick up a pilot abreast the Father Point pilot station, where Andersen was to take command for the most difficult part of the voyage, but at the time the collier was under the command of the first mate, thirty-three-year-old Alfred Toftenes. Toftenes had been at sea for nearly twenty years and for seven of them had held his master's ticket. Though loaded to within a few feet of her freeboard, the ship steered easily enough and, as it was a fine clear night, the Father Point lighthouse could be seen.

Then across the black water a pair of masthead lights were spotted in the distance. A few minutes later, when the stranger was about three miles away, her green navigation light was seen. Judging from the glow that came from her, she was a big ship and probably a transatlantic liner. The *Empress* was steaming at about seventeen knots and she could see *Storstad* approaching at around ten knots, which gave the two captains about fifteen minutes to execute whatever manoeuvres they intended. The masthead lights seen from the *Empress* were dead in line about forty-five degrees off the starboard bow, which indicated that the liner was crossing the other ship's course. There was plenty of time to get clear and settle on a new track, and Kendall ordered the quartermaster to put the wheel over so that they were on a course almost parallel with the other ship. He then checked his bearings and, satisfied there was no danger, expected to pass the other ship on her right-hand side, with his green navigational light to the stranger's green navigational light.

But now, moving from the shore, came a low bank of fog and, with the strange ship only about a mile and a half away, the oncoming lights began to grow misty. As the fog closed in, Kendall rang for 'full astern' and sent three blasts of the siren roaring through the night to indicate what he was doing. As he put the engines in reverse, a long single wail came back through the fog and Kendall assumed that the other ship was acknowledging his signals and holding her course.

With the fog now all round him, he satisfied himself that his ship had lost way and sounded two blasts to indicate the fact. The single blast came again and, moving to the standard compass to make sure his ship did not swing, Kendall satisfied himself that her head was still on the east-north-east course he had been following. As he stepped back, though, he saw red and green lights approaching him. They could only indicate that the strange ship was still moving and that she was heading straight for him.

If her crew are to be believed, *Storstad* first saw the *Empress*'s white masthead lights and the single green of her right-hand navigation light. Satisfied that they would pass her safely, Toftenes saw the lights alter and began to change his mind. The masthead lights, which had been apart, indicating that the other ship was on a diagonal course, now came together, indicating that she was heading straight for the collier. Then the green side light was replaced by a red, while the white masthead lights opened. The men on the collier became convinced that the liner, instead of passing them green to green, was now going to pass them red to red. Toftenes signalled 'Stop' and, as the throb of the engines died away, only the hiss of the water could be heard. With the fog thickening around them, Toftenes ordered the wheel a little to the right but the ship didn't answer because she had lost way and, to give her steerage, Toftenes rang for slow ahead. Calling the captain, he warned that the fog was growing thicker and Andersen reached the deck just in time to become aware of the bulk of the *Empress* looming out of the fog. He immediately rang for full astern and yanked at the whistle cord.

Nothing in the world could have made *Storstad*, with her 11,000 tons of coal, lose way completely and, vibrating madly from the reversed engines, she slid like an enormous chisel into the side of the liner at an angle of about thirty-five degrees. The shock was only slight. There was a ragged flash as metal ground on metal, but the *Storstad*'s bows had gone between the liner's steel ribs like a knife into butter. Knowing that the only hope for both ships was to keep his bows jammed into the other ship's side, Andersen rang for full ahead and for a while she remained locked there, but then, slowly – because, Andersen thought, the liner was still moving ahead – the collier began to slide out of the hole and her bows were wrenched free. The *Empress* slipped away in the fog, leaving the collier wallowing astern, badly damaged, her forecastle swept clean of fittings. Her tremendous frames had saved her, and the reaction to the collision was largely one of indignation that the bigger ship had failed to return to offer assistance.

Trying to find out where the mysterious ship had gone, Andersen kept the siren going and it was only after ten minutes of peering into the misty darkness that he became aware of the sound of screaming coming from the water.

The *Storstad*'s stem had sliced deep into the liner's side, forty-six feet of reinforced steel cutting her open almost to her double bottom. As *Storstad* drifted astern, water began to pour into the liner at the rate of 60,000 gallons a second. The collier's bows had almost certainly crushed the bulkhead between the two boiler rooms, so that they were both open to the river and, while she had been designed to stay afloat with one of the boiler rooms flooded, now both had been laid open. As she listed beneath the weight of water, more of the gash vanished below the surface and the flow increased. Almost at once the great ship began to slide over on to her right-hand side.

It was the practice for stewards to close portholes at night but some passengers objected to the lack of fresh air and many were left open; as the water poured in, the list increased. Within seconds a tremendous surge of water was crashing through the lower decks, drowning people in their beds before they were even aware of what had happened. Those who survived were those who had not been asleep or who had reacted at once and begun to struggle to the open deck. Of the three night-duty stewards in third class not one survived. The second-class stewards just had time to race along the lines of cabins, hammering on doors and yelling a frantic warning. Some passengers found life jackets, but in the dark and the panic many never found them at all, and when they did, because the liner had not yet got itself organised and there had not yet been any boat drills, they did not know how to put them on.

Aware of the danger, Kendall telegraphed the engine room to close the two watertight doors and repeated this order on the engine-room telephone. He was reassured that the message had been received and that below the waterline the doors were closing, and Kendall himself ran to the boat deck and began loosening the fastenings of the first boats on the starboard side. Returning to the bridge, he again reached for the engine-room telephone. 'Give me all you can,' he said. 'I'm going to try and beach her.' The reply that came back destroyed all his hopes. 'The steam has gone,' he was informed.

Informed that an SOS had gone off, Kendall told his second-in-command to get the boats away as fast as possible. The boat deck was already swarming with passengers, who got in the way of the crew as they tried to clear the boats and prepare the massive blocks and tackles for lowering. They worked well and Kendall saw three boats lowered smoothly to the water. Others were certainly lowered, though no one was certain how many, and one full of people reached the water intact only to be overwhelmed as the ship rolled over on top of it. The lowering of boats soon became an impossibility, however. The boat deck, normally forty-five feet above the waterline, had canted so much that the water had reached the foot of the davits, while the left-hand boats, rising higher and higher as the ship listed, probably never left their blocks.

Within ten minutes of the collision, as nearly as could be established, *Empress of Ireland* lurched and fell over. Kendall saw her funnels hit the water; then, with scores of other people, he was flung into the river. The dying ship lay on her side for a few minutes before lifting her stern and sliding beneath the dark waters. It was no more than fourteen minutes since the collision. Trapped inside her were some 800 people, most of whom had never even got out of their cabins. Their voyage had lasted just nine hours and forty-two minutes.

Approximately another 700 people had been clinging to the ship's superstructure as she wallowed in the water, or were standing on her hull plating as it lay horizontal. Because she lay so still in the calm water, some even thought she was aground. Then, as the ship rolled over, the few boats afloat had to fight to get clear. One had to fend off with oars as the funnels came close, and the ship's wireless aerials entangled others as they tried to struggle free.

As the ship sank there was a terrible cry from those who were still alive. Those still clinging to her leapt or were thrown into the water. The temperature was only a few degrees above freezing, and where the ship had been was now a struggling mass of people, some with life jackets, some without. Many who had life jackets were dragged under by those without. Others literally had to fight their way through the drowning people. Then the fog rolled away and the survivors for the first time saw the ship that had sunk them, brilliantly lit, the light from her portholes streaming across the black water.

A radio message had gone out from the *Empress*, but the operator had been unable to give a position before the power had failed. Receiving the message, the operator at Father Point sent out a general alarm, knowing that the German Norddeutscher Lloyd ship *Hannover* ought to be near. The government postal tender *Lady Evelyn* was despatched, together with the tug *Eureka*; this doubled as pilot boat, had just returned from taking off the *Empress*'s pilot and knew roughly where the liner was. *Eureka*'s captain, Jean Baptiste Belanger, had four years before lent his uniform and cap to Chief Inspector Dew so that he could be smuggled aboard *Montrose* to confront Crippen. The manager of the Great Western Telegraph Company ran on to the pier shouting, 'For God's sake, get downstream. The *Empress* has gone under,' and without hesitation Belanger cut his mooring ropes and left. *Lady Evelyn*, running blind through the fog, found the first evidence of the tragedy when a lifeboat appeared from the fog and a voice yelled, 'For God's sake, hurry up! There are thousands drowning just ahead!' But the two little ships were too late. By the time they arrived there was nobody left alive in the water.

Storstad, finally aware of what had happened, had lowered four boats and a gig. The first of the boats reached the survivors within minutes and started dragging people aboard, half frozen and gasping, and as the boats became dangerously crowded some of the rescued shouted to their rescuers not to pull any more on board. But *Storstad*'s second mate, who was in charge, was in a terrible dilemma. He knew he ought not to leave anyone in case they died of cold, and he was right. On his second trip he found only about a dozen still alive; on his third trip just a little knot of people standing on an upturned boat. The third mate, Jakob Saxe, in charge of the gig, found his little boat so full of survivors that she was in danger of capsizing, but when he heard a woman's cry he turned towards it and she was hauled aboard. They made it to *Storstad* with no more than a few inches of freeboard.

Captain Kendall was dragged into one of the *Empress*'s own boats, where he immediately took command and started directing the rescue work. With around sixty people on board and more clinging to others who were hanging on to lifelines, the boat pulled slowly towards *Storstad*. Unloading his passengers, the soaked and exhausted Kendall called for volunteers and took the boat back to the spot where the *Empress* had disappeared. He and his crew spent three hours rowing back and forth and saved around seventy-five lives. By that time there were no more living, just dark shapes in the water, and, returning to *Storstad*, he came face to face with Andersen for the first time. 'You have sunk my ship,' he accused. 'You were going at full speed, and in that dense fog.'

Andersen turned his words round to accuse Kendall of going full speed and it was *Storstad*'s pilot, who had arrived from *Eureka*, who separated the two men.

Of the 700 who had been flung into the water only about 490 were dragged to safety. Around 200 were later found floating and dead. The dead included the Irvings and their travelling companions, and most of the Salvation Army travellers. One of the survivors, an Irishman named Clarke who had escaped from the *Empress*'s stokehold, only two years earlier had had the same experience aboard *Titanic*. *Titanic*, he decided, was the more awful because the waiting had been so terrible. 'There was no waiting with the *Empress*,' he said. 'She just rolled over, like a hog in a ditch.'

Shocked by what had happened, the crew of *Storstad* did all they could for the survivors. Andersen and his wife, who had bought new clothes for the trip, ended up with little more than what they stood up in because they gave the rest away. Armed with coffee and whisky as she moved among the survivors, Mrs Andersen gave away even her shoes. Tablecloths and curtains were used. One man's only garment was a pillowslip, others used newspaper, one was clad in one of Mrs Andersen's new petticoats. Below decks, in an attempt to get warm, dozens crowded into the engine and boiler rooms. Some were so frozen that they couldn't even remove what little clothing they wore and Mrs Andersen had to undress many of the women, who were then packed into bunks in twos for warmth.

By this time the boats from *Eureka* were searching the water in the hope of finding a few last survivors. *Lady Evelyn* went alongside *Storstad* and took off over 300 and a few of the dead. *Eureka* took most of those left. Among them was Kendall, in a state of collapse. People continued to die of cold and exhaustion. They were put ashore, half-naked, at Rimouski where they were met by residents with handcarts of food and clothing. Those able to travel were put aboard a train for Quebec but, as it pulled out, it became derailed and the wretched survivors had to wait for another one to be assembled.

The dead were laid on the quayside, most of them naked or almost naked. Among them were many children. A train load of coffins arrived from Quebec and on 30 May the Canadian government revenue cutter *Lady Grey* arrived, carrying 188 bodies. Sailors from the British cruiser *Essex* carried the coffins ashore.

The details of the disaster were appalling. The dead numbered 1012, of whom 840 were passengers and 172 were crew. The number of passengers lost was greater than those of *Titanic*. When it became known that 80 per cent of passengers were lost against 41 per cent of the crew there were suspicions that all was not well and, as with *Titanic*, there was an imbalance in the number saved from first class and third class, but this was inevitable considering the positions of their quarters and the speed with which the ship had sunk. Of 138 children aboard only three girls and one boy survived. Of the 200 or so people from Toronto in the ship only about thirty escaped. Liverpool was also hit by the disaster because *Empress* was a Liverpool ship and about 90 per cent of her crew came from there.

Lloyds were heavily involved in the insurance, and the disaster occurred only two years after *Titanic*, since when the best legal brains and the finest technicians of the shipbuilding industry had tried to devise means that would ensure it could never happen again. Could there be something wrong with a system that built bigger and bigger ships but could not ensure that they would stay afloat for a quarter of an hour in calm water within sight of the shore?

The big ships continued to pass the spot where *Empress of Ireland* had sunk, among them *Empress of Britain*, her sister ship, which had been in fog almost all the way. The Allan liner *Victorian*, which also battled through the fog, had wisely kept the news of the sinking quiet. Passengers in *Calgarian*, having learned of it, refused to go to bed. Hardly more than two weeks after the disaster the American *New York* collided with the Hamburg–Amerika *Pretoria*, and a week later the Norddeutscher *Kaiser Wilhelm II* collided with a freighter off the Isle of Wight. It was a bad summer for fog and it affected Atlantic crossings heavily.

The accusations started, among them one that the crew had saved themselves at the expense of the passengers, a charge that had been levelled at *Titanic*. The answer was probably that so many of them had survived because they were still awake and because they knew their way around the ship. Because of their differently placed quarters, there were also no convincing grounds for suggesting that first-class passengers had received preferential treatment.

The public enquiry that opened in Quebec on 16 June was largely overlooked in Europe. War was just over the horizon and most people's thoughts were concerned with that event. The enquiry was conducted by John Charles Bigham, the first Baron Mersey, the man who had been chairman of the court of enquiry into the *Titanic* disaster. Within a year he was to complete the hat trick with an enquiry into the loss of *Lusitania*, sunk by a German torpedo off the coast of Ireland with a loss of 1198 lives. He wasn't the only man connected with all three. A stoker called Tower survived the three sinkings and was willing to try again but, not unnaturally, he found that when he walked on to a ship his fellow stokers walked off.

Kendall insisted that the collision was caused by *Storstad* putting her wheel over and making a right-hand turn which had taken her into the *Empress*'s side. *Storstad*'s lawyers put forward exactly the opposite view – that it had been the *Empress* which had swung in front of the Norwegian ship. Neither side would give way and one Canadian newspaper observed sarcastically that the ships had apparently collided violently while lying motionless two miles apart.

Jakob Saxe, the Norwegian third mate, insisted that while still visible the liner had first shown her green light, then both red and green and finally only her red light. But he also admitted that because the ship's head was being carried to the left by the current he had taken the wheel himself, and that when Toftenes had ordered a little left wheel he had put it hard over. It virtually destroyed the Norwegians' case because all along they had been insisting that *Storstad*'s course had not altered.

Technical evidence was given by Percy Hillhouse, a naval architect who had helped design *Empress*. He explained that although the ship would theoretically stay afloat even with both boiler rooms flooded, the assumption was that the ship would not be listing, and that the portholes would be closed. He calculated that the collier had cut a hole in the liner's side 350 feet square, so that the ship took in initially about 265 tons of water a second, increasing as the gash sank deeper.

The court's report criticised Kendall for stopping his ship, and it was felt that he should have given the Norwegian a wider berth. But the report was harder on the Norwegians. It could not accept that *Storstad* had no way on her, and the fact remained that she had put her wheel over and changed her course. Toftenes was considered negligent in not calling the captain sooner. Conducting their own enquiry under Norwegian maritime law, the Norwegians exonerated *Storstad*'s officers.

With the war, the *Storstad* carried relief stores for Belgium, with Andersen still her master. In 1917, she was torpedoed and Andersen showed great seamanship in steering the boats containing the survivors to safety. Kendall went as marine superintendent for Canadian Pacific's migrant traffic to the port of Antwerp, and when Antwerp was in danger from the Germans he again showed the initiative he had shown in the Crippen case. There were two Canadian Pacific liners in the port, one with her engines out of action but a full load of coal, the other in good working order but with no coal. Kendall transferred the coal from the broken-down ship to the sound one; then, with both ships full of Belgian refugees, he set off for England, the sound ship towing the other. He served during the war with the Navy, was torpedoed twice and went back to Canadian Pacific after the war as the company's marine superintendent in London. He died in 1965, aged ninety-one. Professor Hillhouse, the expert who had given evidence, was also not yet finished with the sea and was in the news again in 1917, when he was personally caught up in another disaster.

The disaster was pushed out of sight in Europe by the events which followed. Even as the court delivered its verdict, the heir to the Austrian throne was assassinated at Sarajevo and from then on European minds were less concerned with the deaths of a thousand people in a river in Canada than with their own survival.

There is still a question about why competent seamen had allowed the collision to occur. But there are always questions that are never really answered and it is possible that, like many long liners which were never easy to steer, while swinging on to her new course the *Empress* had been allowed to swing just too far to the right so that for a brief moment she *had* shown her left-hand side to *Storstad*. It is also possible that, with her decks so brilliantly lit, her weaker navigational lights were not easy to see and the Norwegians might well have lost sight of them altogether. The real cause, of course, was the fog.

As a direct result of the collision the soft-bow system in ships, which gave vessels a raking bow, was introduced, and such bows were soon adopted so that in most cases of collision the damage was limited to injury above the waterline. Nowadays bulbous bows – bows that extend forward below the water – are in fashion, not only as an aid to higher speed but as a safety factor in collisions. According to one expert, they are as effective in reducing damage as 'the button on a fencing foil'. But *Jupiter*, with her load of schoolchildren, sank in a mere forty minutes after an eighteen-foot hole was torn below her waterline by the bulbous bow of *Adige*, and another expert promptly claimed that the bulbous bow was just 'a ram protruding below the surface of the water'.

CHAPTER 2

Fire down below

Lakonia

Disasters at sea come in all shapes and sizes. Sinking is bad enough, but for a ship to be on fire first is one of the most horrifying things that can happen. At sea there is nowhere to run for safety, and the blaze and smoke can prevent the launching of the boats. Such fires invariably start and spread because of a high wind and, once away, they become difficult to control.

When the 1530-ton East Indiaman *Kent* sailed from England in February 1825, carrying a total of 640 persons, she ran into a gale almost at once. Then one of the ship's officers, going below to check that water and spirit casks were not working loose, dropped his lantern which set fire to leaking spirits. The blaze was soon out of control but by the grace of God a small brig, *Cambria*, bound for Vera Cruz with Cornish miners on board, appeared and began to rescue *Kent*'s complement. The number lost was eighty-one and only daring seamanship by *Cambria*'s master saved the rest.

Because of its construction, like the lift shaft in a skyscraper, the interior of a ship causes a tremendous draught, and as the flames increase so they cause the draught to increase also. This is still the case with steel ships and vastly improved methods of fire fighting; with timber-built ships containing wooden bulkheads and only hand pumps and buckets to fight the flames it must have been hopeless. Where breech-loading guns were carried, to add to the perils there was a powder magazine. With lighting only from lanterns fuelled by oil, their wicks contained only by glass, the danger was always present.

Emigrant ships with their crowded quarters were especially vulnerable, and all too often outbreaks aboard them occurred far out to sea. *Ocean Monarch*, however, was barely out of the river Mersey in 1848 when a blaze broke out in an after store room. The sails caught fire and the burning canvas prevented boats being lowered; 178 people died.

The dangers were intensified by the introduction of steam machinery, and the loss of a brand new liner in 1852 drew attention to the undesirable combination of wooden hull with engines and boilers. Shipowners expecting to carry mail or troops tried to fall in with the current Admiralty distrust of iron hulls. For some reason it was also preferred that mail should be carried in paddle steamers, and these obsolete views explain the pine hull and paddles of the 3000-ton Royal Mail ship *Amazon*, which sailed on her maiden voyage in January 1852 for the West Indies, with a crew of 110 and fifty passengers. Several times the ship had to be stopped for overheated bearings, and then fire broke out. One version of the disaster was that it was impossible to stop the engines, another that they were kept going to hold the ship's head to wind in a gale. In any event, the ship was still moving ahead when attempts were made to lower the boats, and in the only boat that got away there were only three passengers and eighteen of the crew. Overheated bearings or boiler lagging which caught fire was the cause of the disaster, and it caused the experts to look into the relative merits of iron as opposed to wooden passenger ships.

On their journey to the Crimea in 1854, the Inniskilling Dragoons were in the transport *Europa* when it caught fire 123 miles off the Scillies. Though the soldiers behaved with discipline, in the holocaust of flames, smoke and falling rigging they lost fifty-seven horses, their veterinary surgeon, twelve men and two of the women who had accompanied the regiment, to say nothing of every scrap of equipment they possessed. Screaming horses were hoisted out of the inferno below and dropped in the sea to take their chances.

Sarah Sands was one of the few cases where a serious fire was mastered in a ship with the primitive fire-fighting appliances of the day. She was a four-masted iron steamer with auxiliary sails, and when the Indian Mutiny broke out in 1857 she was chartered to carry the 54th (Dorsetshire) Regiment to Calcutta. After rounding the Cape of Good Hope smoke was seen coming from the after hatch, which was close to the magazines containing cartridges and gunpowder. Her crew deserted her but the troops set to work to clear the magazines. There were no smoke helmets and they could work in the choking fumes only for very short periods; but the barrels of ammunition were hauled on deck one by one and rolled overboard. After about sixteen hours the magazines were almost empty so that when the remaining few barrels did explode they merely blew a hole in the ship's side above the waterline.

Controversy was already raging about the respective merits of wood and iron for shipbuilding, and the loss of the teak-hulled *Cospatrick* in 1874 hastened the change. Carrying 429 emigrants on their way to New Zealand, when she caught fire there was only a light wind, but the blaze was in the forepeak where inflammable material was normally kept. It might have been possible to master the flames if the ship could have been kept stern-on to the wind but, because the head sails burned away, the after sails acted like a weather vane and kept the bows into wind. Only two lifeboats containing eighty-one people got away and ten days later one was picked up. It contained only five people, one insane from his sufferings.

With the final change from wood to iron it was expected that fires would be less devastating, but when in 1913 the liner *Volturno*, carrying emigrants to New York, caught fire 900 miles west of Ireland, despite having enough boats to accommodate everyone on board, the emigrants, most of them with no knowledge of English, panicked and 103 of them lost their lives with thirty of the crew.

Still the fires came. It has been said that every passenger liner, every cargo vessel, every tanker built before the Second World War represented a fire risk of 'awful severity'. This seemed true even in port. The French liner *Normandie*, taken over after the fall of France in 1940 by the United States government, was being fitted out as a troop transport when fire broke out in the main saloon. Though the fire was mastered, so much water had been pumped into the ship that she became unstable and capsized.

Cruise liners are particularly vulnerable to fire. Though they carry large crews, many are involved only with the passengers and the number of actual seamen is often small. In addition, they carry large numbers of people who are unfamiliar with the working of ships. The result in the event of a disaster is that lifeboats have to be lowered with more than their normal share of non-seamen, such as stewards and cruise officials. When disaster struck the cruise liner *Lakonia* in 1963 she carried 646 passengers, 630 of them British, and the appropriate number of non-seamen to attend to their wants. Altogether there were 1022 people on board.

A 20,000-ton ship, *Lakonia* began her career in 1930 as a passenger liner in the days when travellers had to depend on a long sea voyage to move about the world. She had started as the Dutch liner *Johan van Oldenbarnevelt*, and was employed on round voyages to the Dutch East Indies. After the fall of Holland in 1940 she was converted into a troopship and carried soldiers and supplies, emerging from the war unscathed and once more under Dutch ownership. She was given a major refit and used to take emigrants to Australia; then in 1959 she had another refit to become a single-class cruise ship for round-the-world trips.

By the end of 1962 her career seemed to have come to an end when she was withdrawn from service, but the Greek Steam Navigation Company bought her for little more than scrap value and spent half a million pounds on another refit. The short-voyage cruise trade had started, and she was named *Lakonia* and prepared for her first cruise under her new name. Her crew included British, Canadians, French, Belgians, even Chinese, but were mainly Greeks, Italians, Germans and Cypriots. She sailed on Thursday, 19 December 1963, on an eleven-day Christmas cruise, and moved down the Solent for Madeira, Tenerife and Las Palmas. A cruise director was aboard to arrange entertainments, and there was no lack of stewards and waiters. Most of the passengers were delighted with her.

But there were things that were not as they should have been. Some cabins were too warm or too cold. Hot-air blowers did not always work and people waiting for the ship to sail found the tea they were served was tepid because of an electrical fault in the galley. Others complained of no hot water in their showers, that stewards' bells failed to work and that lights by the beds repeatedly went out. On the morning after departure a lifeboat drill was held. All those on board were supposed to go to their lifeboat stations, but not everybody went and of those who did some had drinks in their hands. The holiday spirit had taken over and only a few had their life-jacket fastenings checked by a ship's officer or seaman, while the crew seemed to regard the exercise as something to be done only to comply with the regulations.

Extensive rules and regulations to ensure safety at sea had been laid down by the International Conventions of 1948 and 1960, and in each of *Lakonia*'s twenty-four lifeboats – which together could accommodate 1500 people – equipment, provisions and water should have been stored and a deck officer or a certificated member of the crew allocated to take charge in an emergency.

Before *Lakonia* sailed, a marine superintendent from the British Ministry of Transport had examined her safety certificate and watched a lifeboat drill which included the lowering of lifeboats. The British superintendent had no jurisdiction over the Greek ship, and the drill had been carried out largely as a gesture of courtesy by the captain, Mathios Zarbis. And although *Lakonia* was sailing under the Convention of 1948, she was not subject to the regulations governing structural materials and fire precautions because she had been built before they came into force. As a result, she had more flammable materials in the form of ornate woodwork than is found in modern ships, and instead of the usual sprinkler system of fire prevention, she was fitted with fire hydrants and fire extinguishers because it was felt that in a minor fire they caused less damage.

Fitters, carpenters and electricians continued to check fuses in the corridors, and cabin bells that wouldn't work. Some passengers still had no hot water, but these were only a few and the majority were enjoying life aboard. By Saturday afternoon, the ship was beyond Cape Finisterre.

On Sunday evening elderly people retired early and parents with young children put them to bed before going to the Lakonia Room, on the promenade deck amidships, where a ball was being held. Fairy lights were strung across the stern and by 10 p.m. the ball was in full swing. While the winners of a fancy-dress competition were waiting to be crowned, a Mrs Loyst slipped away to make sure that her husband, who was not well and had decided to go to bed early, was all right. Their cabin was on the upper deck near the purser's office, the ladies' hairdresser and the barber's shop, and one deck below the Lakonia Room. Having made sure her husband was all right, she stayed with him for a few minutes before returning to the ball at about 10.45 p.m. As she walked along the corridor, she saw two stewards kicking in the door of the ladies' hairdressing salon and realised that thick smoke was seeping out from under it.

Chief purser Antonio Bogetti had been just about to leave his office when he was warned about the fire. He had alerted the fire squad and, under his orders, members of the crew had begun to break down the door of the hairdressing salon. As the door fell in, clouds of smoke poured out and Mrs Loyst saw one of the men reach for a fire extinguisher attached to the bulkhead wall. He was unable to free it because it was stuck in position with paint, and she hurried back to her cabin to warn her husband to get dressed. By the time he had thrown his clothes on and they had opened the door again, they found themselves trapped by a black wall of smoke.

Dragging his wife back into the cabin, Loyst tried to open the porthole, but it was thick with paint. Ships live by their paint, because it preserves steel and iron, and every mate and every bosun makes it his job to see that it is plentifully and skilfully applied. But when the job is done by inexperienced or indifferent seamen or dockyard workers it is often simply plentiful. On *Lakonia*, there were years of paint on and around the screw that held the porthole and the deadlight above it. It was only after a great deal of struggling that the Loysts managed to open the porthole and hang out of it trying to breathe.

In the Lakonia Room the stewards were just laying out a cold buffet, and the entertainment was just coming to an end, when thick black smoke began to curl through the open doors. As soon as the fire was reported to the bridge the officer on watch sounded the alarm bells. Unfortunately, they didn't alarm. Passengers thought that they were part of gala night, or that there was a practice on for the crew. One even thought it was the tea bell which had gone off by mistake. In one bar the stewards said that it was for a minor matter and that the 'all clear' would go soon, but as he closed the bar the passengers grew uneasy.

As crew members began to unroll hoses from their glass cases in the corridors, the entertainments director, George Herbert, called for calm. People who had been in their cabins began to appear in night attire. The fumes and smoke were rousing them, and as cabin doors were flung open the draughts roaring through from open ports helped fan the flames, which began to take hold of the paint and woodwork. By the time the firemen arrived the fire had become serious.

Captain Zarbis had wasted no time. He had ordered his radio operator to send out an SOS, and two of his officers were now moving among the passengers reassuring them, but contradictory orders were being given by other members of the crew. The steward of one bar closed it down, while another went on serving drinks. Many passengers did not have their life jackets and many had not bothered to find out where spares were kept. Passengers on the promenade deck were instructed to go to the dining room three decks below, but those who went down realised that there might be danger and began to make their way up again. It caused confusion and the crew became infected by it.

Officers, seamen and stewards were struggling to reach trapped children and adults. One man went to fetch his youngest child and found it impossible to get through, but then he saw a seaman wearing an oxygen mask carrying the boy in his arms. Another passenger realised his son was trapped in his outside cabin, but a young Cypriot steward, Adree Vasiliades, went over the side of the ship on the end of a rope and pulled the boy to safety. Two German stewards wearing gas masks, also hanging over the side on rope ladders, were working their way along the portholes.

By now the fire had obtained a good hold and the fire-fighting crew, wearing helmets, skin-diving goggles, gas masks or merely wet cloths tied round their mouths, were beginning to be driven back. There was still time for an orderly evacuation. The sea was calm and the night was clear, the ship's lights were still blazing and there was enough space in the lifeboats for everybody on board. The SOS had been picked up and five ships were driving to the rescue, the first two expected in three hours' time.

Around midnight Captain Zarbis ordered the boats to be lowered. The engine-room staff were still at their posts and he tried to make a lee for the boats. Things were still in order, but in disasters at sea there are always unexpected developments. The public-address system had broken down by now, and some of the passengers didn't hear the order to take to the boats until later; those whose boats were on the port side could not reach them for the flames, while the boats already being lowered were descending with difficulty. On liners boats are sometimes under the control of men with little experience. It was so on *Titanic* and other ships. On *Duchess of Atholl*, torpedoed off Freetown in 1942, many passengers owed their lives to the fact that there happened to be a large number of small-boat men on board; they were members of the RAF Marine Section on their way to Freetown and in many cases they took over the boats and handled them skilfully until they were picked up.

On *Lakonia* those with experience were often fighting the fire, and the boats went down erratically. It also became clear that the lowering gear was in a terrible condition. Like the extinguishers and the portholes, it was jammed by layers of paint and, handled by inexperienced stewards, the result was disastrous. One boat capsized as it hit the water. Another was upended as it was lowered, flinging everyone into the sea. Nevertheless, within half an hour seventeen of the twenty-four boats were safely away, filled in the old tradition of women and children first. These days it is considered better to keep families together.

Some of the boats had had to be hammered loose from the davits. One passenger saw a seaman standing perilously on the ship's rail wielding an axe to chip a boat free from the paint that jammed its tackle. As it descended, it went down in fits and starts and as soon as it touched the sea it started filling with water. Some boats were fully loaded, some half empty. Some had an officer in charge, others had no one in charge. The state of affairs was chaotic and passengers, unable to reach their own boat and feeling that they might be left behind, piled into any boat they could find. With the loudspeaker system not working, the language problem also contributed to the confusion. Some elderly people refused to enter a boat and when all the boats had gone there were around 150 passengers and fifty crew still on board. Above them they could see the twinkle of fairy lights and the illuminated name of the ship glowing between the funnels.

However, the radio operator's message had been picked up – 4000 miles away by the US Coastguard Headquarters on the Atlantic Coast of America – and computers were in action. The system, called Atlantic Merchant Vessel Report, had been extended early in 1963 to include the entire North Atlantic, and *Lakonia*'s appeal for help was the first time it had been used for a major disaster. The ships of sixty-one countries contributed to the system, which was a mutual-aid idea operating through the voluntary daily reporting by radio of position, course and speed. Within minutes Coastguard Headquarters had a picture of almost all the ships in a radius of 100 miles from *Lakonia*'s position, and the massive rescue operation included the US 57th Air Rescue Squadron stationed in the Azores.

It was probably the fastest and most widespread operation ever mounted for a ship in distress and it was well under way by 01.30. The first ship to sight *Lakonia*, at 02.40, was the British freighter *Montcalm*, a 5000-ton vessel making for Casablanca. Her radio operator had actually been in bed, off duty, but the automatic alarm had called him to his set. The Argentinian liner *Salta* arrived at about the same time. It was still dark, and on their radar screens the two ships picked up lifeboats spread over a wide area. Since there might have been people swimming or clinging to wreckage in the water it would have been dangerous to approach any nearer, and it was decided to wait for daybreak.

The fire in *Lakonia* seemed to have stopped spreading. Those passengers who had decided that it was safer aboard the ship gathered at the after end of the promenade deck. Some sat in deck chairs. A few gathered round the piano in the disco room and tried singing Christmas carols. Then two men, seeing stewards helping themselves to drink, joined in. Exploring the Lakonia Room, others found the food that was being set out when the fire started and began to share it round. With rescue apparently close, it seeemd that the danger was dwindling and someone suggested tea. Somehow it appeared and cups were handed round in the best British manner. A few people actually started dancing.

As Captain Zarbis, his uniform torn and his face grimy, appeared to reassure them, however, there was a tremendous explosion that shook the deck. Further explosions followed and the passengers were driven to the ship's starboard quarter. Meanwhile, the wind had risen and, as the lifeboats began to heave up and down, many of the occupants were seasick. Some of them were scathing about the crew, who were said to have made no attempt to do anything to help passengers. But many of them were stewards with no more experience of the sea than the passengers themselves, and other passengers spoke well of the men in their boats.

Though the lights of two or three rescue ships were now visible, the lifeboats had nothing they could signal with. In one boat built to carry eighty people but containing only thirty-three a torch and a flare were found. But the torch died almost immediately and no one knew how to use the flare. Cigarette lighters were lit and handkerchieves set on fire. Captain Kempton, of *Montcalm*, manoeuvred his ship to windward of the boats and allowed her to drift towards them; she dragged her first boatload aboard at about 04.45. *Lakonia*, meanwhile, had been shaken by more explosions and the hopes of the people on the stern were fading rapidly. Rope ladders were dangled over the side and tables and chairs were thrown into the water. People began to descend the ladders in the dark but at the bottom many couldn't bring themselves to drop into the sea and queues formed. A few jumped from the ship, some breaking their necks as their life jackets struck the sea and jerked their heads back. Others injured themselves when they hit floating obstacles or landed on swimmers. Some fell, knocking others into the water, while the suction caused by the movement of the ship drew people to the hull and some were too weak or too old to swim clear.

Little mats of bobbing heads formed round any floating debris, and Vasiliades, the young steward who had already saved several lives, dived in to help. He dragged three people to the ropes hanging from davits and, finding a floating table, steered it to them before climbing back aboard *Lakonia*. A man who had lost his wife and son in the capsized boat went down a ladder only to find that two men were hanging on at the bottom who refused to move. Then a man trod on him from above and in he went. He was thrown three times against the stern but was able to push away from it. Forty or fifty people around him were screaming for help that couldn't be given.

The last people went overboard just as dawn was beginning to show. At about this time the first of the American aircraft from the Azores flew over the scene, dropping life rafts and dinghies. Its crew could feel the heat from the burning ship through the open door of the plane. One dinghy fell close, but on the wrong side of the ship for those still on board, and Vasiliades once more came to the rescue. Going into the sea, he pushed the dinghy round the stern from one dangling rope to another until he had collected sixteen people. Only Captain Zarbis and a few of his crew now remained on board.

With full daylight, more aircraft arrived with three more ships and, with five ships now available, *Montcalm* moved in close and launched her own lifeboats. The last survivor to be rescued by her was dragged from the water at 4 p.m. Altogether she rescued 236 people, some of whom died from exposure or exhaustion. The seriously ill were transferred to the P. and O. liner *Stratheden*, which was equipped with a sick bay. After putting them aboard, *Montcalm*'s boat brought back 240 loaves of bread from the liner to help feed the many extra mouths on board and, because they were short of blankets, the American Air Force parachuted 400 down.

Soon after dusk, *Montcalm* handed control of the operation over to another ship until the carrier *Centaur* could arrive from

Gibraltar, and set course for Casablanca. When *Centaur* arrived, a helicopter lowered an officer to *Lakonia*'s after deck to make sure there were no living people left on board. He reached a strip of deck that was still intact, but on either side of him he could see through three decks which had been burned away as if by a giant blow lamp. The string of fairy lights above the stern was still intact.

Stepping ashore with nothing but their dried clothes or garments provided by the rescue ships, the *Lakonia* passengers had nothing but praise for their rescuers and little but criticism for the *Lakonia*'s crew; 128 people, ninety-eight of them passengers, had lost their lives.

The enquiry in Piraeus blamed Zarbis for an inadequate fire-fighting organisation, but the owners were exonerated because they claimed to have supplied sufficient appliances and life-saving equipment. The cause of the fire was never known for certain. Insurance companies sent a team of analytical chemists to Gibraltar to investigate, and two tugs started to tow the derelict vessel there on Christmas Day. By this time the fire had burned itself out and for four days the two tugs struggled with her. They had covered nearly half the distance to Gibraltar when a gale blew up from the west and *Lakonia* began to sink by the stern. Minutes later she disappeared, taking with her any evidence that might explain her last hours.

Morro Castle

The *Lakonia* disaster should never have happened, particularly as it was a virtual repetition of another disaster which had occurred only thirty years before when another cruise ship, *Morro Castle*, was destroyed in similar circumstances. But if the *Lakonia* disaster was the result of carelessness and indifference, the *Morro Castle* fire was a weird affair that occurred under the most bizarre conditions imaginable with people behaving in an extraordinary fashion. The incident belonged to the America of that strange period of the Thirties so accurately and so often recorded by Hollywood – the Great Depression – when the poor grew poorer and, because they were obliged to accept lower wages to get a job at all, the wealthy who employed them grew richer. It was a period of graft, corruption, recklessness, the yellow press, bootleggers, gangsters, racketeers, the quick buck and the razzmatazz of publicity; and what happened in *Morro Castle* seemed to symbolise all that was reprehensible about the era.

1934 was a good year for taking a cruise from America. In 1929 a deep financial slump had hit the United States. After years when the market had been saturated with consumer products and inflationary pressures had been concealed, although the boom was clearly over a stock exchange surge continued. Deluded by propaganda, investors maintained an orgy of crazy speculation in overvalued stocks, and as the American banking structure was unsound, grafters, swindlers, imposters and frauds were involved. In the autumn of that year the crash came.

It was no gradual decline from prosperity, giving time for adjustment, but a sudden fall down a precipice. It brought a worldwide recession and the United States was deeply involved. By 1934, the worst was almost over and there were people with money available again who saw cruising as a wonderful opportunity to forget the Depression for a week and, what was more, to get away from Prohibition.

Prohibition was the result of an Act brought before Congress in 1919 that banned all alcoholic liquors. It was impossible to enforce and became the period of the bootleggers, or illicit vendors of liquor, giving rise to the great gang wars. Gin was made in bath tubs and cases occurred of death, blindness and paralysis from drinking whisky made from wood alcohol. It was always possible to obtain a drink, but it was a shifty business and people were more than glad to leave the shores of the United States for places where they could have an honest drink in peace.

Morro Castle was an 11,520-ton passenger-cargo ship of the American Ward Line and on Friday, 8 September 1934 she was drawing to the end of a cruise to Havana and back. She was a good ship, a comparatively new turbo-electric liner designed expressly for the cruise trade, which meant that, in common with most similar ships of the period, her lavish interior fittings and decorations carried a great deal of wood and flammable material. To counter this she had fire doors, a system of hydrants with hose attachments at points about the ship, and portable extinguishers. She had been launched in 1930 and had been under the command of the same captain ever since. She had spent her days shuttling between New York and Havana, always with plenty of passengers, all anxious for a good time in what was in effect a floating gin mill, and all eager to get away from Prohibition and the Depression for a week.

They were able to enjoy a cruise of three days on the way out and another on the way back, with a day's roistering at Sloppy Joe's or La Tropicana in Havana in between. The trip was not expensive, costing around eighty dollars, except for a few more expensive first-class staterooms. It seemed a good bargain, but though the accommodation was comfortable enough and the cruise director, Robert Smith, made sure that there was never a dull moment in the entertainment, the food and service were indifferent. This, however, probably didn't matter much to many of the people aboard, who were classed as 'a fast crowd – men with other people's wives and that sort of thing', and women on the look-out for a husband. They had come for a good time with plenty of cheap booze.

By contrast, the crew were poorly paid and men carried as able seamen were often not qualified as such, while others who *were* qualified were paid as ordinary seamen. They were also overworked because, although the passengers enjoyed themselves in Havana, the crew were always very much involved in preparing for the return voyage, and when *Morro Castle* docked in New York she was due to sail again for Havana the same evening with another crowd of passengers. In addition, unattached women passengers persisted in making advances to members of the crew, which didn't lead to good discipline.

The noisy enjoyment of the passengers highlighted the discontent among the crew. Wages of thirty dollars a month wasn't much for a deckhand who doubled up as a waiter, but it was better than the dole and there were plenty ashore who were willing to exchange places. There were compensations, too, of course. Good booze fetched high prices in the States and smuggling and bootlegging went on all the time. The suggestion in the company brochures that *Morro Castle* was manned by the cream of American seamen was nothing but a fable. The owners were taking advantage of the times to get their labour cheap. Many of the men were of poor quality and many could not even speak English.

Morro Castle had done the trip many times before, but this one was to be different. Before she left the crew had changed, as it invariably did between trips because the Ward Line had a bad reputation for hiring and firing. At the end of the previous voyage around fifty deckhands and stewards had been sacked for a variety of offences including drunkenness, theft and assault, and when the ship returned another score were due to go. With the Depression ashore, replacements weren't hard to find.

There were other odd things about the *Morro Castle*. In addition to carrying holidaymakers, she also secretly carried arms and ammunition. In the days before Fidel Castro, American interests had dominated Cuba politically and economically since 1903, and the US had acquired military bases at a peppercorn rent. But there had been revolutions in 1917, 1924, 1931 and 1933, when the country was run by what was supposed to be a provisional government but was in fact a dictatorship by a junta, backed by powerful US business interests concerned that Communist actions would threaten their profits. In return the Cuban authorities did not mention independence.

But Communists were increasing their activities in the hope of overthrowing the corrupt régime in power, and the arms that *Morro Castle* carried were for the government to use in suppressing the rebellion. They were classified as 'sporting goods' and were always unloaded at night by Cuban soldiers. But they had almost certainly come to the knowledge of the Communists, who had recently grown more aggressive, and there had been an outbreak of fire in a hold containing explosives only the week before, started, it was believed, by use of a chemical device.

During the First World War, German agents in New York had produced mysterious fires at sea in ships carrying American arms to Europe, by means of a device invented by a Dr Walter Scheele. It consisted of a lead tube containing picric acid in one half, sulphuric acid in the other. The acids were separated by a copper disc and the timing was arranged simply by varying the thickness of the disc. The sulphuric ate away the disc, then reacted on the other acid to produce a tremendously hot flame.

This was almost certainly how the fire had been started, but it had been impossible to decide whether the device had been planted in New York while the ship was loading, or later by a Communist member of the crew. The fire had been discovered as a result of the ship's smoke-detecting system, a very sophisticated design for the time, and the flames had been extinguished by an automatic fire-fighting mechanism.

Among the crew the general attitude was to say nothing. Communism had already infiltrated the seamen's union and it was always considered better not to talk. When making a living meant not being difficult, no one was difficult – not even the officers. Yet an ex-Scotland Yard man, Harold Brust, who worked for Cuba's tourist office, had warned in 1930 that *Morro Castle* was 'at risk'. Nothing was done, however, though on her present round trip, before the ship had left Havana for the return run, the ship's master, Captain Robert Wilmott, had been warned by the Havana chief of police that a Communist agent was believed to be on board and that an attempt at sabotage would be made. Wilmott kept the warning to himself.

The fifty-six-year-old captain had not been well for some time, and even felt that someone was trying to poison him. His behaviour after leaving Havana became very odd. Instead of entertaining passengers at his table and being generally friendly, as was expected, he had kept to his cabin and kept in touch with his senior officers only by telephone. In addition, he had given orders for the smoke-detecting system which had saved the ship on her earlier trip to be switched off and to remain off, because, he said, the smell from a cargo of salted hides taken aboard at Havana would spoil the trip for the passengers. He had also cancelled lifeboat drills because they 'upset the passengers', who were there for a good time.

There were men aboard *Morro Castle* who were aware of the dangers and one of them, Arthur Spender, a licensed first mate who had been forced by the Depression to accept the job of ship's watchman, had checked all the breaches of safety rules and even compiled a 'potential disaster dossier'. He had noticed a lack of training and information among the crew, the absence of emergency equipment, and that faults in the buoyancy tanks of some of the lifeboats had been covered with paint. He had also noticed that the Lyle gun, a line-throwing apparatus carried for emergencies and fired by explosive powder, had been removed from the bridge and stored in a space above the ceiling of the first-class writing room. These weren't the only flagrant breaches of rules, because the other two watchmen had been sent to help with the cabin services and Spender found lockers full of useless life belts. It was obvious that the bridge officers, every one of whom held a master's certificate, were aware of the faults but, afraid for their jobs, preferred to look the other way.

At nine o'clock on the evening of Friday 8 September after a grey day with the weather deteriorating, Captain Wilmott was found dead in his cabin. There is some confusion about who exactly found him, but there is confusion about a lot of things which occurred that day. One version says that it was William Warms, the first officer, who found him, another that it was Howard Hanson, the fourth officer. Whichever way it was, the captain, whose poor health was known, had last been seen by Warms about to start eating from a tray. Fifteen minutes later he was found slumped over the side of his bath – dead.

The ship's surgeon, Dr De Witt van Zile, and the purser, Robert Tolman, were sent for and with them came the chief engineer, Eban Abbott, whose visit was purely fortuitous. He wanted to report that a faulty boiler had been closed down, something which would affect the ship's speed and reduce water pressure. He had tried telephoning but, getting no reply, had set off in person. He showed no surprise at hearing that the captain was dead, because there had been several strange events lately and the captain had been ill after a meal a month before when food poisoning had been suspected.

As the body was lifted to the bed, Abbott, who had been at sea for more than thirty years, noticed that the skin was becoming blue.

He looked at the doctor bent over the corpse. 'Do you know the cause of death?' he asked.

The doctor decided that Wilmott had died of indigestion and heart failure, but Warms, the first officer, felt that the superficial examination which had been given was insufficient to determine the real cause.

'I am assuming command,' he said, and told the purser to prepare the necessary documents. Warms had been at sea for thirty-five years since the age of twelve and had had several commands, but each time he had been demoted for failing to heed safety precautions. Following a mysterious fire in a cruise liner he had been commanding, he had spent a whole year 'on the beach' before obtaining his post as first officer of *Morro Castle*. He had a contempt for poor seamen, and a reputation as an excellent cargo officer who knew how to keep his mouth shut, a useful asset in view of what the ship carried. It was Warms who had given *Morro Castle* her first fire drill in three months, but even that had been something of a charade as the hose was not connected and nothing was tested.

Warms's first order as captain was to Abbott – to seal Wilmott's cabin. Giving orders to Abbott gave him pleasure because during the four years that they had been in the ship together they had cordially disliked each other. Abbott was a very different man from Warms. He enjoyed appearing in full dress uniform and sometimes took his duties as a social performer more seriously than those of senior engineer. Yet he was experienced and had held his chief's licence since 1909, when he had joined the Ward Line. He and Warms had always been at loggerheads, however, and Captain Wilmott had decided to recommend Abbott's removal to another ship.

As he helped to dress the body, Fourth Officer Hanson was startled to notice that the captain's face was now turning black. It could have been the result of a heart attack, but it could also have been a sign of poisoning. Meanwhile, returning to the bridge, Warms informed the officers of the watch of what had happened and gave orders for the head office of the line to be informed by radio. At this time the ship was moving at twenty knots through the dark night into a strong north-easter with rain, and Warms decided to stay on the bridge until the ship docked in New York in a matter of twelve hours' time. He was determined to remain alert but, despite this, he failed to notice that Wilmott had switched off the smoke-detector system.

While Warms was effecting the changeover, passengers in the first-class dining room were awaiting the arrival of the captain to preside at the traditional farewell dinner and gala, but instead the cruise director, Robert Smith, appeared to announce his death.

'Out of respect for him,' he said, 'I ask that all the usual festivities for tonight should be cancelled.'

The passengers could only agree, but they were aboard to have a good time and, as the evening wore on, a number of impromptu parties started in the bar and in cabins. Some of the passengers had cheap rum bought in Havana, and mixed groups on the promenade deck started singing. This was the last night, after all, and all they could look forward to on docking was Prohibition once more. Stewards tried to encourage them to go to bed, but with little success, and Smith had to go round expressing his disapproval.

While this was going on, Chief Engineer Abbott had done what had been ordered in the captain's cabin. Returning to his own cabin, he telephoned the engine room and, on being informed that all was well, turned in for the night.

By this time the weather had calmed a little, but the ship was rolling as she pushed through the dark water. Soon after midnight the lights of the New Jersey shore resorts began to be seen to port, and at 2 a.m. the navigating officer, Clarence Hackney, reported the ship thirty miles south of the Scotland Lightship. Still on the bridge, Warms acknowledged the information, knowing that it would soon be time for the last change of course which would take the ship into the New York channel. He was elated by what he had done and expected the ship's owners to confirm him as captain, but he was tired and Hackney suggested that he take a rest.

Warms agreed and left the bridge. But he had a sense of foreboding and all he did was prowl through the public rooms and inspect the promenade deck, lounge and smoking room. Only one drunken party still remained, watched by disgruntled stewards.

After half an hour, Warms was back on the bridge and within minutes he received a report of a fire in the writing room on the promenade deck, just forward of the lounge through which he had just passed. He sent Hackney down to investigate.

Hackney found the writing room full of smoke and was told that the seat of the fire was in a locker. As Hackney snatched the locker door open, a mass of flame burst out at him. Running for a fire extinguisher, he emptied it into the locker, but it had no effect whatsoever and the flames roared towards the deckhead and raged about the room. This was no ordinary fire, and the intensity of the flames had all the signs of being caused by an incendiary device.

Running to the nearest telephone, Hackney warned the bridge and, giving orders to rouse the crew, Warms rang the engine room for all possible water pressure. He was reminded that a boiler was still out. Chief Engineer Abbott's reaction on learning of the fire was as strange as everything else that occurred that night. Instead of putting on overalls, as he should have done, and going to the engine room to take charge, he put on his full dress uniform and took up a position on the bridge.

By now the writing room was an inferno and the flames were spreading to the lounge. As smoke filled the corridors, stewards went round hammering on doors to wake sleeping passengers. Although some hoses had been broken out and were being directed at the flames, the pressure was so low that they were virtually useless. There had also been some delay in rigging them. A month previously a woman passenger had sprained her ankle after falling on a deck made slippery by passengers fooling about with the hoses. She had claimed heavy damages and, to stop drunken passengers using the hoses for fun, Captain Wilmott had ordered them to be locked away, the stations capped and the operating spanners removed.

One of the first lessons to be learned about fire at sea is the vital necessity of positioning the ship to the wind so that the flames blow overboard by the shortest possible route. Warms had turned *Morro Castle*'s head into wind to reduce the effect of the squall, and he kept it there for far too long. He also failed to reduce speed and, with the ship moving at nineteen knots into a twenty-knot wind, the passage of air was as strong as if it came from a giant bellows. By Wilmott's orders no fire drills had been held and, as Hanson had not closed the fire doors or shut off the forced ventilation, in no time the entire superstructure of the ship was a mass of flames. As Second Officer Ivan Freeman made for the bridge, he became aware of how bad the fire was. 'We should run for the beach,' he advised Warms. 'In case we have to get the passengers off.'

Warms examined the fire-detecting system. Not a single light showed red, but the system did not cover the public rooms and he had no idea that the smoke-detecting system was switched off. Passengers were also unaware of the danger. Groups were singing, and some were drunk and determined not to waste their last night on board.

Pungent and acrid from the heavy layers of paint and the highly flammable panelling and upholstery, the smoke which enveloped everything crept down passageways and up staircases. It was still raining hard and Warms assumed that the smoke he could see from the bridge was a sign that the fire was being put out. But then, as he turned to check the ship's course, the entire fire-detection system suddenly flashed red and he immediately ordered a turn towards the shore.

In the radio room, just forward of the fire and two decks above the blazing writing room, the two operators were waiting for an order to send out a distress signal, aware that the room was already filling with smoke. George Alagna, the twenty-two-year-old senior radio assistant, had been on duty when the fire started and had roused his chief, George White Rogers. Unknown to anyone on board, Rogers had psychopathic tendencies and a minor criminal record, and Abbott had suspected him of the earlier poison attempt on the captain. Warms thought him the Communist saboteur who was believed to be aboard, but had allowed himself to be persuaded by Wilmott that the Communist agent was Alagna.

Rogers was an enormously fat man. The pituitary disorder which accounted for his size had also produced a social maladjustment. His voice had never deepened and he had been teased about his size. As a boy he had been accused of stealing from other children and had been sent for correctional training to an institution. Even there he had committed petty thefts, was known to be untruthful and a moral pervert, and to have a bad influence on other children.

When the *Titanic* disaster brought about the compulsory placing of radio operators aboard ships, however, he was able to get a job at sea. He had joined the Navy but had been discharged after only a few weeks, and when the Depression arrived he found it hard to make enough to live on. He joined *Morro Castle* in 1934 as a junior operator and promptly set about getting his senior removed. By September he had managed it and was rated senior operator himself.

Neither he nor Alagna had served in *Morro Castle* for more than three months and both were due to be dismissed, Alagna because he had tried to get the crew to take strike action against the conditions they worked under, and Rogers because his dubious past had been discovered. Nevertheless, both radio men knew their duty in an emergency. With no orders coming from the bridge, Rogers sent Alagna to find out what was happening. He returned within minutes, unable to make it to the bridge.

'The flames are roaring up,' he reported, 'and everything is chaos out there.'

When Rogers tried to call the bridge he could get no reply. He sent Alagna off to try again, and when he went to the door himself to look out all he could see was black smoke. Turning to the set, he switched to the distress frequency as Alagna reappeared. 'Come on, chief,' he said. 'Get out of here. We'll die like rats in a trap.'

'What are the orders from the bridge?' Rogers asked. 'Am I to send the distress signal?'

'I don't know,' Alagna admitted. 'They're running around like a bunch of madmen up there.'

Rogers sent him back yet again and he reached the bridge just as Warms gave the order to bring the ship round on a heading for the New Jersey shore. Warms still did not think the situation critical and seemed to believe that he could bring the fire under control, despite the low water pressure and the hamhandedness of new members of the crew. His alteration, however, changed the direction of the fire and now, instead of driving towards the stern, it began to sweep across the ship. As the ship swung, there was a muffled explosion as the powder for the Lyle gun, stored above the writing room, exploded. The roar started a new panic, and seamen started to chop up chairs and tables and stack them near the rails to be flung overboard if necessary for use as rafts. They were working entirely on their own initiative and no officer had appeared to give instructions.

By now, with the water pressure dwindling, the fire had gained a disastrous hold and the upper decks were crowded with terrified passengers, some still the worse for drink. Others, trapped in their cabins, had scrambled through the portholes to fall into the sea. Even though the ship was still moving, the order was given to launch the starboard boats. With the flames sweeping across the deck, it was impossible to reach the port boats.

One steward made for his lifeboat, but it was burning and so was the next. Number 10 boat was undamaged and he put in it three girls who were standing dazed on the sun deck. Then the lights went out and the panic became intense. Drunks were singing and hysterical women were screaming. Others were praying. 'You never heard such praying in your life,' one of the crew members said. 'They were huddled together, kneeling on the deck, calling out loud for deliverance.' When a boat was lowered, dozens tried to fling themselves into it, many falling in the sea and drowning, while crewmen, driven back by the flames, simply abandoned their hoses without turning off the hydrants so that gallons of desperately needed water drained away.

Ten miles away, coastguard stations saw the burning ship. She was also visible to fishermen on shore and was seen by the freighter *Andrea Luckenbach*, steaming on a parallel course to seaward. The freighter's radio officer had heard no SOS and called up the nearest shore station to ask if they had a report of a ship on fire. He received a negative reply.

Rogers heard the question and answer on his own set and decided to take action without waiting for orders. Three times he sent out a stand-by call, and at around 03.18 he sent the same call again to keep the lanes open. The smoke in the radio cabin had become so thick by this time that it was almost impossible to see. The emergency lighting system had failed, but he found a large flashlight and managed to start the auxiliary transmitter. He then realised his feet were burning with heat and, putting his hand to the deck, discovered that it was too hot to touch. Paint began to peel from the bulkhead, and a shift of wind sent flames through the after porthole to set fire to a curtain.

A little after 03.20, nearly an hour after the fire had been reported, Alagna came hurrying back. 'Okay,' he said. 'Send it.' The delay was undoubtedly caused by Warms's awareness that an SOS which proved unnecessary could be expensive and would undoubtedly dim his promotion prospects.

Rogers began to tap the key. 'SOS *Morro Castle*. Afire twenty miles south of Scotland Light. Need immediate assistance.' Halfway through the message, he saw the corner of the table burst into flames.

The room had now filled with what Rogers described as 'some sort of sulphuric gas from the batteries'. Probably, he thought, the hot deck was causing the acid to boil as it bubbled out of them. The receiver was completely out of commission by now, but the transmitter was still functioning and Rogers continued to send the SOS.

He had just finished when the small auxiliary generator stopped because, he said, the connection between it and the batteries had melted. He rose from the table and staggered to the bulkhead, a damp towel to his face. Hardly able to breathe, he had to hang on to the bulkhead for a while to recover, then he rejoined the connections and continued to send the SOS.

Meanwhile, when Alagna reached the bridge once more, he heard that the ship was being abandoned. She had finally been brought to a stop – not by Warms or Chief Engineer Abbott, who was still on the bridge, but by the engineers who had thrown the machinery into neutral and left the engine room.

Learning what had happened, Alagna dashed back to the radio shack. 'Come on, chief,' he yelled. 'Get out of here! The whole damned place is on fire!'

Dragging Rogers towards the bridge, he found Warms apparently in a daze. The splendid ship of which he had taken command only six hours before was now an inferno drifting under the power of the wind and the sea. Only eight lifeboats had been put into the water, but there were already more people in the sea than in the boats, some trying to swim towards the nearest boat, some clinging to debris, some – the strong swimmers – making for the not far distant shore. Many had already drowned.

Chief Engineer Abbott, who had still not been near the engine room, stepped into one of the earliest boats to be made ready and ordered it to be lowered. With a capacity for seventy people, it held only eight, six of them members of the crew. Of the first eighty people lowered away, in fact, over seventy were crew members. But while most of these were stewards with no knowledge of the sea, Abbott was the second most important officer in the ship. Even in his boat, Abbott did not behave with much credit. He claimed that he couldn't help with the rowing because he had cut his hand, when it was obvious to everyone that he had not.

There was panic everywhere now. Injured and burned people lay about, some of whom had been crushed or trampled in the rush for safety. Occasionally a figure burst through the smoke, clothes and hair on fire. The few still aboard were in two groups – one in the bow, consisting of two deck officers, the two radio operators, a few seamen, two passengers and Warms, whose only hope now was to beach the ship. Another group by the stern consisted of passengers, stewards and Smith, the cruise director. The flames were being driven towards the stern group by the wind so that several people jumped overboard, only to be dragged under by suction caused by the movement of the ship's stern.

Charles Wright, the chief steward, was carrying a young girl he had rescued from a blazing cabin. Ducking through the flames, he jumped into the sea with her and, swimming steadily, was carried away from the blazing ship. Then Smith, the cruise director, grabbed a screaming woman passenger and also jumped overboard. Others also jumped, to find themselves in the middle of a mat of struggling people, so that they had to swim hard to draw clear. With the lights of the shore tantalisingly near,

talk to newspapermen, he set off up the beach, tears streaming down his face.

As dawn arrived, the rescue work was well under way, though some of the people in the water had been carried so far by the current that the rescue ships had difficulty finding them. The coastguard vessel picked up seventy survivors altogether, taking the loads to *Andrea Luckenbach* before turning back to pick up more from the water. *Paramount* rescued about another sixty. Among them was Charles Wright, who had supported the young girl he had rescued for two hours until she died. The last person picked up by *Paramount*, at about 10 a.m., was a woman who had been in the water for seven hours. By this time aircraft had joined in the rescue operation and, flying low over the area, were spotting people in the water and signalling their position with smoke bombs.

Robert Smith and the woman passenger he had kept afloat for several hours were picked up by a boat from *Monarch of Bermuda*, whose final count was seventy-one. Her boats saved people hanging from ropes at the stern of the blazing ship and offered to take off the group clustered on the forepeak. Only the two passengers elected to go – Warms, Rogers and the other members of the crew deciding to stay. They had managed to drop an anchor and the ship had finally stopped moving. Warms even had hopes of getting a tow into harbour.

By this time survivors were arriving ashore at various points along the coast, some in lifeboats, some of them swimmers who were helped ashore by watchers on the beach. Thousands of people were lining the New Jersey shore staring out at the burning cruise ship about five miles away, and restaurants and cafés at Asbury Park, Spring Lake and other resorts began to do an unexpectedly lively trade. It was the era of blossoming radio networks, and they had mobile units out to broadcast on-the-spot accounts of this tremendous scoop. Local reporters were also sending copy to newspapers across the country and the *New York Herald Tribune* was able to print an eye-witness account of the arrival of the first boatloads of survivors. Lurid stories of their struggles appeared, and private homes along the shore took them in, put them to bed and fed them hot drinks until medical aid arrived.

But as the Sunday newspapers had already been printed, it left the new medium, radio, with a clear field. It handled the subject brilliantly and, alerted by their radios, people rushed to the beach and began to move in a huge crowd along it, keeping pace with the pall of smoke out to sea. It grew all the time until the tragedy was almost forgotten in the carnival atmosphere that began to prevail, particularly as few of the watchers saw anything of the heartbreak in the shape of a survivor. Yet while people were struggling for life, the impression was still being given by the media that all passengers had been rescued.

As the morning advanced and the wind rose again, the sea increased. A coastguard vessel circling the cruise ship hailed the group of exhausted, grimy men on the bow, asking if they wished to be taken off. Once more they refused, although by this time the ship was little more than a red-hot wreck and was dragging her anchor. Soon afterwards the coastguard cutter *Tampa* arrived and her captain, Lt.-Commander Earl Rose, offered Warms a tow. A hawser was hoisted aboard entirely by manpower and secured with great difficulty. Then the anchor, which would have impeded progress, had to be released as, without steam, there was no mechanical power to hoist it. Taking it in turns to struggle with a hacksaw, the men cut through the three-inch links of the anchor chain.

It was several hours before *Tampa* could take the strain and start to move. A tugboat, hooking on to one of the ropes trailing over the side of the burning ship, acted as a jury rudder, and in the end, with the wind increasing to gale force, Rose insisted on Warms and the other men transferring to his own ship. They were worn out and had been without food and water since the start of the fire.

Throughout the Saturday afternoon, *Tampa* fought to bring the burning hulk into harbour. They had struggled along the coast as far as Asbury Park, one of the coastal resorts, when the stern line, caught by the flames blowing back along it, burned through. For two more hours they fought on, trying to tow the *Morro Castle* into the calm water of New York harbour where the fireboats could get at her, and they finally got the ship's bows pointing seawards in an attempt to offset the wind blowing on to the shore. Taking soundings, however, they discovered that the two ships were drifting towards the beach.

By this time the sky was full of planes carrying newsreel cameramen filming the drama, and the crowds were still on the seafront, staring. The newspapers were having a field day as reporters scoured all the areas where survivors were landing to get their stories. It was a period when American newspapers were not noted for their veracity and, while some gave honest accounts, women were photographed by others with children they claimed to have rescued from the fire. The children had certainly never been aboard *Morro Castle* and probably the women hadn't either. There were lurid stories of looting and bullet-riddled bodies washed ashore, and heroes were created overnight, many of them totally fictitious. One newspaperman who flew out in a hired plane said that flames a hundred feet high were roaring from the ship and the steel hull appeared to be red hot. As they flew over her, he claimed, he saw the funnels melting like lead soldiers on a stove.

It was the day of the quick buck, publicity and razzmatazz and, as the burning ship moved closer to the resort of Asbury Park, a few officials stood on the promenade watching it. Keeping pace with the moving cloud of smoke were around 50,000 people, and one of the officials started estimating their value to the town.

'Just supposing they beached her here,' he said.

In 1884, a journal in the area had considered in a leader that a first-class shipwreck would make the place a famous winter resort and had suggested that it could best take place between the fishing pier and the Asbury Avenue Pavilion. 'We need,' it insisted, 'a spectacular ship.' It was about to have one.

Tampa struggled on for another hour or so, then, as the engine revolutions were increased, the towing hawser broke and the end whipped back to foul *Tampa*'s propeller. Helpless, the crew dropped anchor to avoid drifting back on to *Morro Castle* or grounding on the beach. A few minutes later, through the driving spray, they saw the cruise liner, now nothing but a derelict, blot out the lights of Asbury Park as she came to rest on the beach. She was hard aground right in front of the promenade and the Convention Hall, just where she was wanted, and only a few hundred yards from the local radio station. The announcer took advantage of the scoop of a lifetime. 'She's here,' he yelled into the microphone. 'The *Morro Castle*'s coming right towards the studio!' It was just twenty hours since the fire had been reported in the writing room.

Asbury Park did well out of the wreck. By Sunday morning someone had erected a banner on the Convention Hall: '22 cents to see the *Morro Castle*.' It was a fine day, with the gale gone, and with hurriedly erected signs outside the town to direct them, around 25,000 people turned up, filling the shops and cafés and crowding the hot-dog and soft-drink stands. Primo Carnera, the former world heavyweight champion, who was training in Asbury Park for a South American tour, suddenly found twice as many people paying to watch him spar.

By midday, to the music of hired steam organs, 10,000 visitors had paid for a close-up view of the burnt-out wreck. A breeches buoy had been rigged from the stern to the Convention Hall and scores of newsmen took advantage of it, paying five dollars to be allowed aboard. Fast-talking salesmen were on hand to persuade them that they would need a gasmask, and offered them one for five dollars, with a flashlight thrown in, for – guess what! – another dollar. The money was supposed to be for the firemen on duty, but one newspaperman at least noticed that there were no firemen to be seen.

For two days a group of men searched the wreckage for Captain Wilmott's body. They found nothing but charred bones. Eager to cash in on the disaster, householders let rooms, garages, even lawns, and the Mayor was put under pressure to make the hulk a permanent exhibit. To his credit he refused. Among those who got aboard were looters. One man posing as an underwriter was allowed to search the ship and got away with diamonds he had known were there.

A total of 134 people had died, most of them passengers, and many more had serious injuries. Those who were saved were not slow to condemn the crew who, they claimed, hadn't understood the first principles of fire-fighting. The failure of the coastguard wasn't missed either, but New York papers blamed the inefficiency on the low wages which they said could never induce good men to join.

Meanwhile, Rogers had become the hero of the day and as he was taken to hospital the ambulance was chased by a convoy of cars containing reporters and photographers. Alagna went in a car with the novelist Damon Runyon, at that time a journalist with the *New York American*, who wrote that Alagna believed there might have been a chronic pyromaniac on the ship. Alagna was remembering that after leaving Havana two bottles of acid, one picric, one sulphuric, had been found above his bunk, and he was beginning to suspect that Rogers had put them there. Certainly Rogers had bought acids in Havana, and he had also watched as the Lyle gun with its keg of powder had been placed in the locker over the writing room.

But no one took any notice of Alagna. There had all along been talk of a Communist plot, which was given strength by reports from Havana that the police there had arrested six men they suspected of sabotaging the ship, and officials preferred that story to Alagna's theory. Alagna continued to insist on a firebug, and Rogers promptly denounced his junior operator as a troublemaker.

When the official enquiry began on 10 September, various theories were advanced as to the cause of the fire. Warms, Hackney and Freeman all supported the theory of a fire-raiser, and Rogers again pointed the finger at Alagna. Although the enquiry officials seemed to discount the theory, the cargoes of arms, the lack of boats and fire drills, Warms's earlier suspensions and Abbott's behaviour all came to light, and it was shown that flammable polish had been used by stewards because they found it easier for cleaning brass and woodwork. The enquiry seemed to accept that the fire might have been started from this source, but there was also talk of wild parties and sex orgies, and the suggestion that drunken passengers might have caused the fire. Useless lifeboats were mentioned, and not a day passed without the passengers censuring the crew, or some member of the crew accusing passengers of being too drunk to understand orders.

The court decided that the cause of the fire was spontaneous combustion among cleaning fluids, and that contributing factors were delays in sounding the alarm, lack of training and the poor discipline of the crew. Without doubt, poor discipline and training, and the delay in sounding the alarm and sending an SOS, had a lot to do with the loss of life, but the intensity of the flames suggested more than spontaneous combustion. Was there a cover-up? Prohibition was a period of corruption in many American cities and it is possible that someone had been paid to influence the verdict.

Very few of the ship's staff emerged from the ordeal with credit, and Warms and Abbott were charged before a federal grand jury with 'misconduct, negligence and inattention to duties'.

Frank Rushbrook, a distinguished fire chief and consultant on fire and fire safety, who made a particular study of fire at sea, had no doubt about what caused the disaster. He blamed the ill-organised and haphazard fire-fighting, the panicked behaviour of the acting master, Warms, who failed to slacken speed, and the failure of the crew to help passengers. As he pointed out, number 1 lifeboat, the first away, contained one of the most important of the ship's officers, Abbott, the chief engineer, and of those on board her, only one was a passenger. On the other hand, he also firmly blamed the heavily combustible furnishings of the luxuriously equipped ship, which, he said, had a 'fire load' of the highest order.

One of the few to come out of the affair with credit was Rogers, the wireless operator. He was considered to be a hero and was given a medal by his home town, Bayonne, New Jersey. His dismissal was withdrawn by the Ward Line, and he was offered jobs by a dozen other lines.

Prison terms were imposed on Warms and Abbott but, on appeal, their convictions were set aside and in the end Warms had his master's certificate restored and he went back to sea as second officer on a freighter. Under the complicated liability law, the Ward Line had had little responsibility for insuring the passengers, who had had to take out their own coverage. By the end of 1934 claims totalling over a million dollars had been filed. The Line offered $250,000 as a full and final settlement, but with seventy-one insurance companies, including Lloyds of London, involved, they flinched at the possibility of another public hearing and raised their offer to almost $1,000,000.

The charred hulk of *Morro Castle* was towed off the beach and sold for scrap. A hundred thousand people had paid to view her from Asbury Park's Convention Hall, and the disaster had made small fortunes for many people in the resort. Though the story seemed to have ended, in fact there were more revelations to come. Rogers, the heroic radio operator, soon proved to be different from what everyone had believed.

Seized on by publicity men with an eye for a quick dollar, he moved to New York for a series of personal appearances dressed in an officer's uniform and on a $1000 a week salary as a hero. It didn't last long, and he opened a radio-repair shop in Bayonne. In February 1935 it caught fire and arson was suspected. There was insufficient proof, however, and Rogers collected the insurance.

The following year, helped by a local businessman, he joined the Bayonne Police as a radioman. His superior officer was a man called Vincent Doyle, who had also once been a radioman and had always been suspicious of Rogers's tale of heroism. In the months that followed, as they talked in the quiet hours on duty, Doyle learned how Rogers had experimented with delayed-action fuses and studied the famous Black Tom explosion in the First World War, when an incendiary device had destroyed a New Jersey factory. He also learned that Rogers had been suspected of arson by the wireless company where he had worked, and, as a result of newspaper stories about the methods of German agents in 1915, had dabbled with incendiary and explosive devices himself. He had often had enough of them in his room to destroy a dozen factories. They also talked about *Morro Castle* and, after learning about Rogers's interest in incendiary devices, Doyle compiled a dossier on the case in which he stated that Rogers had told him he had planted the device in the writing room. He did it, Doyle said, because he considered 'the Ward Line stinks and the skipper was lousy'.

One theory about the affair was that Rogers was involved with smuggling and used his radio to pass details of pick-ups and landings to accomplices ashore. A drugs- and liquor-smuggling ring had operated for some time, and the belief was that Rogers got rid of Captain Wilmott because he had been discovered, using poison obtained during the stopover in Cuba when he bought the bottles of acid.

Soon after making his discoveries, Doyle was severely injured by a bomb and was lucky to survive. In March 1938 Rogers was charged with planting the bomb, was convicted and given a long prison sentence. He was released on parole during the Second World War to join the armed services, and returned to sea as a radio operator. He was assigned to a ship heading for Australia, but the voyage ended with his arrest in Darwin on a charge that seemed to involve enemy aliens. He left the sea again and went to work in a war plant in New Jersey, but was dismissed on a suspicion of stealing. He tried another job and this time was dismissed after a number of employees showed signs of being poisoned.

After the war, he opened another radio-repair shop in Bayonne, but a few years later was charged with the savage murder of an eighty-three-year-old retired printer and his daughter. He was found guilty once more and sentenced to life imprisonment, dying of a coronary four years later in 1958 in New Jersey State Prison.

In recent years considerable circumstantial evidence has been gathered by writers that indicates that Rogers did start the blaze in *Morro Castle*, and that he had first poisoned Captain Wilmott. In view of his psychopathic background, it seems very possible. But on the other hand, any one of the 500 people who had been on board could have been guilty of the fire which horrified the nation and brought one of the greatest dramas of the sea directly into the homes of the whole United States by radio and film.

CHAPTER 3

Every day becomes a nightmare

Minerva Reef

From the very first day when man ventured on to the ocean in his ill-constructed boats there have been dangers. The sea is a dangerous element and, no matter how much safety is preached, chances are always taken by incautious sailors. But unexpected changes of weather, unmarked shoals, rocks, fog and wind have also constantly destroyed the lives of experienced and cautious seamen aware of all the sea's moods.

Throughout history ships have been wrecked, and every wreck is a disaster and a tragedy for someone.

Even if a man escaped from the wreck of a ship and was flung up alive on the coast during a gale, in the eighteenth century, and even into the nineteenth, he had to take his chances with what he found ashore. Men of the Spanish Armada were murdered after they had struggled from the sea. Castaways on the coasts of Africa were butchered by natives. Even round the coasts of England men waiting for a ship to strike would not have had much compunction about killing if it meant seizing a small fortune. To people who lived in primitive fishing villages jewellery represented untold wealth, and even the gentry were not averse to helping themselves. Men like the Duke of Buckingham thought nothing of extorting sums as high as £3100 from the owner of a ship wrecked at Dover before restoring his cargo. In 1623, when the *Anne Lyon* was wrecked near Sandwich, £9000 in salvaged coins was taken to Deal Castle. Locals blatantly looted the ship and, though Sir Henry Mainwaring was expected to restore order, in fact he tried to persuade the sergeant-at-arms to slit the bags of specie at the Castle so that no one would be able to identify individual property and he would benefit.

Neither the sea nor the people who lived by it were very merciful. There is the story of the *Chantiloupe*, a vessel returning from the West Indies which ran aground near Bantham. All on board were lost except one man. A woman passenger, probably thinking that if she should be washed ashore a good appearance would help, put on her richest gems and clothes. Instead of being helped, she was seized and stripped and the people who dragged her up the beach cut off her fingers for her rings, mangled her ears for her earrings and left her to die.

When Rear Admiral Sir Cloudesley Shovell's body was washed ashore at Porth Hellick, a sandy bay south of St Mary's in the Scillies, after the loss of his flagship *Association* in 1707, it was said that he was still alive but was murdered by two women for the emerald ring on his finger. The body was buried in the sand and when it was later exhumed for a state funeral it was noticed that 'his ring was lost from his finger'.

When the *Wendela*, a twenty-six-gun frigate, was lost in the Shetlands in 1737, gentry and villagers alike fell on her, jostled, fought, bribed and stole among the litter of bodies and broken rigging, and even troops sent to guard the wreck helped themselves. When a Dutch galliot loaded with wine and brandy was stranded on Thurlestone sands in 1783 'there was come not less than 10,000 people who came from remote parts in order to plunder ye cargo'. When *Royal Adelaide* drove ashore on Chesil Beach with a cargo of spirits, kegs of whisky were washing about the shallows and, despite large numbers of coastguards and customs officers, the entire foreshore was littered with drunken men and women, making love, sleeping where they fell, fighting or just staggering around.

From time to time there was talk of false lights being displayed to lure ships ashore, but little real evidence of wrecking. In a fishing village in Yorkshire in the Thirties, however, there was a tale of a coaster groping its way in thick fog some years before, about to run ashore, and the villagers doing nothing to stop it. It was in fact warned away by a group of city-dwellers fishing from the rocks, who lit a fire of driftwood and banged empty oil drums. When they boasted of their success in the village pub that evening they couldn't understand the sudden silence that ensued.

Despite the absence of real evidence of wrecking, however, after the wreck of the *Charming Jenny* in 1773 three wealthy local citizens were charged with piracy. The captain and his wife, who struggled ashore on a piece of wreckage, were the only survivors and when they were found exhausted on the beach the wreckers cut the buckles from the captain's shoes and stripped him naked. Recovering consciousness, he found his wife, who had carried two bank rolls of considerable value and seventy guineas in her pocket, a half-naked plundered corpse.

Yet sometimes there was reason. The parish was responsible for removing bodies, and after a series of gales in the eighteenth century Dorset newspapers refer to a 'foreshore littered with broken ships and corpses – over a thousand dead to be taken care of by the parish'. In 1796 the foreshore at Porthleven, Cornwall, was strewn with the bodies and belongings of 600 men of a dragoon regiment from a wrecked transport. When the *Annie Jane*, an emigrant ship, was wrecked in 1853 at Barra in the Hebrides with the loss of almost 400 lives, because there was no timber on the bare island to make coffins, the dead had to be carried slung over men's shoulders for ten long miles to the nearest burial ground.

Without doubt, survival depends on luck; it also depends on one other important thing – the determination to survive. There are many examples of people who have survived because they were determined not to die, among them, of course, Captain William Bligh, who steered his single boat a matter of 4000 miles to save the lives of those cast adrift by the mutineers of the *Bounty* in 1789. Courage and an ability to improvise seem to be the key factors.

A group of Tongans marooned in the South Pacific in 1962 endured for three and a half months because they never lost heart and used what skills they possessed to save themselves.

During a gale, the cutter *Tuaikaepau*, with seventeen men

aboard, ran on to the South Minerva Reef. Under the battering of the sea she was reduced to floating planks within hours, so that the men found themselves in darkness without a ship on a bare reef which in a few hours would be beneath the tide. They had neither food nor water and their condition was as hopeless as any of the luckless mariners of history, but most of them survived, keeping themselves alive for 102 days on the bare coral by taking advantage of a wrecked Japanese fishing vessel which lay on the reef on her beam ends. They were able to live on the high side of the ship not reached by the sea, and even managed to find a few items which enabled them to catch fish and make fires. As in many cases of survival, they were blessed with a strong character, David Fifita, the skipper of the cutter, whom they accepted as leader. They were almost all men with strong and sincere religious beliefs, some Catholics, some Methodists, some Mormons, and they held regular prayer meetings.

They were a mixed lot. Apart from the crew, there was a widower travelling just for the trip, a copra planter, a carpenter, a taxi driver, a retired heavyweight boxing champion of Tonga, the current heavyweight and light-heavyweight champion and four other young boxers. The cutter was going to New Zealand for repairs, stopping at islands *en route*, and of the boxers some were hoping to pick up money by fighting in Auckland while others just wanted to see more of the world than their own native island.

From the stranded hulk they cut mild steel to make harpoons and hooks for fishing, built a raft and, with some paint they found, painted an SOS and their position on it; they then launched it into the current in the hope that it would be seen. They also painted an SOS on the exposed aside of the ship in case an aircraft flew over. They constructed a still to give them a few ounces of drinking water a day and even managed to make diving goggles for an attempt – vain as it turned out – to recover tools from the lost cutter.

The first man to die was the widower, and they managed to scratch a shallow grave in the hard coral to lay him in. When the next two died within a short time of each other, they realised that they could no longer bury them. Instead, they buoyed them up with floats found aboard the wrecked fishing boat and, wrapping them in blankets or canvas, wrote an SOS with their position on them and launched them into the sea. Again and again they launched planks, small rafts and drums with their position marked on them. They were strengthened by their faith and, though some of them weakened and broke the rules they devised for survival, they had a splendid sense of loyalty that brought most of them to safety. In the end they encompassed their own rescue by building with a handful of inadequate tools a small decked outrigger of which a boat builder could have been proud. They had to build their boat, which weighed all of a ton, high out of the water on the side of the capsized ship, then lower it carefully down. In their weak state, it was a tremendous task, but seamanship and a knowledge of ropes and tackles enabled them to do it.

Four men altogether died on the reef and one died as the boat – in which three of them, David Fifita, his son and the *Tuaikaepau*'s carpenter, set out to fetch help – was wrecked on the island of Kandavu after a week-long voyage across the empty spaces of the Pacific. As they approached the reef, exhausted after their ordeal, their little boat was capsized by a huge wave and, as they began to swim for the shore, Fifita had to watch his son drown, knowing perfectly well that, with the carpenter also tiring, if he turned back to help his son, he might drown himself and there would be no one to get ashore to bring help to those men still on the reef. The twelve survivors were finally rescued by a flying boat.

The Baileys

The Tongans found that their religion sustained them, but Maurice and Maralyn Bailey – who survived for an incredible 118½ days in a small rubber dinghy four feet six inches in diameter, to which they attached a small life raft – were not in the least religious – indeed Maurice was an atheist – and they never fell back on prayer. They were utterly dependent on the resources that were offered by the ocean and the sky when their yacht was sunk by a whale near the Galapagos in the Pacific on 4 March 1973. The area of the sinking was full of fish and bird life, but to devise ways of catching the creatures and of living and eating required outstanding qualities of ingenuity and determination. Heat and cold, hunger and thirst, storms, capsize, damage to the raft and loss of equipment were all faced and overcome, and the fact that they were passed seven times by ships – none more than one and a half miles away – which failed to see them added to their sense of despair and hopelessness. Finally they were rescued by Korean fishermen.

Their survival after almost four months of incredible hardship must stand as a feat of unparalleled fortitude. They survived by using their brains to make up for lack of physical abilities – Maralyn could not even swim – but they also remained keen observers who kept notes of what went on around them. They did not even have a sea background but had lived in the centre of England. Yet their account of their ordeal was of considerable scientific significance, and for coolheadedness they take some beating; even in the moment of their distress as they lost their boat, they took a series of photographs that showed it sinking. They remained calm enough to scramble a sensible assortment of tins of food into their dinghy, and there were no recriminations – only an instant decision to survive.

They set out from the Hamble river in 1972, crossed the Atlantic, then set off to face the Pacific. It was then that the whale, wounded by a whaling ship they had noticed earlier, smashed a hole in their boat. They made fish-hooks out of safety pins, and caught turtles, sharks and birds. They made themselves a pack of playing cards to pass the time, but because of their flimsy nature they could only play on fine days. On one occasion a ship actually stopped no further than a mile away, then continued. The fact that it did not see them did not lead them to give up and they passed their time planning the boat they would build to take the place of the one they had lost. They suffered a puncture to their dinghy, a violent storm and illness for which they had no cures. When picked up they could not understand the sensation they caused.

With little to do but think, they had no secrecy, no privacy, no inhibitions, and when their morale was low they found themselves saying hurtful things to each other, before immediately apologising. 'I would rather serve a prison sentence,' Maralyn felt when at her lowest ebb. 'At least there would be a . . . date of release.'

'Every day becomes more of a nightmare,' she wrote in the diary she kept.

Endurance

There are of course dozens, hundreds, of accounts of survival from wrecks or founderings. Some are more remarkable than others but, for sheer determination, the survival of Sir Ernest Shackleton and his men tops the lot. The explorers and crew of *Endurance* disappeared from human ken in the Antarctic on 5 December 1914, until they reappeared on 10 May 1916. For eighteen months they had been feared dead, but they had kept themselves alive in appalling conditions by their own efforts after their ship, beset by the ice on 18 January 1915, had broken up, finally effecting their own rescue by a tremendous seventeen-day journey by small boat through some of the worst seas in the world.

It was Shackleton's third expedition to the Antarctic. He had gone there first in 1901 as a member of an expedition led by Robert Falcon Scott. In 1907 he led the first expedition to declare the South Pole as its goal, and they had struggled to within ninety-seven miles of it when they had to turn back because of the shortage of food. The return journey was a desperate race against death, but they made it and Shackleton returned to England a hero and was knighted and decorated by every major country in the world. In 1912 Scott was beaten to the South Pole by the Norwegian, Amundsen, the sadness of the death of Scott and his companions compounded by the fact that Britain, whose record for exploration was unparalleled, had to take a humiliating second place to Norway.

Shackleton then devised a plan to take a ship into the Weddell Sea and land a sledging party of six men and seventy dogs, while at the same time another ship would put into McMurdo Sound at the other side of the continent and lay down caches of food which could be picked up by the sledging party who would reach them by living on the rations they carried, so that they could cross the continent. The scope of the enterprise is indicated by the fact that the crossing remained untried for forty-three more years until Vivian Fuchs led a Commonwealth team on the trek in 1957–8. But Fuchs had heated, tracked vehicles and radio, and was guided by reconnaissance planes and dog teams, and even so was strongly urged to give up. He succeeded only after a tortuous journey lasting nearly four months.

Shackleton was forty years old, with broad shoulders and a strong jaw, and a face that was handsome but often brooding. He had never settled to ordinary life and, with a character that always demanded something daring, he also had an undoubted talent for leadership. *Aurora*, a sealing vessel, was acquired for the Ross Sea party while Shackleton commanded the Weddell Sea group in a ship bought from the Norwegians who had built it for the Arctic. It was christened *Endurance* and Shackleton had no difficulty finding volunteers. He was deluged by applications, including three from girls, and almost without exception they were motivated by the spirit of adventure, because the salaries offered were little more than token payments.

By the end of July 1914 everything was ready, but on the very day that George V presented Shackleton with a Union Jack to carry on the expedition, Britain declared war on Germany. Shackleton placed the entire expedition at the disposal of the Admiralty, but the reply was a one-word telegram: 'Proceed'. *Endurance* sailed five days later.

The crew list contained the names of twenty-seven men but in fact there were twenty-eight on board, an eighteen-year-old called Perce Blackboro, who had been hired to help the cook while the ship was at Buenos Aires, managing to stow away at the last moment. Shackleton was furious. 'If we run out of food, and anyone has to be eaten,' he said, 'you will be the first.'

Endurance reached the Grytviken whaling station in South Georgia, a dependency of the Falkland Islands, on 5 November to learn that ice conditions in the Weddell Sea were the worst in the memory of the Norwegian whaling skippers who operated in the area. The Weddell Sea was roughly circular in shape, so that much of the ice formed there was prevented from escaping into the open sea, and a strong current moving in a clockwise direction tended to pack it tightly against the western side of the sea.

Endurance left South Georgia on 5 December and they spent Christmas Day in the Antarctic Circle, then on 18 January, as they moved south, the ship was beset by the ice, as one man put it 'frozen, like an almond in the middle of a chocolate bar'. The northerly gale had compressed the pack ice against the face of the land, and no force on earth could open it up except a gale from the opposite direction. As the southern winter days grew shorter, the ship was a tiny speck embedded in nearly 1,000,000 square miles of ice slowly being rotated by the clockwise sweep of the winds and currents.

In May they saw the last of the sun, then, after a period of half light, they were left in darkness. In the polar night, there is no warmth, no life, no movement, but Shackleton's men made their own amusements, keeping diaries and playing cards, kept warm by a coal-burning stove and the insulation provided by *Endurance*'s thick sides. As spring arrived, they began to hope for the break-up of the ice, but instead it began to build up a tremendous pressure against the ship. All this time, they were being carried in a clockwise direction round the south side of the Weddell Sea, and as the pressure mounted the ship began to groan.

Anyone who has seen ice floes building up can vouch for their power. Floes four feet thick and as big as tennis courts, moving inexorably along a coast on a tide towards the sea, are heavy enough to carry with them boats, moorings and anything else in their path. The ice of the Antarctic is immeasurably thicker and in vaster floes, so that the pressure was tremendous, and on 27 October, after being beset for ten months, *Endurance* began to break up. She sank on 21 November and the men were left in the middle of the ice with nothing but the ship's three boats, the dog teams and sledges and what they had been able to salvage, marooned on a huge floe with no hope of rescue.

They were all well aware of what had happened to Sir John Franklin's expedition in 1845, when his two ships had been beset. Not a single man of the 127 who were with him had survived. They were also not unaware of what had happened when Adolphus Greeley's American arctic expedition of twenty-five men was stranded in 1881. Three separate expeditions were sent after him; the third found only Greeley and six of his men alive, on the point of starvation. All the rest had perished.

They were obviously going to have to save themselves and, telling his men they must be ruthless in getting rid of excess weight, Shackleton added point to his words by taking out a gold cigarette case and several gold sovereigns and tossing them on to the ice. Men with diaries were allowed to keep them, and one man who had made a zither banjo was ordered to take it along. They were aiming for a point 346 miles north-west, where they knew food had been cached in 1902. The floe they were on was more than half a mile in diameter and made up of ice ten feet thick with five feet of snow on top of that.

On 30 October, stripped down to absolute necessities, they set off north, the sledges pulled by the dogs, with two of the three boats on runners, pulled by the men. In the first two hours they covered a scant three-quarters of a mile and, realising the boats and sledges would not last very long over the confusion of tumbled ice, Shackleton decided on another plan. Their advance hardly merited the effort they had put into it and, since the floe they were on was strong and spacious, he decided that it would be wiser to stay where they were and let the drift of the ice carry them closer to land.

Salvation was going to take a long time, so he sent dog teams back to the camp they had established when they had abandoned the ship to bring back anything that might be of value, including the third boat. In less than a week they had gone from a well-ordered life aboard ship to one of primitive discomfort, unending wet and inescapable cold, crammed together in overcrowded tents and lying in sleeping bags on the bare ice.

They managed to salvage a few stores from the wreck, and, to save their rations, began to live off seal and penguins. By January they expected to find open water by which they could escape in the boats. If the pack stopped moving, rather than spend the winter camped on the ice they would abandon the boats and dash for the nearest land, using a small punt they had built to ferry them across any open water in their path. The third prospect was grim indeed. If the pack drifted eastwards, they would have to spend the winter adrift on the floes, trying to survive the polar night with its paralysing cold and violent storms.

Shackleton suffered an almost pathological dread of losing control of the situation. It arose out of his sense of responsibility. He had got his party into its present fix and, feeling he must get them out of it, he was careful to allot possible troublemakers to tents where there was a balancing personality.

By 13 November they had been carried by drift about 275 miles north-west, and Shackleton announced that if the pack ice would only open they would launch the boats. He was careful, nevertheless, to issue an emergency-stations plan so that everyone knew exactly what to do if their floe broke up unexpectedly. Meanwhile the carpenter, Harry McNeish, began to raise the low sides of the boats for their journey across some of the worst waters in the world. Largely thanks to Shackleton, the men retained an astonishing optimism. He was known always as the Boss and he *was* the Boss.

On 20 December 1915 Shackleton tried to make a survey of the ice to the west in the hope of finding a way to land. The results were disappointing and the men were now living entirely on seal meat and blubber. With the possibility of having to endure another winter as the food situation grew worse, the thoughts of the men were once more on the fate of the Greeley expedition and Shackleton was growing anxious. They were still drifting northwards, but the opening in the ice they expected refused to come.

1916 arrived and they were no nearer salvation. It was now five months since *Endurance* had broken up. Their tea and coffee were finished and they were reduced to one ration of very diluted powdered milk a day. On 23 March the drift took them within sight of land; then suddenly on 27 March the floe which had supported them so long began to split. The last of the dogs were shot and everybody moved to the largest part of what was left of the floe. By 3 April the floe which had once been a mile wide was now less than 200 yards across, and on 5 April they realised that the drift had carried them straight towards the open sea. On 6 April they again sighted land, Clarence Island, and then the floe broke again. And then again, and the following night Shackleton gave the order to launch the boats.

The oarsmen were hopelessly out of practice, but they gradually put the soot-blackened floe which had been their home for nearly four months behind them. Caught in a tide rip, they were almost overturned but, threading through the ice in a cross sea, they made their way north-west. One boat carried eight men, one nine and one eleven, but they were uncomfortably crowded because of the equipment they were obliged to carry to survive. They camped that night on a floe, but it split beneath them and they were only just in time to rescue one of the men who had been flung into the water still in his sleeping bag. With no means of drying his clothes, he was walked up and down until they dried, his companions listening to the crackle and tinkle of the ice crystals that fell from him. Though he made no complaints about his clothes, he grumbled for hours about losing his tobacco.

They continued to move north, unable to take sightings because of the weather, until eventually they realised they were in the open sea and that somewhere just to the north was land. Camping on a floe-berg, praying it would last the night, by daylight they realised it was crumbling beneath them, but with the gale that was blowing they dared not launch the boats, which would have been smashed within minutes by the ice.

At last a pool opened and they launched the boats. Using sail and oars, they continued northwards until on 12 April they discovered from a sighting that they were twenty-two miles further from land than when they had first launched the boats. An easterly current had been carrying them away from their goal, Joinville Island.

Tired and discouraged, they sat in silence in the boats. Once again they moored to a floe, but once again they had to make a hurried departure and for a second night running were without sleep. Their clothes set stiff, and when dawn came cheeks were drained and white and eyes bloodshot from the salt spray and the fact that they had slept only once in four days.

With daybreak, they decided that they must run for Elephant Island, and they worked their way through the floes. Just before noon, they broke into the open sea again and found themselves faced with enormous swells, three tiny boats packed with twenty-eight suffering men in a final desperate bid for survival. There was no turning back. If this leg of the journey didn't succeed they would all die.

That night the temperature dropped lower and lower and the wind increased with the darkness. It was so cold that the seas which broke over them froze at once. As the hours dragged on, their agony deepened and at times they were sitting almost knee-deep in the water. Blackboro, the stowaway, began to suffer from frostbite.

Then, as the sun appeared, they saw Elephant Island ahead of them. The sleeping bags were sheathed with ice and the boats were thick with it. It took more than an hour to chip away enough to make them fit for sailing. They had had no sleep for more than eighty hours and their bodies had been drained by exposure of the last vestige of vitality.

It was decided that the boats should make their way independently, and they lost touch with each other as they struggled in a ferocious tide rip. They were on the brink of exhaustion with the wind screaming to new heights but, as dawn broke, they saw Elephant Island rising out of the mists ahead. They were facing tremendous offshore gusts of wind sweeping off the cliffs but, bailing frantically, they survived. The following day by a miracle they all found each other again and one after the other touched land. For the first time in 497 days they were on solid earth. It was the merest handhold, 100 feet wide and fifty feet deep, a meagre grip on a savage coast exposed to the full fury of the sub-antarctic ocean. But there were seals and a rookery of penguins and, standing on the beach, they drank hot water and milk powder and ate seal steaks. Then they unrolled their soaked sleeping bags and slept 'as they had never slept before'. Shackleton allowed them to sleep late the next morning, but at breakfast he announced that they would have to move because the spit where they had landed was tenable only in good weather and while the tides were moderate. Yet for the first time they were aware that – comparatively at least – there was no imminent threat of disaster.

They broke camp at dawn and managed to land again seven miles further along the coast. The spot was no more hospitable but it was safer, and once more they were all on land and safe. The wind was so strong, however, that they could not use the tents and a blizzard started. On 20 April Shackleton announced that he would take a boat and a party of five men and sail for South Georgia to bring relief. Nobody was surprised. They knew perfectly well that not a soul knew where they were and that there was no likelihood of a rescue. With the prevailing winds generally astern South Georgia would be the best place to aim for, but it was a terrifying prospect because they were proposing to sail nearly 1000 miles in a twenty-two-foot boat in icy storm-wracked waters.

The planks which had raised the sides of the boats were removed to make decking for the boat they intended to use. The discomfort was now so intense in winds that reached 120 miles an hour that sleep was almost impossible. Faces were cut by flying ice and rock and most of the group spent all their time in their sleeping bags.

The party to leave – in the boat they had christened *James Caird*, after one of the sponsors of the expedition – were to have six weeks' supply of food and a primus stove, and everything that could be spared in the way of clothing was rounded up. As soon as the weather moderated on 24 April, the *Caird* set off and the remaining twenty-two men turned away, knowing that they were now quite helpless because the *Caird* had taken the best of everything they possessed. The two remaining boats were inverted to form a hut. With the arrival of May they knew that winter was once more only a matter of weeks – possibly days – away, and they were suffering from salt-water boils that refused to heal, toothache and abscesses. The most serious invalid was Blackboro, in whose left foot gangrene had attacked the toes. On 15 June it became necessary to perform an operation. They had a little chloroform and, using the cooking pot to sterilise the instruments, the toes were removed. Midwinter's day arrived on 22 June and by 19 August they had to accept that it was no good deceiving themselves any longer.

But in fact the *Caird* had reached land. The occupants had had to endure an unbelievable journey through the ice, but within two days had travelled 128 miles. They faced dreadful winds and enormous waves, living in a grey world of overcast skies and sombre seas with no sound but the hissing of water about them. By the 28th they were all suffering from puffy dead-white feet, but by 29 April they had covered 238 miles and were one-third of the way. On 2 May they lost the sea anchor, which was essential for giving them some sort of rest from the incessant labour of sailing, but by 3 May they had put 403 miles behind them. Several times they were certain that they were lost, but they always managed to survive, and on 8 May they saw the land they were seeking. For nearly two more days they struggled to reach it, and on 10 May *Caird*'s keel ground against the rocks and once more they were on dry land.

They had reached South Georgia, but were still not finished. On 18 May Shackleton set out with two men to cross the island, leaving the remaining three men living under the overturned boat. After another incredible journey, at times struggling through snow and ice at over 4000 feet, they found themselves on a ridge so sharp that Shackleton was able to sit on it with a leg on either side. The light was fading fast and it was essential that they move lower down or they would freeze. Their descent was maddeningly slow, and Shackleton finally suggested sliding. Sitting down in a row, the man behind Shackleton locked his legs round Shackleton's waist and his arms round his neck, while the third man did the same to him and, looking like tobogganers without a toboggan, they shot down the slope at a tremendous speed, faster and faster, until the slope eased off and they ended up in a bank of snow. What had been a terrifying prospect two minutes before had turned into a tremendous triumph.

They had to cross more ridges, and then, as they started down, a faint sound that could only be a steam whistle reached them. It was the signal for the men at a whaling station to wake. It was the first sound they had heard from the outside world for seventeen incredible months.

At four o'clock in the afternoon of 20 May the whaling station foreman saw three gaunt figures approaching. Their faces were almost black, their hair hung to their shoulders, and they were not wearing the clothing sailors wore. The factory manager knew Shackleton well, but as he stared at the three ragged figures he said, 'Who the hell are you?' The man in the centre stepped forward. 'My name is Shackleton,' he said.

A whale-catcher was sent to pick up the remainder of the boat party, but as Shackleton set out for Elephant Island, a series of maddeningly frustrating rescue attempts began which lasted more than three months, during which it seemed that the pack ice was determined to let nothing through. But on 30 August they finally made it and the rest of the party were reached.

Shackleton had achieved something that was almost unbelievable. Though the expedition had failed, he had brought out every man alive and, apart from minor injuries, sickness and one heart attack, reasonably well.

Despite the war that was raging, their return became a worldwide sensation. Shackleton's face was everywhere and the story caught the imagination of the world. Shackleton's influence on his party had been incredible and at no time had he lost control. He could not stay still, however, and in 1921 he left once more for a three-year tour of Antarctica, but died of a heart attack on the way. He was only forty-eight.

CHAPTER 4

'Rich the treasure, sweet the pleasure'

Among the oldest of the legends connected with the ocean is that of lost treasure.

Talk of treasure has always excited the imagination of land-bound people. Most boys are brought up on *Treasure Island*, Captain Bones' gold and the song 'Fifteen men on the dead man's chest'. The seventeenth and eighteenth centuries provided pirates in plenty, and since pirates hoarded gold it was assumed that caches of treasure, the loot from captured galleons, lay on islands all over the world. Everybody has heard of William Leach, who went by the name of Blackbeard, of Sir Henry Morgan and Captain Kidd, and many a boy dreamed of finding one of their buried chests. Blackbeard's treasure has never been found. Nor was that of Henry Morgan. William Kidd's treasure was different and a big question mark hangs over it.

Kidd, born in 1645, was a Scot who emigrated to America as a young man. In 1691 he was awarded £150 by the council of New York for his services as a privateer against the French. He was put in command of a ship in 1696 with orders to seize the pirates who at that time infested the eastern seas, and reached Madagascar in 1697. In 1698–9, however, news reached England that, instead of ridding the seas of pirates, Kidd was associating with them and plundering trading vessels himself.

He was heard of in the West Indies and a naval squadron was sent there to hunt him down, and he was finally caught. Charged with the murder of one of his crew and with piracy, he was found guilty and hanged at Execution Dock, London, in 1701.

He was reputed to have amassed and hidden away somewhere a vast treasure acquired from his depredations of shipping in the east, and the night before he was hanged he was said to have given his wife a slip of paper bearing a number of figures. The figures meant nothing to the prison authorities, who were all landsmen, but to a navigator who saw them they immediately meant a position on a chart. The name given to the spot was Deer Island. The figures, however, were incomplete, and whether Kidd's wife ever did anything about using the paper, and whether it *did* in fact indicate the position of the treasure chest, was never discovered, but intriguing stories emerged.

In 1932 an Eastbourne solicitor called Hubert Palmer, who was a keen collector of antiques, came into possession of an old sea chest which he discovered had belonged to Kidd. In a secret panel he found a map of an island. He thought little of it beyond the speculation that it might be a treasure map, but pirates were notorious for keeping their hoards secret, even for making false maps to throw off the scent any of their crews who might have ideas about sharing them. But then he came across a desk which he learned had been on Kidd's ship and this also contained a map which was an exact copy of the one he already possessed.

Unfortunately, neither map mentioned an ocean or gave a position, because doubtless Kidd kept the secret of its position in his head, and the map seemed to indicate simply a position on an island known to the owner of the map, who could only have been Kidd or one of his henchmen. Numerous maps have been found since, but no treasure has been unearthed and Palmer died before he could set up an expedition. He had taken advice from the Royal Navy, however, and his island seemed to be in the area of the China Seas.

Other expeditions were set up, but nothing was found. Then in 1952 Japanese fishermen reported finding drawings of a goat in a cave on an island near Formosa – in the China Seas – and Kidd was known to have used the sign of a young goat (or kid) as a signature.

Nothing was heard of the fishermen ever doing anything about their discovery, but an astute Japanese student did. He learned where the cave was and later reported finding treasure worth, in 1952 values, £30,000,000. He had no money of his own but he approached a wealthy businessman to act as backer. Money was raised for an expedition and the treasure was supposedly taken to Tokyo. But it was noticeable that nothing further was heard of it and the Japanese police, pushed into action by the wealthy backer, were reported to have been looking for the student who had vanished into thin air.

Kidd undoubtedly had a treasure hoard somewhere. But did the scholar really find it, or was he just a clever swindler who took advantage of the fishermen's discovery of the drawing of a goat to extract money for the expedition and then quietly disappear?

Because there *is* treasure, from other than pirate hoards – bullion being carried from one country to another, to finance wars, to bail out a failing friendly nation, to pay debts or to buy weapons. One of the greatest hoards of sunken treasure still waiting to be found went down with the *Merchant Royal*, lost in September 1641 with a king's ransom taken from the Spanish. There were no survivors and the loss to the Treasury was such that Samuel Pepys felt it necessary to interrupt proceedings in the House of Commons to pass on the information. *Egypt*'s bullion – £1,054,000 of it – was raised after she sank off Ushant in 1922. Five tons of gold being carried in HMS *Edinburgh* from Russia to England to pay for the weaponry which helped the Russians destroy the invading Nazi divisions was lost when the ship was torpedoed in 1942. It was raised in 1981.

In 1985 porcelain from Nanking valued at £10,000,000 was salvaged from the wreck of *Geldermalsen*, which sank in the South China Sea in 1752. It wasn't gold, but it was treasure, nevertheless, and it is accepted these days that treasure can be mere artifacts which not only have a value but also enrich the knowledge of the period in which they were made.

In 1982 a whole ship, *Mary Rose*, was raised. She was the only survivor of a period of rapid but poorly documented change in ship design, and her sinking in 1545 was so sudden and unexpected that everything inside the hull was trapped and preserved – not only fittings, guns and weaponry, but personal objects like clothes, jewellery, books, even a barber-surgeon's medical kit. These were all in everyday use and made the ship a perfect time-capsule of ordinary Tudor life. Because she wasn't carrying treasure, however, she held no interest for those seeking only wealth and she was never ravaged by greedy hands.

Britain is surrounded by wrecks, and treasure from Spanish, Dutch and English ships almost beyond counting, sunk by treacherous rocks and protruding headlands, still lies waiting to be raised. Ships from Plymouth to the Orkneys, from Cardigan Bay to Norfolk; from Roman barges dating from AD 100 to *Annie Jane*, the emigrant vessel lost with 348 lives at Barra in 1853; from *Association*, and three others lost with around 2000 men in a matter of minutes off the Scillies, to *Laurentic*, 14,892 tons, mined off Ireland in 1917 with £6,000,000 in gold aboard, almost all of which was recovered, and *Empire Politician*, which sank off South Uist, carrying a cargo of whisky, the salvage of which by the locals was the inspiration for Compton Mackenzie's uproarious story, *Whisky Galore*.

One of the differences in treasure-seeking these days is that sunken ships can now be explored, and wrecks have become a challenge to underwater explorers. Thousands of silver and gold coins have been recovered, but the 'treasure' modern divers seek is not just bullion but a knowledge of the past, and the challenge is not just in the diving but in piecing together the identity of the lost ships.

Roland Morris, a Cornishman with the sea in his blood, had always dreamed of finding the treasure of Sir Cloudesley Shovell, Commander-in-Chief, Mediterranean, in the days of Queen Anne. Ordered home to England with a fleet of twenty-one ships, he headed north in his flagship, the ninety-four-gun *Association*, aboard which was a vast shipment of gold and silver intended for Spain but captured after a battle in Vigo Bay in 1702. On 22 October 1707, in a gale off the Scillies, Shovell ordered his ships hove to, to confer with his sailing masters who all reported good depths ahead of them. Shovell decided that the fleet was in the latitude of Ushant and ordered three of his ships to sail with despatches for Falmouth. He was wildly wrong, and they were barely out of sight when they found themselves among the treacherous outcrops of the Scillies. Two managed to survive but the third ran ashore. Beyond signalling distance, there was no way they could warn the following ships and, driven by a howling gale, the eighteen following ships pitched and rolled towards disaster. Within minutes four ships and 2000 men had been lost, among them *Association* with Shovell and the treasure.

For years people thought of the wealth lying off the Scillies without trying to reach it, then, in the late 1960s, Roland Morris picked up at a sale an old map which he realised showed not only *Association*'s position but also the position of two of the other ships. In 1967 he began to bring up a number of gold and silver coins; the media seized on the story, with the result that almost immediately there were others on the site. Morris continued his researches, then a silver plate with Shovell's crest on it was brought up to prove that what they had found was definitely *Association*. Once again the media thought up stories of a £3,000,000 treasure, and brought more treasure-seekers to the Scillies.

At the time Britain was one of the few countries in the world with historic wrecks which had no legislation to protect them, and people seeking to enrich themselves used crude methods, including dynamite, that often destroyed what was, if not treasure in the conventional sense, treasure in the sense that it was knowledge.

The Crown at one time saw shipwreck as an opportunity to swell treasury funds at no expense to authority, and a legal controversy has always revolved round what is termed 'right of wreck'. 'Right of wreck' refers to the legal beneficiary of shipwreck in a particular area, regardless of whether it be cargo, ship's stores, part of the fabric of the vessel or a complete ship. In the twentieth century the word 'wreck' embraces not only ships and cargo but anything unnatural to the sea, including such things as crashed aircraft, dead animals, and dinghies, provided it is on or under the surface, within territorial waters, or ashore below the highest spring tide mark. Ownership of items of shipwreck has been the subject of countless orders in council, proclamations, acts of Parliament, high court injunctions, writs, legal wrangles and prosecutions. When *Beulah* was stranded near Barnstaple, Devon, in 1764, the tide surveyor looking after the wreck to prevent looting was attacked over the contents of a chest of drawers which had floated ashore. Mrs Budd, wife of the tenant of the land where the ship was lying, beat him over the head with an iron ladle, claiming that whatever was washed ashore belonged to her husband, and before she could be restrained the surveyor was badly injured. The drawers contained nothing of value.

In 1970 John Nott, MP for St Ives, proposed an amendment to the existing Act for protecting historic wrecks and in 1973 the Act gave legal rights to a wreck to its discoverer. It led to Roland Morris and others recovering hundreds of items, not only from *Association* but from other ships, and finally to his finding of *Colossus*, a seventy-four-gun ship which Nelson had put at the disposal of his good friend, the diplomat Sir William Hamilton, husband of Nelson's mistress Emma and an expert on Greek and Roman antiquities. Badly in need of a refit, *Colossus* was sent home with wounded and with French ship fittings captured at the Battle of the Nile, and Nelson also ordered a consignment of coin and eighteen crates of Hamilton's collection, one of the finest of Greek and Etruscan pottery in the world, to be put aboard. In a winter gale, the ship ran aground on the Southern Wells reef off the island of Samson.

Fortunately, Sir William had commissioned folios of drawings and paintings of the pottery so that when shards of pottery were brought up it wasn't difficult to identify them. Over £1,000,000 came from the Scillies wrecks, among them the Dutch East Indiaman *Hollandia*. Another wreck in the area, the *Princesse Maria*, produced little because of the pillaging that had occurred at the time of her foundering. Even James II, the reigning monarch, had sent his yacht to the islands and had had delivered to him 13,000 pieces-of-eight.

Grosvenor

Some treasures have a particularly poignant interest. The East Indiaman *Grosvenor*, wrecked on the coast of Pondoland, south-west of Natal, on 4 August 1782, has never been forgotten in the 200 years since it happened.

The story of *Grosvenor* began in March 1782, when she sailed from Madras for England. Her departure had been delayed by the East India Company, who had intended that she should sail with two other Indiamen. But one of these failed to arrive and the other was condemned as unseaworthy, so, instead, it was decided that she should sail as a single ship with the naval squadron lying in Madras Roads.

The arrangement didn't please Captain John Coxon, the master, as it meant that he had to wait on the instructions of Admiral Sir Edward Hughes, commanding the squadron; and he had little love for the Navy which had recently pressed into service eighteen of his best seamen and one of his midshipmen. It also meant that the ship would meet with bad weather in the region of the Cape of Good Hope through leaving so late in the year. He protested vigorously, stressing that the 'owners of the said ship *Grosvenor* shall not be responsible or accountable for any damage . . . to the said homeward-bound cargo'.

What was the cargo the captain was so concerned about? In February, while waiting in Madras, the ship had taken on a cargo of 'coast goods'. The value of these and a consignment of diamonds received later was given in a letter which still exists. The total amount came to about £75,000, but this was the purchase price and the East India Company reckoned that the value of the goods when they reached England would be in the region of £300,000. In addition, some of the passengers were carrying their wealth back to England with them.

Grosvenor was a fine ship of English oak, square-rigged on three masts, her length almost 140 feet, her beam just over thirty-five feet, and Coxon first took her over in 1778. In his early forties, he was a capable, much respected captain who had been at sea since the age of seventeen, always in ships owned by or on charter to the East India Company.

The ship sailed from Madras with Admiral Hughes's squadron on 30 March 1782 for Trincomalee, where she remained for nearly two months, finally setting sail for England alone on 14 June. There were eleven adult European passengers on board, some of whom had made fortunes in India. There were also six children and several servants. William Hosea, of the East India Company, the most prominent of the passengers, was returning to England with his wife and daughter after seventeen years' service.

Due to a mistake in navigation, during a gale the ship struck a reef just south of where modern Durban lies. There were 123 survivors, of whom twenty-five were Lascars, but they were a frightened, demoralised lot, and when large groups of natives armed with assegais began to appear it was decided that they should try to reach the nearest white settlement, about sixteen days' march away. Coxon divided the company into three groups: one, consisting of Lascars, led by Shaw, the second mate; one, which included the passengers, under Beale, the third mate; and one, under the leadership of Coxon, consisting of the rest of the officers and crew. Logie, the chief mate, was so ill that he had to be carried in a hammock in Beale's party. The provisions were shared out and two men decided to stay behind and take their chance.

The orderly march lasted only a few days and covered only thirty to forty miles. By Sunday 11 August the provisions were nearly all gone and morale was low. The stronger people decided that they must forge ahead, leaving the women and children, and try to bring help. Several passengers and crew put themselves under the leadership of Shaw and parted from the rest of the group. With them went a small boy passenger who had become fond of the ship's steward and could not be separated from him.

There remained forty-seven people, including Coxon, Mr and Mrs Logie, Mr and Mrs Hosea, and all the children except the one with the steward. Of this party, only six men and two women – Mrs Logie's coloured maid and Mrs Hosea's maid – reached friendly territory. Of the rest nothing was ever seen again.

The story of the terrible journey was set down by William Habberley, a young sailor who was one of the six male survivors who reached a friendly Dutch settlement on 14 January 1783. All that was known of Coxon's party came out later. Mrs Logie's maid and Mrs Hosea's maid were found in different parts of the country. Mrs Logie's maid said the captain's party had split up and that Logie, her master, was almost dead when she left.

Others were equally bad. She had left in the hope of catching up with the Lascars, and eventually she joined some natives, with whom she lived for a time. One of them, she said, was wearing Coxon's coat.

There was one exception among Coxon's party, a man who travelled on at least 150 miles before dying. Habberley mentioned meeting him. 'At low water we went to the rocks at the mouth of Stone river [actually the Great Kei river, just north of present-day East London] and found on them George McDonald, carpenter's mate.' McDonald preferred not to continue with Habberley's group, although he was so weak he could not stand.

Rumours that the women were captured by natives and had settled down with them persisted. A rescue expedition found skeletons wearing scraps of clothing, and heard that a number of half-castes – descendants of Europeans who had been shipwrecked – were in the area, but these proved to be castaways from a much earlier wreck.

The expedition never reached the scene of the wreck, but in 1790 another expedition did reach what was believed to be the site and found five cannon and a quantity of ballast. The leader wrote an account but didn't give enough detail to identify the site. Meanwhile, Habberley and the other British survivors had been giving evidence at the enquiry into the loss of the ship conducted by the Official Hydrographer to the East India Company, Alexander Dalrymple, who tried to establish the position of the wreck. The latitude given by the seamen varied considerably, and Dalrymple came to the conclusion that the wreck occurred 'nearly in twenty-eight degrees thirty minutes south'. He was about 200 miles out.

The differing opinions about latitude led to a great deal of confusion. Professor P. R. Kirby of the University of Witwatersrand, the foremost modern authority on the wreck, concluded that the site found by the second expedition was certainly the site of a wreck, but it was not necessarily that of *Grosvenor*. In any case, by this time the real mystery was: did *Grosvenor* carry treasure?

The story has never died that she sailed with gold bars and silver ingots worth around £3,000,000; chests stuffed with diamonds, rubies, sapphires, emeralds and ivory; together with the valuable luggage of the wealthy passengers, and the load of silks and spices an Indiaman normally carried. There were certainly diamonds. There is also mention of miscellaneous goods and of a 'present' Coxon was taking home.

After the wreck gold coins were picked up from the sand by natives who, not realising their value, preferred the metal and copper cooking pots they snatched from the survivors. In 1800, 2000 gold coins were said to have been found. In 1852, more coins of gold and silver turned up. In 1880 Sidney Turner of Durban, who decided to dynamite the rocks round the site, produced more coins, some of them minted in India and all of the right date. It was this find and a newspaper reference to possible bullion which led to the idea that *Grosvenor* contained immense riches. But nothing more substantial than the coins, some bullets, cuff-links, part of a ring and other small objects appeared.

In 1905 the Grosvenor Recovery Syndicate was formed to search for the treasure, but they did not even find *Grosvenor*. In 1907 another attempt, using a dredger and divers, was made by a company whose articles stated that its intention was to recover and market 'all the treasure whether in bullion, precious stones, bar gold or silver bars'. In 1921 a bigger and better syndicate was formed, whose prospectus gave mouth-watering details of gold, silver, tin, ivory, emeralds and rubies, and corroborative evidence such as quotations from *Grosvenor*'s log. Most were the work of a lively imagination, and the syndicate found nothing of interest or value.

The greatest *Grosvenor* legend was born in 1923. An anonymous writer in the *Cape Times* produced an article describing the work of the last syndicate, quoting the fictitious log and adding that besides the bullion there were indications that the *Grosvenor* had carried two priceless golden peacocks, looted from the Peacock Throne made for Shah Jehan, builder of the Taj Mahal. The throne was said to be constructed round two peacocks, tails spread and thickly encrusted with sapphires, rubies, emeralds, pearls and other jewels. It was valued at £6,000,000.

Later expeditions in search of *Grosvenor* all appear to have had the golden peacocks in mind. The organisers wanted to believe the story. Was the throne the 'present' Coxon was supposed to be bringing home, and was the reference a way of mentioning something too valuable to name? Or was the writer merely trying to improve the chances of the syndicate?

As late as 1938, another salvage company was formed and its prospectus stated the value of *Grosvenor*'s cargo at approximately £5,000,000. One of its promoters stated firmly in a letter to the press that after Hyder Ali had been defeated, his treasure, amounting to £3,000,000 was shipped to England in *Grosvenor*. This sum did not include the two golden peacocks with their diamonds, rubies, sapphires and pearls whose value, it stated, had been fixed at £6,000,000. If they were not in *Grosvenor*, it asked, where were they?

In 1950 yet another expedition made an attempt and announced that the wreck had positively been located off the Pondoland coast. But as the company ran out of money little further was done. Are the diamonds still in the wreck? As recently as 1954 frogmen tried diving, but the discoveries of cannon claimed to be *Grosvenor*'s were suspect because the area was a noted spot for wrecks and the guns may well have come from other ships. There has never been any real proof that there was treasure in *Grosvenor*, and many of the prospectuses and the companies that were formed for its recovery smack of fraud.

And yet . . .

More than 1000 uncut diamonds were found in a sandy plot of land near the Great Kei river, just above high-water mark. Experts decided that the stones could not have originated in South Africa and that they must have come there by human agency, possibly from a wreck. Professor Kirby made a strong case for them coming from *Grosvenor*. His researches revealed that Hosea, while still in India, made arrangements to insure rough diamonds valued at £7,300 and gold and silver bullion worth £1,700, which he had intended to send to England but in the event took with him in *Grosvenor*. It is not too much to suppose that when the ship was wrecked Hosea and Coxon, who also had a consignment of diamonds in his charge, took their valuables ashore with them. Later, when the castaways split up, both men realised that their only hope of survival was in some strong man reaching civilisation with the stones and persuading the Dutch to send a rescue party. This, Professor Kirby thought, might account for the presence of George McDonald at the mouth of the Great Kei river and for his unwillingness to accompany Habberley's party up the river.

This treasure trove gave credence to the reports of *Grosvenor*'s wealth. The salvage attempts of the Fifties were concentrated 500 yards from the traditional site and resulted in iron fittings, lead and ballast being found. But no treasure. Professor Kirby was of the opinion, in fact, that it was nothing but idle dreams. Yet hardheaded businessmen persisted for years in investing money to search for it. And why was the East India Company so keen to establish the exact site of the wreck? It even went to the extent of asking the Admiralty to send a ship to search that part of the South African coast. Other East Indiamen had been lost – eight in 1783 alone – yet the company never showed so much interest as it did in *Grosvenor*. Did its Court of Directors have more knowledge of *Grosvenor*'s cargo than they admitted?

HMS *Lutine*

Another great treasure ship of the period was *Lutine*, a thirty-two-gun French frigate captured in 1793 during the French Revolutionary Wars and incorporated into the Royal Navy. She left Great Yarmouth, Norfolk, in the early hours of 9 October 1799, with a crew and passengers numbering around 240 and a cargo of British government specie valued at over £1,000,000, and headed for Hamburg under the command of Captain Lancelott Skynner. She was seen leaving by a fishing boat which passed her quite close and noticed that, instead of the silence and darkness normal in a king's ship, there was a lot of light and 'much joviality in the State cabin'. She was seen briefly during the following day off Texel but then, as she approached the Dutch coast, a tremendous nor'-nor'-westerly gale broke.

Caught on a lee shore, she struggled to claw off the West Friesians, a long string of islands that were originally part of the coast of the Netherlands, but in the early hours of the 10th she struck a sandbank off the island of Terschelling, where she became a total loss. A British sloop, *Arrow*, manned by twenty of the crew of the corvette *Wolverine*, under the command of a Captain Portlock, arrived at Terschelling from Vlieland, another of the islands, and demanded that the skippers, pilots and seamen should take their boats to the spot immediately. A few corpses, including those of *Lutine*'s captain and two of her officers, and one solitary survivor were picked up with various items of the ship's equipment.

Lutine was not the first ship to fall prey to the treacherous currents off the Dutch coast and the sandbanks which are always changing their position, but this ship was different, and what she carried became known very quickly. The value of the treasure was rumoured to be as high as £1,400,000, though other figures were mentioned. The highest estimate, from a Dutch government source, was £1,666,666, while an agent of Lloyds of London in 1858 rated the value at £1,200,000.

Lloyds had started around 1685 as a coffee house in Great Tower Street, where Edward Lloyd had made the place a centre for anyone who had an interest in shipping and shipping insurance, and brokers met there to talk business over a cup of coffee. That *Lutine* had carried bullion was not denied. By 1799, when the French revolutionary armies were ranging across northern Europe, Hamburg, then one of the most important ports on the Continent, had become a commercial centre of the first rank, but because of the war and the British blockade of Europe the city faced a crisis. More than 200 ships were lying in the port unable to discharge their cargoes because the warehouses were full. Money was short and, because firms were going bankrupt, an appeal for help was made to London.

Over a million pounds was raised in bullion and *Lutine* was placed at the disposal of the bankers for its transportation. Several important people joined the ship and Lloyds undertook the insurance. In addition to the bullion for Hamburg, money was said to be on board to pay troops stationed on the island of Texel, another of the Friesian group. Various sums have been mentioned – £140,000 for the pay of the troops, £160,000 for the city of Hamburg – but these seem small and, though the money for the troops is in some doubt, the money for Hamburg, whatever its value, is not. There was also said to be gold bullion for the Continent and – so it was claimed – diamonds belonging to the Prince of Orange. According to Dutch newspapers in 1869, these diamonds were part of the Dutch Crown jewels which the Prince had sent to England to be reset and polished, and they were in a sealed chest. It was also said that there were many rich people among the passengers, enough in fact for the 'joviality in the State cabin' mentioned by the crew of the fishing boat, to be assumed to be a party being held. Whatever the truth about what *Lutine* carried, its value must have been substantial.

The news of the ship's loss had to pass by boat from island to island to the mainland and then by men on horses or by post-chaise, and news of the sinking did not reach the Admiralty until 19 October. It was reported that the inhabitants of Vlieland and Terschelling had their hands full with interring the washed-up corpses, and about 200 were buried in a pit near the Brandaris lighthouse. Nevertheless, the islanders were not so busy that they didn't notice the opportunity presented to them. Captain Portlock was given the job of salvaging anything of value and the Sheriff and Receiver of Wrecks at Terschelling advised haste as vessels were regularly moored over the wreck, which lay in only three fathoms, hauling up anything they could.

Although the official operations were well organised, nature did not co-operate and the winter of 1799–1800 was a very bad one. But by August cordage, cannon and cannonballs had been brought up. Then came a cask containing gold bars and a chest containing Spanish piastres. Altogether, the operation brought up fifty-eight gold bars, ninety-nine silver ones and 41,000 silver coins. As work went on it was found that the packing round the bars and coins had proved unequal to the movement of the sea and fell apart at a touch, so that the contents of the ship had become scattered and the divers had to grope blindly at a depth of about twenty-five feet through rotten rigging and rusty guns.

During the winter of 1803 the weather changed the shallows so much that the place where all the treasure had been discovered was found to be covered with the side of the ship which had fallen away, though it was noticed that strange boats still made for the wreck on moonlit nights. After the end of the Napoleonic wars, Lloyds began to hope to recover more of the gold and obtained half rights to the wreck, but with the Dutch insisting that all salvage be handed over to them in return for a reward, operations halted until 1857, when a fisherman hauled in a buoy which had come adrift. With it came a piece of the *Lutine*, and this set things moving again. Divers brought up a lump of rust and with it numbers of *louis d'or* and two silver spoons. Dutch maritime laws allowed competitors on the scene, and vessels stuck so firmly to their positions that a gunboat had to be sent to move them. More gold coins were recovered, and then in 1858 bars of gold and silver. The following year, 1859, a piece of wreckage which proved to be the stern part of the ship, where the treasure had been stowed, was opened and more gold, silver and coins recovered.

The wreck was found again by divers from Lloyds, and in 1862 a diver discovered a floor in which there were regular seams between hard objects one and a half decimetres across. He was convinced that they were silver bars, but when he went down again the next day he found the floor buried under a mass of sand. By this time Dutch museums were full of relics from the ship in the shape of cannon, gold and silver coins, uniform buttons, gold rings, etc., but the bullion that was always expected never fully appeared. Further attempts were made in 1907, 1910 and 1911, but always the mud and sand defeated them and nothing was found beyond a few gold and silver coins, anchors, cannon and iron ballast, from the sale of which no more than about £135 was raised.

Work continued, using a variety of methods including suction pumps, grabs, dredgers and an enormous tower which was placed over the wreck. It was designed to project above the surface of the sea and even included a lift. Then the *Karimata*, which, it was claimed, was the biggest tin dredger in the world, was brought to the scene in 1938. Even if it did not bring much to the surface it certainly gave Dutch holidaymakers something to see, and boat trips were organised to the site. A few things were recovered, then a diver brought up a gold bar. It led to the expectation that more gold was to be found. It was – one large coin dated 1797, and that was all. It was suggested that the salvage team had planted the bar.

It was the last attempt. Effort after effort, some quite extraordinary, had been made to salvage the cargo. On two occasions half a million guilders' worth of bullion had been brought to the surface, but for all the other syndicates who operated divers and their apparatus the rewards were negligible, and the tin dredger got no recompense for her incredibly expensive, blundering and archaeologically disastrous efforts.

Perhaps the best known recovery was the ship's bell, dated 1779. It was brought up on 17 July 1858, and was presented to Lloyds. It was hung in the Royal Exchange in London and in 1957 was transferred to the underwriting room in the new Lloyd's building in Lime Street. It is rung to obtain silence whenever there is important news to announce, once for good news, twice for bad. During the war the German propagandist, Lord Haw Haw, William Joyce, asserted that it was rung non-stop to announce the vast losses at sea. In fact it rang only once – when the German battleship *Bismarck* was sunk.

Despite the disappointments, *Lutine* is far from forgotten and every now and then new plans are formulated, while holidaymakers still point to the surf off the island of Terschelling and say, 'That's where she went down, a ship laden with pure gold.' Near the ferryboat landing stage are two ancient bronze cannon from the *Lutine*. There is also a Lutineweg (Lutine Way) and a Lutine Café and in that part of Holland fine weather is referred to as *Lutine* weather, while a particular type of sand like that removed from the wreck is called *Lutine* sand. There are also songs and witticisms, but by now the stories of the treasure that was there for the taking have begun to take on the appearance of fairy tales.

But the treasure *had* existed. It was established in 1894 from the numbers stamped on the bars of gold and silver that many have still not turned up, and it is more than likely that some of them disappeared clandestinely, because there were strange stories that hitherto poor people unlikely to receive inheritances several struck out, helping each other to keep afloat, and several made it.

There had been confusion ashore. Coastguard stations had been receiving calls that a large ship was blazing a few miles out to sea but they could see nothing and decided to wait until there was something more definite. Then Rogers's SOS was picked up and by 3.40 a.m. the media were all aware and were preparing their reporters, radio commentators and film cameramen. On paper, a small fleet of vessels were available for rescue, but their radio operators failed to pick up the order to go to the rescue. Other patrol boats were not equipped with radio, and four larger boats were trailing a liquor smuggler north of New York. The coastguard station at Cape May, only eighty-eight miles south-west of the *Morro Castle*, had seven aircraft but four were not in service and only one was suitable for rescue work offshore.

Ships at sea reacted more quickly. *Andrea Luckenbach*, having picked up Rogers's SOS, arrived at about 04.30 and stood off from the blazing ship to lower her boats, which immediately began to snatch people from the water. The Furness Line ship, *Monarch of Bermuda*, was also near and hurrying to the scene of the disaster. *City of Savannah* and *President Cleveland* had altered course and were also drawing near.

In fact, it was a coastguard surfboat from Sea Girt that was first on the scene. It had put to sea to investigate a 'ball of flame' that had been seen. More might have set off but the local radio station had announced that everybody had already been rescued. One man, however, the skipper of the thirty-ton *Paramount*, decided that nobody could be certain that the rescue was as complete as it was claimed and he put to sea with a crew of other captains.

One of the first lifeboats to reach the shore was Abbott's. It now contained thirty-two people but only one of them was a passenger. Abbott was in a strange state of mind, and as the boat arrived near the beach he tried to persuade the rowers to turn away, saying that the shore was too rocky. In fact, the sea took matters in hand and deposited them on the sand. Still in full dress uniform, Abbott was the first man to step ashore and, warning the men with him not to had suddenly struck out to buy cattle and properties, and jewellers had been offered 'family heirlooms' in gold, to be melted down, by the most improbable types. And there is still a mystery about some of the big houses which came to be built in the area, and in some cases still exist. Because of the number of wrecks cast up on their shores the islanders knew a great deal about salvage and were far from inexperienced at diving. With the ship in such shallow water in 1799 it is more than likely that they got their share.

The Tobermory Galleon

A treasure even older than that of *Grosvenor* or *Lutine* is one that has haunted people since the sixteenth century. According to rumour, the ship that carried it groaned with the weight of silver from Mexico, gold coins, ornaments, holy images studded with jewels, even a crown supposed to have been given by Pope Sixtus in 1588 to be worn by the new Catholic ruler of England. Above all, £30,000,000 in gold alone. And it is all supposed to lie within a stone's throw from the houses of Tobermory, the little township at the north end of the island of Mull in the Hebrides. Originally a mere scattering of fishermen's cottages, it did not exist as a town until 1788, but for four centuries it has been the centre of a continuing treasure hunt – and practically all for nothing.

The lost ship, which lies beneath the water of the little land-locked bay, is one of the 130 ships – the Invincible Armada – sent by Philip II of Spain to conquer England. The vast fleet was a crusade against the northern heretics and, since it caught the imagination of the Spanish aristocracy, many members of noble families wished to be part of the great adventure and took with them their retainers and the jewels, gold chains, inlaid swords, silver plate and ornaments they considered necessary to their image.

Flying the flags of half the great houses of Spain, the fleet gathered in the ports of Portugal and Philip controlled its gathering in the same way in which he controlled everything – from a small whitewashed office in the Escorial Palace near Madrid, but with a bureaucratic passion that produced mounds of paper which to this day show in the minutest detail exactly what his ships contained and what they cost.

To command the fleet, Philip chose not an experienced sailor but the nobleman the project demanded, the Duke of Medina Sidonia. Aware of his shortcomings, the Duke begged to be excused but the King ignored his protestations. He was determined to add England to his possessions. With this in mind in 1554 he had married Henry VIII's elder daughter Mary, daughter of Catherine of Aragon, and when she died had proposed to Elizabeth, his daughter by Anne Boleyn. But Elizabeth preferred to keep foreign potentates dancing to *her* tune, and enjoyed stirring up discord in Philip's possessions in the Netherlands, where Philip's troops were commanded by the Duke of Parma. A late conspiracy to put the Catholic Mary of Scotland on the throne was exposed by Elizabeth's secret service and Mary was executed, so Philip had no alternative but to invade. It was decided that Parma's army should cross the Channel, aided by the mighty fleet that Philip had raised.

Supplies were brought from all over the Mediterranean to Portugal, where the ships were assembled, and if Medina Sidonia was no sailor at least he was an administrator; every ounce of supplies was accounted for, every coin that was paid out on bills or in wages for the seamen and soldiers. Eventually, on 20 April 1588, the great fleet set sail for the English Channel, huge ships flying the banners of their captains and the noblemen they carried.

The first day's skirmishing in the Channel ended with a disaster for the Spanish when the *San Salvador*, which carried much of the Armada's loose cash, exploded, killing over 200 men. During the night, Drake, a man feared almost as a supernatural by the Spanish for his feats against them, cut out the crippled *Nuestra Señora del Rosario* with her commander. For two days the two fleets moved up-Channel, driven by the prevailing westerly winds until they managed to anchor in Calais Roads to wait for Parma's troops. Soon after midnight fireships were sent among them, their double-shotted guns firing at random as they became red-hot. The Spanish tried to put to sea, but many were damaged in the manoeuvring for sea room and the following morning the English moved in like a wolf-pack. As the Spanish fought to avoid the shoal water off the Dutch coast, they were caught by a changing wind and blown northwards. In the end orders were issued to return home north-about round Scotland and the west of Ireland.

Defeat was accepted, and on 23 September Medina Sidonia returned to Spain with the news. Many of the commanders and noblemen who had set out with such high hopes were dead, and of the vast fleet sixty-three ships never returned to Spain. Some were lost on the Irish coast. Others were smashed on rocky shores from Fair Isle to Devon.

One ship, lagging behind the rest, found its way into Tobermory Bay in the Isle of Mull, at the time supporting no more than a tiny fishing community.

That much is fact. After that it is often hearsay.

Dutifully Lachlan Mor MacLean of Duart, the clan chief in the area, sent word of the ship's arrival to the Scottish king, while a member of the English Embassy to the Scottish court, William Asheby, on 23 September described it to London as a 'greate ship of Spaigne of 1400 tons, having 800 soldiours and there commanders; at an Iland called Ila (Islay) on the west part of Scotland'.

On 6 November he wrote that she was off Mula (Mull) in MacLean's country and, 'unable to sail . . . is supplied by the Irish people (the MacLeans) with victuals'. The natives had been friendly at both her anchorages. Many Spaniards who had come ashore or swam ashore from wrecks had been murdered and robbed by those to whom they appealed for help, but there were too many men in the ship for MacLean to capture her, so he compromised by offering her safety in return for 100 men to help him settle a dispute he was having with the MacDonald clan.

Soon afterwards Asheby reported the ship destroyed. 'Almost all the men is consumed with fire,' he wrote. 'It is thought to be one of the principall shippes, and some one of great accompt within; for he was alwais, as thei saie, served in sylver.'

The story went that MacLean had sent a foster son on board, who had been taken by the Spanish and held as a hostage for MacLean's good behaviour, but that in his fury he had managed to get at the magazine and blow up the ship. Another story was that a supplier of victuals, John Smollett, whom Tobias Smollett, the author, claimed as an ancestor, had won the trust of the Spanish and it was he who laid the device which destroyed the ship. About both these stories there was great doubt, but either way there was now a Spanish galleon lying at the bottom of Tobermory Bay.

The name of the galleon was said to be *San Juan di Bautista, San Juan di Sicilia, San Francisco* or *El Galeón del Gran Duque di Florencia di Nombre San Francisco*, and she was said to have been loaned to Spain by the city of Florence, her commander Captain Don Antonio Pereira. Around her grew the legend that she was the principal treasure ship of the Armada with the paymaster general and the pay chest for the whole Armada aboard.

Paymaster and treasure (said to be over £30,000,000 in gold doubloons) were reported to have been aboard *San Salvador*, damaged in action and abandoned, and her treasure then distributed among other ships of which *Duque di Florencia* was supposed to be one. The 7th Earl of Argyll was supposed to have heard the story from a descendant of Captain Pereira, whom he met in Spain where his wife's relatives were prominent at court. However, there is evidence that *Florencia* never reached Tobermory but was captured off the west coast of England and brought as a prize into Weymouth Bay.

As a reward for his father's information about the galleon, the 8th Earl of Argyll received a deed of gift from Charles I allowing him salvage rights, but he never exercised his rights as he was executed for treason in 1661. When Archibald Campbell, the 9th Earl, wanted to exercise the rights he was told that they only applied to the reign of Charles I and were now extinct. The Earl took the case to court and won, and an attempt at salvage was made in 1661 when half a dozen guns were brought to the surface. In 1665 another attempt was made and more cannon were retrieved. By this time the story of the vast treasure had begun. The 9th Earl's memorandum on the situation said that the wreck was 'reputed to have been the *Admirall of Florence* . . . a ship of fifty-six guns and that there was aboard 30,000,000 of money'.

In 1683 a diver called Archibald Miller went down. He was

working for James, Duke of York, later King James II, after the
Argyll family had been dispossessed of its rights to the wreck. His
report, which is in the Bodleian Library at Oxford, called the ship
'*the Florence of Spaine*' and in it he claimed to have seen a paper 'of
Lattin Extractes out of the Spanish records that there were thirty
millions of cash on board . . . under ye sell of the Gunroome'.

He reported the ship's position, not more than nine fathoms
deep at low water, and brought up guns and a silver bell, and
claimed to have hooked an object he thought was a jewelled
crown, but was unable to get it out. He made his statement after
diving had stopped, however, and, probably having heard of Pope
Sixtus's promised crown, was no doubt trying to talk himself into
another job.

By the time James II was overthrown by William of Orange, it
had become accepted that the ship in Tobermory Bay was a rich
prize indeed. The 9th Earl of Argyll had also gone to the scaffold
on a charge of treason in 1685, but his son had joined William of
Orange and was created 1st Duke of Argyll. His younger son, who
became the 3rd Duke, decided in 1740 to try again for treasure and
under his directions gold and silver coins were brought up, with a
bronze cannon wrought at Fontainebleau by Benvenuto Cellini.
It is today at the castle at Inveraray. It bore no ship's name.

Various other attempts were made, then a man called Jacob
Rowe took over. His divers used drags and explosives and, if
nothing else, destroyed much of what was left of the ship.

During the nineteenth century a diver reported that the wreck
had disappeared under a mass of silt and sand, but a Glasgow
treasure syndicate was formed in 1903 after the chance discovery
of a gold coin and an ancient sea-encrusted anchor. A Captain
Burns found more cannon, weapons and some coins, but not the
wreck. Suction pumps and steam shovels were used.

A new group was formed in 1909 under the leadership of a
Colonel Kenneth Foss, who declared that Archibald Miller had
misled everybody about the position of the wreck so he could
cash in on it for himself, and Foss found it under thirty feet of
silt eighty-four yards from Tobermory pier. His men located the
captain's cabin in the stern and brought up two small cannon, some

silver coins and pewter plates, crystal and fragments of arms and armour. They also found a silver medallion which was presented to Princess Louise, Duchess of Argyll.

Foss was convinced that the ship was *Florencia*, an Italian ship full of Portuguese soldiers, commanded by a Captain Pereira. He persuaded more people to invest in the hunt, and the collection of cannon, pieces of timber, fragments of crystal, silver and copper coins and a few human bones continued to grow – but still no treasure. So far the value of what was recovered was estimated at no more than £1000.

Foss was interrupted by the First World War, but was back in 1919 with a new group of investors and a powerful pump and water jet called a Sykes digger to blow the silt away from the search area. For four weeks the work went on, then a silver peso and a broken piece of silver plate were brought up. The next day four more silver coins appeared. The excitement grew, especially when they were followed by an ornamental handle, wrenched by the Sykes digger from the silver wine flagon to which it had been attached. Foss's methods would have made a modern underwater archaeologist weep. No object larger than a matchbox was likely to come to the surface, because his digger not only sliced through the sea bed but probably also through what remained of the ship.

Foss was still there in 1926, by this time with divers who had made their name salvaging the scuttled German High Seas Fleet at Scapa Flow, and more fragments of silver, pewter, glass, china, armour and weapons were brought up. In 1927 there was an accident with a high pressure hose which flung Foss into the scuppers, breaking several ribs and causing serious internal injuries. It was the end of his involvement, though he tried to interest the Italian salvage company which had raised more than £1,000,000 of gold from the sunken P. and O. liner, *Egypt*. But they had heard of the Tobermory operation's ability to swallow money and weren't interested.

Foss's pulley-hauley methods had worked no better on the Tobermory ship than those of *Karimata* on *Lutine*, but if Foss had done nothing else his enthusiasm had caught the public imagination, and there were always hopes that the gold would be found.

Two more syndicates were formed, but war again intervened. In 1949 the 11th Duke of Argyll resumed the search, and the Admiralty lent two small craft and a fishery protection vessel. On 8 May 1950, naval divers found the wreck of an oak vessel, sixty feet below the surface and buried twenty-four feet in silt. It was in pieces and there were indications of fire. In 1955 the team, under the command of a retired rear admiral, was joined by Commander Lionel K. Crabb, the famous frogman and wartime hero who disappeared while diving under the Russian cruiser *Ordzhonikidze* in April 1956. It has been assumed that he was doing some freelance and unofficial diving work for military or naval intelligence which entailed examining the hull of the Russian cruiser or her accompanying destroyers, and that something went wrong. Though not officially a member of the naval team at Tobermory, he was welcomed.

A few artifacts were brought up and once again the press had a field day guessing at the size of the treasure. Two silver medallions were found and photographs of them were sent off for expert examination, but when they were dropped in the bay 'by accident' a hoax was suspected; the perpetrator suspected was Crabb, who was known to indulge in underwater pranks.

The following year the hunt continued, and if nothing else the publicity was good for local tourism. The problem now was getting at the ship through the silt. A long metal pipe was lowered from compressors to suck up silt at the rate of thirty-five tons an hour. As it came up, it was sieved into a hopper ship. The first loads produced a rusty sword blade, more weapons, fragments of weapons, pottery and coins. There were no chests of gold and silver, no jewelled crown as described by Miller.

In 1982 an approach was made to the salvors of the gold of the *Edinburgh*. Its divers had taken tremendous risks to raise the £45,000,000 in gold sent by the Russians, but while they were prepared to take risks they were not prepared to waste money, and the project was abandoned after five weeks.

It was left to a young Scots writer and broadcaster, Alison McLeay, who was married to a former diver and had learned to dive herself, to bring some sense into the operation. She found that great trenches and pits – 'as if some demented underwater dog had been grubbing about' – had been carved across the floor of the bay, so, instead of blundering blindly about below water, she went to the roots of the affair, deciding that it was first necessary to identify the ship. For this she went to old records and documents kept by Philip of Spain in the fitting out of his fleet.

The records showed exactly how much everybody had been paid and where the gold of the fleet was carried. She soon disposed of the names *Florencia, Florida* and *Admirall of Florence*. Sir Julian Corbett, the naval historian, had pointed out that there were two captains called Pereira commanding Armada vessels, which probably led to the confusion about *Florencia*; and also that a ship of *Florencia*'s size could not possibly have carried the weight of troops, crew, armour and over 750 tons of coins alleged to have been aboard. Alison McLeay took the view that Andrew Lang, the Scottish historian, had taken in 1912, and identified the ship as *Santa Maria de Gracia y San Juan Bautista*. But since there were other *San Juan Bautistas* in the fleet, and as the ship came from Sicily, she was commonly called *San Juan de Sicilia*, from Ragusa, now known as Dubrovnik in Jugoslavia, and was captained by Luka Ivanov Kinkovíc, translated in the Spanish records to Lucas de Juan. There were vast amounts of documents concerning the ship and every item of her supplies, all meticulously recorded by Philip's clerks. They showed exactly what guns she carried and what weapons, but the elusive treasure still evaded the researchers.

She now took her ideas to Geoffrey Parker, Professor of Early Modern History at the University of St Andrews, who had explored the shelves of documents on the Armada. Parker had cracked the code of Philip's clerks and was probably the one man capable of pursuing the sixteenth-century Spanish accounts through their meticulous records. He was engaged on an account of the Armada and made available to her some of the documents he had seen. These showed at once that the ship wasn't destroyed by MacLean of Duart for revenge, or even by Elizabeth's agent Smollett. The ship's magazine exploded when powder for the guns was being moved in an effort to dry out waterlogged kegs.

Further search of the accounts showed a last payment to Captain Kinkovíc. It concerned the handing over of 36,866 gold *escudos*, nine *reals* and seventeen *maravedis*, all sums large enough to turn the head. For a moment the researchers thought they had at last found proof that treasure had been aboard, but then they realised that the figure paid to Captain Kinkovíc, written into the accounts in a flourishing Spanish hand and dotted with ink spots, in fact concerned money which had been paid *from* a sum of 36,866 gold *escudos*, nine *reals* and seventeen *maravedis* held by the Governor of Portugal. The vast treasure chest that had been sought for centuries seemed finally to have vanished. If there had been a treasure, the Spanish accountants would surely have mentioned it somewhere, because large sums put aboard other ships were all recorded, and any large sum in the *San Juan de Sicilia* would inevitably have been put on paper. In any case, the ship made her way up the North Sea in a sinking state, and if she had been carrying gold the Spanish commanders would have made sure the money was transferred to a sounder ship.

No gold was discovered and is not now likely to be, and the treasure hunt over the centuries destroyed what might have been a treasure trove in other ways. *Trinidad Valencera*, wrecked off County Donegal, centuries later produced hundreds of things like clothes, armour and boots that showed how her people had lived, and the galleass *Girona*, wrecked off the coast of Antrim, produced enough treasure to be breathtaking. What started as a trickle became a stream – gold chains, coins, rings, cameos, pearls, crosses, candlesticks, everything imaginable – but no cash beyond what had been the personal belongings of those aboard. When the *Girona* was lost, what was reachable was looted but enough was left to be housed in what are now the Girona Rooms of the Ulster Museum.

How much of this sort of splendour might have been found at Tobermory if the crude methods of syndicates greedy only for wealth had not been used? There is no doubt that the blundering attempts in Tobermory Bay were historical vandalism at its worst, and what might have emerged from an undisturbed ship could have left the *Trinidad* collection in the shade, because it was a better site with a type of mud that was excellent for preserving materials. In 1740 the ship could still clearly be seen at low tide and there is little doubt that, though she might not have carried chests full of treasure, she carried valuable articles belonging to the Spanish nobles who travelled in her. Perhaps even, like the *Mary Rose*, she might have been raised herself.

Though the three millions in cash didn't exist, the wealthy men on board must have taken both money and plate with them to allow them to live in the style they were used to and to set up households in England after the conquest. Undoubtedly, as Asheby said, they would have been 'alwais served in sylver', but it seems unlikely that £3 million in cash was ever aboard.

HMS *Hampshire*

Horatio Herbert, Lord Kitchener, the British warlord who raised a whole army for Britain in 1914 with the poster of his face, complete with bullhorn moustache, pointing finger and basilisk stare, died when the cruiser *Hampshire*, on the way to Russia, struck a mine off the west coast of Scotland during a gale on the evening of 5 June 1916.

A hero in the eyes of most Britons, by 1916 Kitchener had actually passed his finest hour. When war was declared in 1914 he was appointed Minister of War and, one of the few to realise that the war would not be over by Christmas as most people believed, demanded a huge volunteer army – and got it. He saved the country with his foresight, but the shortage of shells in 1915 was blamed on him and, while he never lost popularity with the troops or the general public, moves were made among politicians to get rid of him; the trip to Russia may have been one. Lloyd George, in particular, disliked him and certainly Kitchener was never the man to fall in with the wishes of politicians and the great press barons, all of whom he considered – often with good reason – to be self-interested, tricky and untrustworthy. The trip to Russia was to enable him to confer with the Tsar and his generals, who were becoming perturbed over the way the war was going on the Eastern Front. With the Russian revolution only months in the future, there were murmurings in the country at the inept generalship and it was hoped that Kitchener could put things right.

The weather was bad as he prepared to leave, but he refused to delay. The forecast that had been issued proved to be far short of the truth, however, and the British naval Commander-in-Chief, Sir John Jellicoe, still heavily involved with the after-effects of the Battle of Jutland on 31 May tried to persuade the field marshal to wait twenty-four hours to give the storm time to die down. Because of the weather, minesweepers had been unable to make a proper sweep of the western route round the north of Scotland that *Hampshire* was to take, but Kitchener refused to be put off.

The ship was under way by 4.45 p.m., but by 6.20 the gale was such that the escorting destroyers were unable to keep up and were ordered to return to base. Just after 7.30 p.m., near Marwick Head, *Hampshire* struck a mine laid by the submarine *U75* at the end of May in the hope of catching units of the Grand Fleet when they were tempted to sea by the German High Seas Fleet – the sortie that ended in Jutland.

Hampshire sank in fifteen minutes and, because of the gale, only twelve men managed to struggle ashore at Birsay on the western end of the mainland of Orkney. Every member of Kitchener's party was lost, and Kitchener's body was never found.

At once, rumours began. It was said that Lloyd George had arranged the whole thing, that spies were involved. It was even said that Kitchener wasn't dead, that he had gone on a secret mission, even that he was living in a cave in the Orkneys. The same thing happened when Lawrence of Arabia was killed on his motorcycle. Nations do not like their heroes to disappear before their time, and stories are invariably invented to suggest that they are still alive.

Certainly there seemed to be some mystery, and from it sprang another. Did *Hampshire* carry bullion destined for Russia? Rumours started in 1933 of a secret attempt to salvage the ship, carried out at the instigation of that enigmatic international arms salesman, Sir Basil Zaharoff, who loomed so large in the 1930s.

Born in 1850 in Constantinople of a Greek family that claimed to be Russian, Zaharoff was educated – mostly informally – in London and Paris, and for almost half a century crossed and recrossed the world persuading governments to buy weapons for wars they were not very likely to fight. He was the agent of the arms manufacturers Nordenfelt and Maxim, and finally Vickers, and was prepared to sell anything from automatic weapons to battleships. He profited enormously from the tensions that existed in the Balkans and employed a diplomatist's skill to get rid of his wares. Little was ever known of him, but he was always larger than life, and when he died in 1936 he was still an enigma. However, he amassed an enormous fortune from his interests in armaments, engineering, banking and oil. During the First World War he worked in the closest co-operation with Lloyd George at the Ministry of Munitions as a representative of Vickers, and the relationship became even closer when the Welshman became Prime Minister.

The story started on 26 April 1933, when an Associated Press despatch from New York stated that £15,000 in gold had been recovered from the *Hampshire*. The Admiralty, however, stated quite firmly that they had 'no knowledge of any expedition to salve the *Hampshire*'.

It seemed to kill the story dead, but in December the same year the *Berliner Illustrierte Zeitung* came up with the story again, this time in much greater detail. They claimed to have obtained it from a diver, a Mr Whitefield, who was described variously as a 'German deep-sea diver' and as an American from Norfolk, Viriginia. At the time, the story said, he was in a Berlin hospital.

Whitefield's story was that a German vessel flying the British flag had done salvage work on *Hampshire*, and as a result had recovered £10,000 in gold bars, valuable papers and British signal volumes. The salvage vessel was said to be docked at Königsberg undergoing a refit, but a *Sunday Chronicle* reporter, sent to make enquiries at the port, failed to confirm the ship's presence.

The story grew. Three divers were said to be in hospital with serious injuries received in a mud-slide that had followed explosions as they had blasted their way into the cruiser's strong rooms. The salvage operations, so the story went, had begun two years

1a The White Star liner, *Titanic*, lost with over 1500 lives in 1912.

1b *Titanic* goes down after striking an iceberg.

1c Collapsible boat D comes alongside the rescue liner *Carpathia* with survivors.
This was the last boat to leave *Titanic*.

2a The collision between the excursion steamer *Princess Alice* and *Bywell Castle* in the Thames in 1878.

2b The after part of *Princess Alice*, with engines and paddle-wheel boxes, beached near Woolwich.

3a A contemporary engraving of the sinking of *Mary Rose*. Her topmasts with survivors clinging to them are shown top centre. Henry VIII, who witnessed the disaster, is seen on horseback, lower right.

3b *Royal George* lying on the bottom at Spithead.

4a The officers of *Empress of Ireland*.

4b The sinking of *Empress of Ireland*
in the St Lawrence River.

5a The burning Greek liner *Lakonia*,
abandoned by her passengers and crew.

5b Survivors from the blazing *Lakonia*
being taken on board the liner *Stratheden*.

6a The lounge of the cruise liner *Morro Castle*,
still smouldering when boarded by rescue parties.

6b The ill-fated *Morro Castle*,
beached at Asbury Park, New Jersey.

7a A winter gale on the Goodwins.

7b A tug tries to get a rope aboard a distressed vessel
during a Channel gale in 1881.

8a *Endurance* frozen in the pack ice of the Weddell Sea.

8b Sir Ernest Shackleton.

8c Relief at last. The rescue of the men of *Endurance* 22 months after disappearing.

Articles of Agreement,

Made the 10th Day of *October*, in the Year of our Lord 1695.
Between the Right Honourable *RICHARD* Earl of
BELLOMONT of the one part, and *Robert Levingston* Esq;

AND

Captain William Kid,

Of the other part.

WHEREAS the said Capt. *William Kid* is desirous of obtaining a Commission as Captain of a Private Man of War in order to take Prizes from the King's Enemies, and otherways to annoy them; and whereas certain Persons did some time since depart from *New-England*, *Rode-Island*, *New-York*, and other parts in *America* and elsewhere, with an intention to become Pirates, and to commit Spoils and Depredations, against the Laws of Nations, in the *Red-Sea* or elsewhere, and to return with such Goods and Riches as they should get, to certain places by them agreed upon; of which said Persons and Places, the said Capt. *Kid* hath notice, and is desirous to fight with and subdue the said Pirates, as also other Pirates with whom the said Capt. *Kid* shall meet at Sea, in case he be impowered so to do; and whereas it is agreed between the said Parties, That for the purpose aforesaid a good and sufficient Ship, to the liking of the said Capt. *Kid*, shall be forthwith bought, whereof the said Capt. *Kid* is to be the Commander. Now these Presents do witness, and it is agreed between the said Parties,

I. That the Earl of *Bellomont* doth covenant and agree, at his proper Charge, to procure from the King's Majesty, or from the Lords Commissioners of the Admiralty (as the Case shall require) one or more Commissions, impowering him the said Capt. *Kid* to act against the King's Enemies, and to take Prizes from them, as a private Man of War in the usual manner; and also to fight with, conquer and subdue Pirates, and to take them and their Goods; with other large and beneficial Powers and Clauses in such Commission as may be most proper and effectual in such Cases.

II. The said Earl of *Bellomont* doth covenant and agree, That within three Months after the said Capt. *Kid's* departure from *England*, for the purposes in these Presents mentioned, he will procure, at his proper charge, a Grant from the King, to be made to some indifferent and trusty Person, of all such Merchandizes, Goods, Treasure and other things as shall be taken from the said Pirates, or any other Pirate whatsoever, by the said Capt. *Kid*, or by the said Ship, or any other Ship or Ships under his Command.

III. The said Earl doth agree to pay four Fifth parts, the whole in Five parts to be divided, of all Moneys which shall be laid out for the buying such good and sufficient Ship for the purposes aforesaid, together with Rigging and other Apparel and Furniture thereof, and providing the same with competent victualling the said Ship; to be approved of by the said Parties; and the said other one Fifth part of the said Charges of the said Ship to be paid for by the said *Robert Levingston* and *William Kid*.

IV. The said Earl doth agree, That in order to the speedy buying the said Ship, in part of the said four parts of Five of the said Charges, he will pay down the sum of sixteen hundred Pounds, by way of Advance, on or before the sixth day of *November* next ensuing.

V. The said *Robert Levingston* and *William Kid* do jointly and severally covenant and agree, That on and before the sixth day of *November*, when the said Earl of *Bellomont* is to pay the said Sum of sixteen hundred pounds as aforesaid, they will advance and pay down Four hundred pounds in part of the Share and Proportion which they are to have in the said Ship.

VI. The said Earl doth agree, to pay such further Sums of Money as shall compleat and make up the said four parts of Five of the Charges of the said Ship's Arrival, Furniture and Victualling, unto the said *Robert Levingston* and *William Kid* within seven Weeks after the date of these Presents; and in like manner the said *Robert Levingston* and *William Kid* do agree to pay such further Sums as shall amount to a fifth part of the whole Charge of the said Ship within seven Weeks after the date of these Presents.

A   VII. The

9a Captain Kidd's agreement with the New York authorities to subdue pirates in the East.

9b Personal items recovered from the sunken *Mary Rose*.

10a HMS *Hampshire*, sunk by a mine in 1916.

10b Field Marshal Lord Kitchener, lost in HMS *Hampshire*.

10c The first haul of gold ingots salvaged from the sunken liner, *Egypt*.

11a *left* Captain William Bligh.

11b *right* The *Bounty* mutineers seize Bligh in his cabin.

11c Bligh and the loyal members of the crew of *Bounty*
being set adrift.

12a *left* Hauling down the red flag on *Royal George* after the naval mutiny at Spithead.
12b *right* The mutinous sailors at the Nore turn out in their best rig and line the yards to cheer the King's birthday.

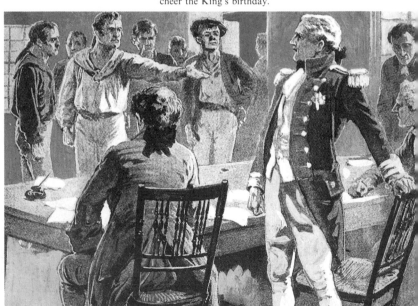

12c Seamen threatening their officers
during the naval mutinies of 1797.

13a Sailors of the Russian battleship *Potemkin*,
throwing one of their officers overboard (a scene from Eisenstein's film).

13b German destroyers resting on the bottom
after the scuttling of the German High Seas Fleet at Scapa Flow.

14a *left* Captain Hugh Talbot Burgoyne, VC, of HMS *Captain*.

14b *right* Captain Cowper Phipps Coles, designer of HMS *Captain*.

14c HMS *Captain* in dry dock. Her huge masts can be seen
with her strange two-deck design and narrow beam.

15a How the French saw the ramming of HMS *Victoria* by HMS *Camperdown*. In fact *Victoria*'s funnels were side by side and her gun was much bigger.

15b Photograph taken from one of the accompanying ships showing *Victoria* in her final plunge to the bottom.

16a *K22*, formerly *K13*, lost in Gareloch during her trials
and, recovered and renumbered, almost lost again during the 'Battle of May Island'.

16b *M1*, the former *K18*, showing her huge 12-inch gun.
She was sunk in collision in 1925.

previously. At the time they were unsuccessful, but the diving team had managed to fix *Hampshire*'s position. The salvage vessel had then returned to Kiel, and a new and successful attempt was made with the latest salvage equipment in April 1933.

The names of the divers were given as Costello, an Australian; Charles Courtney, a master locksmith; and the man, Whitefield, who had already been mentioned. To avoid speculation about what he was up to, the captain of the salvage vessel, which was not named, had taken a roundabout route from Kiel before heading for Orkney. The divers had worked in shifts for a week, clearing away the sand and mud from a great hole in the wreck.

After a lot of discussion it had been decided to plant three time bombs over the wreck, but when the divers descended to view their work a second and unexpected explosion of ammunition in the forepart of the cruiser had hurled them into the mud.

Despite the setback, they stuck at their work, using oxy-acetylene cutting apparatus, and finally succeeded in raising £10,000 in gold. For the weekend, the story continued, they put into Stromness and each diver and deckhand was sworn to secrecy by the captain. Several days later, they resumed the operation and this time the mud-slide accident that injured the divers forced the captain to abandon the salvage in order to rush them to Königsberg.

The story appeared with such detail in the German, American and British press that the Admiralty was moved to intervene with a statement. 'The *Hampshire*,' they announced, 'belongs to Britain and before anyone can begin salvage of her it is necessary to enter into a contract with the Admiralty.'

'If these salvage operations are proved to be going on, or to have been carried out,' the statement went on, 'they are definitely illegal, and action will be taken against the people concerned.'

This was normal enough procedure. The Navy is always anxious to avoid interference with its sunken ships, which are considered to be war graves and sacrosanct. In 1981, the salvage experts who removed bullion from HMS *Edinburgh* proceeded correctly with the Admiralty, and *Edinburgh* was then returned to peace as a war grave.

The Admiralty's statement about *Hampshire* was made to the *Sunday Chronicle*, yet two days later they issued another statement, this time to the *Morning Post*. 'The Admiralty knows nothing about the matter at all,' it said, 'and has issued no statement.'

The only facts known at this time were that Whitefield had been summoned mysteriously at the beginning of 1933 to London, encouraged by a substantial advance. From London he was directed to Southampton and from there to Hamburg and Kiel, where he was told to report to the 'captain of a salvage vessel flying the British flag'. He was told nothing of the salvage plans until the ship reached Stromness. The divers made their last attempt on 24 April 1933.

The story finally died, but in 1951 a man called Charles Courtney published a book called *Unlocking Adventure*, which repeated Whitefield's story in greater detail. Courtney's story was not just a rehash, however. He said he had met Frederick Krupp, president of the Krupp shipbuilding firm, and through Krupp had come into contact with Sir Basil Zaharoff and was invited to Biarritz where, he claimed, he was told of a syndicate which had discovered *Hampshire*'s resting place. Zaharoff insisted that the cruiser had been carrying £2,000,000 in gold bullion to bolster the Tsar's armies.

Courtney's story differed slightly from Whitefield's. He described Costello as a man who had brought up gold from many a famous wreck. The salvage vessel was described as the *KSR*, and her captain's name was given as Brandt. She carried the British flag but the crew consisted of Greeks, Cypriots and Italians. Mention was also made of a diver called Gruber and a man called Max Weissfelt (which, translated, means Whitefield), a middle-aged German said to represent the syndicate.

The descriptions of the diving seemed to be sound and Courtney gave minute details. There was, he said, enough light to see by; every gun on the cruiser, he claimed, was loaded and beside them were the skeletons of their crews with earphones still on their skulls, lying by shells that were never fired. In the forward hatch, the story continued, was a great pile of skeletons belonging to sailors who had been overwhelmed by the water as they tried to come up from below.

It was a wonderful story and filled the newspapers and magazines of the Thirties, to be recounted more than once in books on sea mysteries. But was it true? The book was detailed but to Donald McCormick, who wrote a book on the death of Kitchener, it seemed to be riddled with inaccuracies. As it was repeated, the story improved. On one occasion, so the story went, one of the ship's torpedoes was released by setting off explosives so that it seemed as if *Hampshire* was trying to hit back. Gold coins were found and in one cabin, after opening an airtight door, huge steel safes were seen. To their horror, on the currents released by the opening of the door, the divers saw gliding towards them through the water-filled room pale human faces as the bodies of two officers, the rings of gold braid still on their sleeves, floated past from the desks where they had been trapped seventeen years before. For a moment the divers thought they had somehow survived and one of them snatched at a body as it drifted by; but the arm he grasped came away, and, so it was claimed, a ring on the finger enabled the body to be identified. Eventually, sack after sack of gold sovereigns were hauled to the surface, but salvage was abandoned after an accident which left, out of the four divers who were down at the time, two injured and two dead.

It was stated that one of the dead divers had actually been on the crew of *U75*, which had laid the mine which sank *Hampshire*. It was a nice touch of irony, but the only basis for this fact was that Max Weissfelt was supposed to have been in the German Navy during the war, and had kept a notebook which recorded where every German mine had been laid.

Courtney's story was realistic and ingenious and continued to twist and turn. On the return of the salvage ship to Germany, Courtney himself delivered the gold to the vaults of the Reichsbank, and Hjalmar Schacht, Hitler's financial wizard, was so appreciative he invited Courtney to attend the great May Day celebration at which Hitler was to speak. The British press naturally followed up the story with all the means at their disposal. They achieved nothing and from the Admiralty they were met with the usual noncommittal silence.

Courtney *did* exist, however. He was a locksmith who ran a business in the Bronx district of New York, and he had an international reputation as an expert on locks and safes, so high in fact that he was employed on several occasions by Zaharoff and was even, on the financier's death in 1936, employed to open his safes.

Zaharoff was a sinister figure in the Thirties, a man who was said to have started wars so that he could profit from the sale of arms. He liked to tell tall tales about himself. His birth certificate was said to have been destroyed by fire, while documents concerning him in various capitals of the world had disappeared – as if he had obliterated all evidence of what he got up to. Nevertheless, there is little doubt that he would have been in a position to know if *Hampshire* were carrying gold, because he paid out huge sums for information, and army and navy estimates often reached him from highly placed civil servants or politicians before they were made known in Parliament.

Salvage would hardly have interested him, though, because he believed in safe bets and his fortune was estimated at £40,000,000, which by today's standard would be an astronomical figure. The £10,000 to £15,000 that it was claimed had been recovered would be a trifling figure to him. Perhaps he invented the story and Courtney made much of it. Donald McCormick, however, did come across the suggestion in Germany that he *had* recovered the gold – for the Nazis, in return for a dossier on his dubious activities during the First World War.

And Zaharoff always insisted to his secretary that there *was* gold in *Hampshire*, and he would certainly know. McCormick asked the Admiralty for their views on the matter when he was researching his book, but they were as noncommittal as ever. 'There is no mention in Admiralty records,' they said, 'of any shipment of gold being carried to Russia in HMS *Hampshire*.' But this was not the same thing as a denial.

Yet so much of Courtney's story seems doubtful. Whitefield was never identified, nor was Costello, and neither did the lists of

German merchant navy and coastal shipping captains and divers turn up the names of Gruber or Brandt. The name *KSR* might have been an abbreviation for Kuesten See Rettung (Coastal Sea Rescue Service), with which some vessels were marked, but nothing was identified.

Salvage experts in Britain refused to believe the story. They would, they claimed, have heard of any salvage operations but, they said, *Hampshire* had never been located.

Cox and Danks Ltd, the firm which raised the German warships scuttled at Scapa Flow in 1919, felt that it was impossible to dive in the treacherous seas in that part of the Pentland Firth where *Hampshire* disappeared. The currents were terrible, they said, and a diver would have been taking the biggest risk of his life.

Finally, no one in Orkney believed the story. People in the neighbourhood who looked at the sea every day of their lives claimed never to have seen any suspicious vessel in the vicinity at the appropriate time, and their views on the currents matched those of Cox and Danks and the salvage experts.

Though there are certainly facts in Courtney's story which have been proved correct, it is difficult to tell where fact ends and imagination takes over. And it does seem likely that it was not Courtney who invented the idea of there being gold in the *Hampshire*. Perhaps Zaharoff believed that the gold *was* there and expressed his belief to Courtney at some point when Courtney was with him on his business. Zaharoff's character, in fact, seems to indicate the only possible explanation. Perhaps he personally encouraged the publication of the story to draw attention away from something dubious he was engaged in at a time when the Nazis were becoming a threat to world peace. Despite the Admiralty statements, the story has never been denied. Yet neither has the gold said to have been salvaged ever been identified. Was it there? Did it exist?

There is one other explanation. The bullion might have been put aboard clandestinely. The British had their representatives in Moscow who knew the situation that was brewing there. Russian failure in the East would release German troops to increase the pressure in the West, so who knows what the politicians were up to? Could it be that the gold was put aboard but kept secret because of political in-fighting?

Or could it have been that King George V himself was behind it? It is well known that he was anxious to help his cousin, the Tsar, whom he resembled to the point of appearing almost to be his twin. If so, he would have had help from Kitchener, the 'arch imperialist', and it would not have been difficult to find sympathisers to contribute and not difficult to have the bullion loaded in secret. And, if it were there, no matter who put it there, Zaharoff would be bound to know. Perhaps there was more to Courtney's extraordinary story than has ever been admitted.

CHAPTER 5

Mutiny!

In the eighteenth century, the gallows was a familiar sight to the City of London. 'Enter it at any point,' wrote Alexander Andrews in *The Eighteenth Century*, 'and you have to pass a line of gibbets. Pass up the Thames, there would be gibbets along its banks, with the rotting remains of mutineers or persons who had committed murders on the high seas hanging from them in chains. Land at Execution Dock, and the gallows were being erected for the punishment of some fellow of the same club.'

Mutiny, of course, is as old as the sea, and is mentioned in the chronicle of the *Odyssey*. Drake experienced mutiny in the *Golden Hind*. The special nature of a ship is a considerable factor in its outbreak. A ship is self-contained and carries everything for its survival within it – food, water and weapons. There is a greater disparity between men and officers than on shore and a greater separatism, yet the relationship is inevitably closer. The extraordinary thing about the history of the sea is that mutiny has been as infrequent as it has.

There had always been single-ship affairs, and in 1789 occurred what, thanks to Hollywood, became the most famous mutiny ever – that of the *Bounty*. Hollywood and Charles Laughton have done a great disservice to Captain William Bligh, and the mutiny in his ship was not due to brutality because, by the standards of the time, Bligh was a very moderate captain and a skilled seaman who ended up as a vice-admiral. He had sailed with Captain James Cook and had rescued his remains after his murder in Hawaii.

The *Bounty* was not even a proper warship and she wasn't

employed on naval duties. She was a small merchant ship specially converted to carry out a prolonged scientific mission and, therefore, had the disadvantages of being away from the fleet. In the eighteen months before the mutiny only eight men had felt the lash, and it has to be remembered that flogging was not unusual even ashore and that a man could be hanged for sheep-stealing. Bligh's punishments were never severe and, according to his log, he had hoped to complete the voyage with no punishment to anyone. Of the eight men he punished, three were deserters and their awards were in the region of two dozen lashes – at a time when deserters in other ships were hanged or given 500 lashes. But Bligh had weak officers under him and was making a voyage that made exceptional demands on his men.

During the six months' stay at Tahiti, where the ship collected the breadfruit and other scientific specimens that gave the captain his nickname, Breadfruit Bligh, the men enjoyed themselves with the local women and Bligh's officers failed to exercise control. Shortly after leaving Tahiti, he found that Fletcher Christian, his lieutenant, and Fryer, the master, had allowed the ship's chronometer to run down, a disastrous occurrence for a lone ship in an unknown ocean; and soon afterwards, as far from a sailmaker as it was possible to be, he found that the spare sails had been allowed to get damp and rot. He entered in the log his wish to replace Fryer – and told Fryer so with some force – and without doubt chivvied Christian. Christian was the educated son of a good family which had fallen on hard times, who started life at sea aged seven, in 1762, as a servant – a ploy to ensure rapid promotion later, since a man had to serve six years before he could qualify as a lieutenant. He became an able seaman and in 1771 a midshipman and it was Bligh who promoted him acting lieutenant during the voyage.

Fletcher Christian seems to have suffered from a persecution complex. He was over sensitive to criticism, at times morose, brooding and given to weeping, and he became far too caught up in the life of the islands during the stay there. Bligh, though a splendid seaman, was quick-tempered with a sharp tongue and, though he tried to emulate Captain Cook, who was actually more cruel physically and had the same sort of temper, he did not have Cook's charisma.

When the time came, the *Bounty* men had no wish to leave Tahiti, and soon after departure for the West Indies on 28 April Christian and others entered Bligh's cabin, tied his hands, and put the ship in a state of mutiny. There were only sixteen men involved out of forty-three, and the rest were put into the ship's boat. After a voyage of 4,000 miles, Bligh and the loyal men reached land. Of the mutineers, some returned to Tahiti to pick up women, but there were quarrels with the natives and many of them were murdered. Others settled on Pitcairn Island, where their descendants remain to the present day.

The *Bounty* mutiny set off other mutinies. Hearing of it, sailors thought it a good idea to go to the Pacific and live in peace there and, in hungry or hard ships, that was what they tried to do. It happened several times at the beginning of the nineteenth century, and there were many Europeans with native wives and half-caste children who dared not leave the islands or give an account of how they got there. But in almost every case the mutiny failed to be entirely successful. Though ships quietly disappeared, none of their crews seemed to live happily ever after. The crime seemed to carry its own punishment and always seemed to end in disaster. Mutineers who, by implication alone, were a lawless type of man, seemed to fall out, get drunk or show bloodthirstiness, and few mutinies in the end were victorious.

The mutinies continued late into the century: *Lennie*, 1875; *Caswell*, 1876; *Frank N. Thayer*, 1886; *Ethel*, 1899; *Leicester Castle* and *Veronica*, 1902; *White Rose*, 1908. Crews were usually mixed – British, American, Negro, Filipino, Chinese, Malay, French, German, Dutch, Lascar. Many of them had been shanghaied so that, apart from conditions and food, mutinies arose from thoughts of revenge, jealousy or complaints of preferential treatment. Most mutineers were caught and jailed or hanged, but still they went on – and go on even to the present day. In July 1989 four members of a seventeen-man crew of a Taiwan fishing boat were believed to have been murdered during a mutiny off the Australian coast near Darwin. In August 1989 a mutiny on a

Panamanian freighter, *E. B. Carrier*, had to be handled by the Japanese coastguard.

Single-ship mutinies could always be controlled, however. Fleet mutinies were different, and in 1797 a mutiny occurred in the Royal Navy that actually put the country's safety at risk.

Spithead

When the French revolution started, it set up a feeling throughout Europe that all the old ideas of privilege had been swept away. Because she was separated from the Continent by the Channel, Britain was the last to experience it, but both plain people and the intelligentsia hailed the event with rapture. Although Britain was supposed to be a free country, the British did not enjoy political, social or economic freedom.

Pitt, the Prime Minister, did not want war against the French but, by forcing them to fight for their lives, the allied coalition against the new republic taught the French about war and, since it was no longer necessary to be of noble birth to hold a commission or a command, intelligent, brave young generals were thrown up, and in England there was always the threat of invasion via Ireland or Wales. By 1796, with Napoleon Bonaparte beginning to emerge as a future leader of menace, Captain Thomas Pakenham of the Channel Fleet, warned the First Lord of the Admiralty, Earl Spencer, that the seamen of the Royal Navy were becoming increasingly discontented at not being paid, and that they deserved increases. Spencer felt that the state of the country made such a thing impossible.

British men-o'-war staggered to and fro in the Channel storms, hanging on through punishing months to intercept a French invasion, but there were no longer ships of the line in the Mediterranean because the decrepit fleet there was having to refit in neutral Portuguese ports. Though British seamen had won enormous wealth for Britain, because of the punishing life they led Nelson considered them finished at forty-five, and at this lowest point in their history and totally unsuspected by the government, the men of the Grand Fleet and the North Sea Fleet went on strike. In the four main naval bases of England, about half the lower deck of the Navy and 5,000 Marines hauled down the Royal standard and the pendants of their admirals and raised instead the red flag of defiance. They swore oaths of fidelity to their cause, and established the first government based on universal male suffrage that Britain had ever seen.

At the beginning of the winter British spies were sending alarming reports of a French invasion fleet at Brest, said to be heading for Ireland, always a back-door route to England. On 15 December 1796 the French force sailed, but ran into the sort of weather that had wrecked the Spanish Armada and had to retire. Another force was made ready immediately and actually made a landing in Wales in February 1797. They were defeated largely by hunger.

The two attempts, however, seemed to indicate that more were on their way and the Channel Fleet of Admiral Lord Bridport was the main defence of the country. Bridport, who was seventy years old and anxious to retire, commanded sixteen sail of the line and two dozen smaller craft, within them around 12,500 men, most of them serving unwillingly and as eager to go home as Bridport. Many of them had been taken by the press gang, snatched willy-nilly from the streets and sent into naval vessels. Others were taken off homeward-bound ships just as they were looking forward to seeing their families. A final source of men were the jails and the debtors' prisons, because service in the Navy was always offered as an alternative. Others were whipped away on the information of fathers worried by unsuitable suitors for their daughters, and by magistrates who handed over men – usually rogues, vagabonds and smugglers – under a system by which districts were obliged to supply a quota of men. They were kept in the holds of hulks until they were claimed by the Navy, and when the hired tender *Caesar* ran aground near Pwll Du Head in 1760, the shore was strewn with the bodies of pressed men who had drowned in their locked hold like rats in a trap.

As the demand grew more fierce with the wars, these impressed men began to include some whose Bible was Thomas Paine's *Rights of Man*, of which hundreds of thousands of cheap copies had been printed in five years. One of the things Paine pointed out was that the pay of the Navy was roughly the same as it had been a hundred years before. It was while the Channel Fleet was blockading Brest in February 1797 that a small group met clandestinely in the three-decker *Queen Charlotte*, flagship of the fleet. The leading spirit was one Valentine Joyce, a quartermaster's mate from *Royal George*. The men were dissatisfied with conditions, food and pay. The food was vile and in short supply because victualling officials stole as much as they could, and ship's pursers, who had sometimes paid for their appointments, shortened the rations further. These abuses were known to the Lords Commissioners of the Admiralty but they did nothing to put them right.

The men in *Queen Charlotte* were determined to put things in order, and they drew up a petition drawing attention to the fact that the army and militia had recently received a rise in pay while they had not. Shrewdly, they did not mention food, cruel officers, unseaworthy ships, unpaid prize money or impressment, and confined themselves to the indisputable fact that they were not being paid what they deserved. Copies of the petition were sent to trusted men in every ship for signature, and practically every ship's company gave its full support. Several sent their petitions ashore unsigned, to be posted to the man they considered the sailors' friend – Black Dick, Admiral Earl Howe, the victor of the Glorious First of June in 1794. Unfortunately, though decently expressed, the petitions were all the same and Howe felt that they were fabricated by some malicious individual. Because they were not signed, he could not reply to them, but he did pass them on to the Admiralty.

On the last day of March, Bridport's fleet returned to Spithead, the great naval anchorage between Portsmouth and the Isle of Wight. The huge ships were those that had fought the Glorious First of June but, with Howe sick with gout, Bridport, his deputy, was in command and as soon as the ships anchored Bridport took a coach for London and many of his captains went ashore. Among the seamen only the crews of captains' barges were allowed ashore, despite the fact that many of the men had not been on dry land for three years. From Portsmouth, wives, laundresses and slops-sellers went out in boats to take the sailors' last few coins, and in the boats were forbidden flasks of brandy, radical tracts, republican propaganda and works by Thomas Paine. As the boats went out they passed the main topmast of Kempenfeldt's ship, the earlier *Royal George*, which still lay in the fairway. Bumboats and wherries passed *Queen Charlotte*'s petition to other ships, and the leaders of the movement contrived to meet again. It was now several weeks since the petitions had been sent to Howe, and disappointment had turned to resolve.

Fortunately for the British, the French Navy was suffering from the same stirrings of discontent, and *Rights of Man* was being read across the Channel in French and Dutch as well as in English, because dissatisfaction did not exist only in British ships. But on Thursday 13 April Captain Philip Patton, boarding *Queen Charlotte*, noticed that both the duty and off-duty divisions were gathered in argumentative groups on the foredeck, some even straying on to the holy of holies, the quarterdeck. The ship's officers were not objecting and the boatswains' mates, who would normally be swinging ropes' ends, were mingling with the men. The seamen were talking openly about refusing to sail if their petitions were ignored. The same thing was happening in *Royal Sovereign*, where a Marine brought the information that if the petitions remained unanswered two guns would signal a general mutiny. Patton hurried ashore to the tower of the Church of St Thomas à Becket, which was a signal station. From there he sent a message to the next signal station, from whence it was passed on to the next, and within three minutes it had reached London. The Lords of the Admiralty cancelled their Easter holiday plans and the next morning a message from Portsmouth indicated that several ships' companies intended to refuse duty at noon on Tuesday, the 18th.

Bridport had no reason to think the rumours idle talk. Recent mutinies were well remembered. Bridport, like Howe, was old and in poor health and, without doubt, discouraged by years of government lack of interest in his men. High officials were unlikely to be bothered by sailors' grumbling, and the House of Commons all too often consisted of the younger sons of the nobility, who were interested only in themselves.

The day before Easter Bridport told his captains to encourage the petitions, and instructed that they should be specific in their complaints. His idea was probably to bring the business to a head so that it could be dealt with, or to amass enough evidence to get the complaints attended to by the government. The lower deck replied with a will, and demands were made that officers accused of ill-treatment should be removed. Bridport wrote to the Sea Lords begging them not to order him to sea before some answer could be given, but it was crossed by a letter from the Admiralty ordering him to hold himself in readiness to sail.

The petitions continued to move between ships, and with growing confidence the ships' companies elected speakers. The mutiny wrecked the myth that sailors were just jack tars, mentally inferior but always jolly and loyal.

When the Admiralty order arrived Bridport was convinced that his crews would not sail but he had to obey instructions to send eight men-o'-war under Sir Alan Gardner to St Helen's, the departure anchorage off the east side of the Isle of Wight. But when Gardner issued orders, not a man moved. It had been planned for the disobedience to take place two days ahead, but the order from London had caused it to happen earlier. Nothing that Gardner tried moved the men, but it was all kept highly respectable. Joyce had made his plans over the months and he now firmly advocated moderation. But his instructions remained: all orders were to be obeyed, save the order to weigh anchor. The men behaved as planned and the Royal Marines, traditionally the policemen of the fleet, sided with them. Bridport advised against force being used to check the rebellion, and from the admiral down the officers all said that the delegates appointed by the ships were the best men aboard. The anchors stayed down.

Before the men was the precedent of the successful mutiny in *Windsor Castle*, ninety-eight guns, in San Fiorenzo Bay, Corsica, in 1794. The men had demanded a replacement of their admiral, their captain and two other officers; the captain was removed and the mutineers pardoned.

Ships were still allowed to sail where the delegates felt it was necessary and, behaving always with propriety and sense, they even allowed warships to escort them. Aboard the ships, as a reminder that self-government was no licence for riot and debauch, the lower-deck committees hung ropes from the yard-arms, the traditional rig for a hanging. It was believed ashore that they were meant to intimidate officers, but in fact they were simply an expression of rigid self-discipline, and spirits were kept high by cheering and singing.

On Easter Monday morning, Earl Spencer decided to go to Portsmouth in person, with two of the Commissioners, and Bridport wasted no time in sending the news to the ships. The men were delighted. Though Howe appeared to have failed them, their petitions had produced the mighty First Lord instead. Spencer, who was only thirty-nine, had worked hard at the Admiralty to clean up the muddle left by his appalling predecessor, the Earl of Sandwich. He arrived at Portsmouth, expecting his presence to overawe the mutineers. A proclamation was issued exhorting the seamen to behave, and calling on the spirit of Kempenfeldt. The seamen gave as good as they got with another proclamation, inviting the spirit of Kempenfeldt to come forth and try the scanty allowance on which they were obliged to subsist. They also produced a new petition, this time drawing attention not only to their wages but also to their provisions, the state of the sick aboard and the payment of men wounded in action. Spencer was dumbfounded. Unable to acknowledge the delegates' authority, he refused to consider the new petition, though he did offer a small rise in pay and to look after the wounded. The offer was not enough; the delegates wanted something more realistic.

The Sea Lords became angry, and sent another ultimatum, but the delegates remembered that after the mutiny in *Culloden* in 1794 the delegates had been hanged after being promised a pardon. They wanted a pardon, too, and they wanted it to be official.

The affair had reached deadlock when it was noticed that *Royal George* was flying a red flag. It was a flag that was raised only when the fleet entered battle and someone had taken it from the flag locker and hoisted it as a gesture of defiance.

With the victorious French armies apparently about to descend on the British Isles, the Prime Minister called a meeting of the Cabinet, which recommended that a full pardon be granted but it was felt that the petitions for the removal of officers could only be considered when the men returned to duty. Night riders brought the pardon to Portsmouth and it was shown to the delegates, but there had still been no settlement in writing on wages, victuals, pensions and other demands. Nevertheless, the pardon was considered to have been granted and the mutiny seemed over. However, the Sea Lords refused to consider food, and their message was so blunt that the command at Portsmouth suppressed it. On 25 April, thinking the affair over, Spencer once again sent Bridport orders to sail, but a gale prevented the ships from leaving, and by the last week of April the Privy Council had still failed – through sheer inertia rather than unwillingness – to send the Bill on the fleet's pay to Parliament. Then it was found that one of the ships that had been allowed by the mutineers to proceed to sea had taken news of the mutiny to Plymouth, where there were more men who had not been paid for two years, while signs of deteriorating morale were now also showing in the Mediterranean fleet.

The surrender of Austria to the French had left Britain without an ally and, with a Dutch amphibious fleet assembling at Texel, a new North Sea Fleet was created under the command of Admiral Adam Duncan, a raw-boned Scot who was often more demanding of the Admiralty than his men. The new fleet was based at Yarmouth but, while mutiny simmered in Duncan's ships, fortunately it was boiling over in the Dutch ships. One of Duncan's ships was *Director*, captained by William Bligh, who had already experienced mutiny in *Bounty*. Though his men called him 'the Bounty Bastard', he was in fact held in high regard by them.

While giving way over pay, the Lords of the Admiralty issued a general order which, while it appeared to preface better conditions, embarrassed officers, intimidated the men, and advised vigorous measures against mutiny, and on 3 May Howe admitted that he had misunderstood the petitions he had received. It showed that the Admiralty had received the petitions two weeks before the demonstrations had started, and that two more weeks had been allowed to pass without action. Fierce emotions ran through the forecastles and Spencer hastened to advise Bridport that the men should be convinced that everything promised was actually on its way, but that things took time.

Pitt had hoped to have the matter settled on Friday 5 May, but Parliament went home for the weekend and the Navy was once more in revolt. This time there was even some loss of life when the seamen were fired on, and many unpopular officers were removed from their ships. It ended with the fleet ready to sail, fully manned and provisioned but with almost no officers on board except Bridport, the Commander-in-Chief. Panicking, the government finally decided to do what it should have done weeks before, and appointed the one man the seamen trusted, Black Dick Howe, to win a settlement.

Howe took his wife with him to Portsmouth. Most of the fleet had been with him on the Glorious First of June and, despite the mistake he had made over the petitions, he was still trusted. He had always blamed captains for lower-deck discontent, and he brought the news that Parliament had finally pulled its socks up and passed the Bill for the increase in pay and rations through all its stages in one day. Within three hours he had won the seamen over. He did not berate them for insubordination, merely expressing amazement that they should have struck a second time on the basis of false reports. By the end of the first day, he had had the red flag struck and the yard ropes unreeved, but this was done because of his personal prestige, rather than a belief that the government had changed its ways.

Even the city of Portsmouth was fed up with the government by this time because it had had to support thousands of wives and families who had travelled there to see their men, and felt that a fleet run by seamen was no worse than one run by the Admiralty.

Black Dick Howe was received on board *Royal William* with full honours. The seamen still wanted a purge of unpopular officers and Howe was handed a list of about seventy-five of them, one an admiral. Howe, an admiral of the fleet, coolly removed a fellow admiral at the insistence of an illegally constituted cabal of mutineers.

On Sunday morning, 14 May, four weeks after the mutiny

began, a formal reconciliation was enacted in the great cabin of *Royal William*. Howe promised that in future petitions, properly signed and drafted, would receive prompt attention. Men with no legal rights – kidnapped, oppressed men, for the most part ignorant and illiterate – had won most of their demands. To show his oneness with the men, the old admiral appeared before the people of Portsmouth with the delegates and, accompanied by his wife, Valentine Joyce, ships' and marine bands, set off in a parade through the town. He invited the delegates for a drink and they carried him on their shoulders through the streets. Not to be outdone, Lady Howe invited the delegates in for supper.

The mutiny at Spithead was over and the fleet sailed. But no one had noticed that while it had been going on the fleet had been visited by four men from the fleet at the Nore, who took back to their ships information about what had happened. Having seen the fleet at Spithead satisfied, they thought it was their turn now, but what had been only a breeze at Spithead turned into a gale at the Nore.

The Nore

For a variety of reasons, the mutiny at the Nore was a very different affair from what happened at Spithead. It was conducted in a more arrogant manner by a very different sort of man, was never as controlled as at Spithead, and – what had a considerable effect on the result – it was in a very different place. Spithead was a long way from London, but the Nore command covered the area at the mouth of the river Thames and, because of its position, the mutiny there was always considered much more of a threat to the capital and to the government.

Tens of thousands of vessels passed the Nore on their way to London, and the Navy used the base more than any other because it was there that frigates made rendezvous with merchant convoys for the Baltic or the Atlantic, and ships came in to be provisioned or repaired or to shelter from Channel gales, or were blown in from the squadrons that were sent out to reinforce the blockaders. There were also prison hulks, guard ships, receiving ships, store ships and lesser craft, and they had none of the communal spirit of a proper fleet. The anchorage lay near the town of Sheerness, a small garrison town whose guns were supposed to dominate any invasion course to London.

The officer in command was Vice-Admiral Charles Buckner, and many months before the Spithead mutiny he had received petitions over pay, food, conditions and cruel officers. His flagship, *Sandwich*, was being used as a receiving ship for pressed men, and above her normal complement of 900 she had more than 500 coerced men. The ship's surgeon wrote that they were 'dirty, almost naked and generally without beds'. Sores and scalds would not heal and fevers resulted from air impregnated with human effluvia.

Among the quota men in *Sandwich* was a handsome dark-eyed man of thirty called Richard Parker. He was a Devon man and had come from a debtors' jail, but he had been a carpenter and a schoolteacher, and had once been a lieutenant in the Navy. He had a striking personality and was a good speaker, but he was undoubtedly paranoic and probably unbalanced.

The first moves for mutiny were conducted with commendable secrecy, and the morning of Friday 12 May was chosen for the cheers that would signal the takeover of the anchorage to be given. It was made easier because a court martial was being held, which removed many captains from their ships, among them Bligh, of *Director*. When Bligh returned to his ship, he found the men obeying one of the delegates and learned that they had discharged three of his officers, though there was no complaint about Bligh himself. He held on to his quick temper and, making sure he controlled the side-arms in the ship, defied the demand for the weapons by men from another ship.

The men at the Nore for some reason did not believe Parliament had passed the Act that granted privileges to the Portsmouth men, and from the very first they set up an organisation that was different. There were also differences between ships, and some were reluctant fellow-travellers. A court martial being held in *San Fiorenzo* was interrupted by massed delegates demanding that the *San Fiorenzo*s join the cause, and when the *San Fiorenzo* men showed reluctance, they were immediately fired on by *Inflexible*. No one was hurt, and little damage was done, but it showed at once how different this mutiny was. Parker insisted to the men that the Act of Parliament that had granted the requests of the mutineers at Spithead wasn't permanent, and the Nore delegates demanded that the men should be allowed ashore. As their relatives appeared for seaside holidays, 'frolics and parades reigned at Sheerness', while the seamen's example began to spread to shore establishments.

Though the mutiny at the Nore had now been in progress a week, the Admiralty considered that what they had granted had surely concluded the affair. Admiral Duncan was having trouble at Yarmouth, but there were no delegates and no red flags. Duncan sent a statement of grievances to London, but in Whitehall offices were closed for the wedding of George III's daughter, and soon Yarmouth was in an uproar, the frustrated seamen bullying the inhabitants and breaking windows. For the most part, Duncan was able to handle it. He was an enormous man and, on one occasion when he had been defied, he had grasped the man's collar and with one hand lifted him over the ship's rail.

The delegates were not playing fair, however. They did not announce the Act of Parliament and the royal pardon to the seamen, who continued to think that they were simply supporting the men at Spithead, and they now even began to think that they should show the men at Spithead a thing or two. Parker, the elected president of the delegates, liked to be called 'Admiral of their fleet' and, with his help, a new set of demands were sent to the Admiralty. Buckner could not bring himself to convey the Admiralty's retort, but he tried to make clear to the delegates that nothing but hostility could be expected. His pendant was hauled down and up went the red flag. Gunboats were sent from the fleet to the Great Nore, and as they passed the fort each boat sent a round whistling at the ramparts. They were not courtesy salutes, and the delegates pulled the ships in the Little Nore out to the main anchorage and moved the fleet into two business-like arcs with the gunboats at either end. Loyal seamen managed to send a message to Buckner, begging him to do something to mollify the extremists, and he appealed to the Admiralty to have the pardon made clear in a more solemn manner with full ceremonial.

For the second time in his career, William Bligh found himself escorted to a boat by a mutinous crew, and 'President' Parker informed Buckner that there could be no settlement until the Admiralty Commissioners appeared in person. He was clearly seeking the humiliation of his superiors. Buckner could only request the Admiralty that he be sent no more ships, while the delegates, striking dramatic poses, refused to allow two ships, which had been ordered to take the newly-wed royal pair on their honeymoon, to sail.

Since the royal pardon applied only to events before the Spithead settlement, it did not cover the more recent events and the Sea Lords now heard that longboats full of armed mutineers were pulling towards London. Their object was to take over ships anchored at Long Reach. As they did so, the red flag began to fly only fifteen miles from the court of St James. Two ships which had not mutinied were covered by a disaffected ship's guns and, since there was discontent among soldiers at Woolwich too, the country began to fear revolution. Still uncertain what to do, the Admiralty sent Bligh, with his experience of mutiny, to find out. By this time the government had decided to make a stand. Howe felt that an invasion attempt by the French was the only hope of everyone recovering their senses, and furnaces were prepared at the Thames forts to make ready red-hot cannon balls if 'President' Parker should try to advance upriver. Duncan was chosen as the man to act against the mutineers if necessary.

In the end the Commissioners of the Admiralty went to Sheerness, where they were met by seamen wearing red ribbons. The men were orderly, however and Buckner, through an informer, learned that the organisation at the Nore was fragile and that discipline was being upheld by intimidation. Pardons were offered, but by now the Commissioners were learning of dissension in Duncan's fleet, though there were no symbolic nooses with Duncan's men, no red flags, no cheers and no hostility towards officers. As mutiny disintegrated Duncan's fleet, nevertheless the men did not hesitate to fire a salute to

Restoration Day, commemorating the return of the monarchy after Cromwell's rule. For the occasion, dockyard men replaced their red flag with the loyal standard.

By this time, however, the delegates were quarrelling and the Admiralty and the Army were beginning to behave more firmly. Harbour defences were erected, and storeships and victualling yards were ordered to stop furnishing supplies. Unhappily for the delegates, they had not been provisioned for a long cruise like the ships at Spithead, and when, on 30 May, Parker and another delegate went ashore at Sheerness to induce the authorities not to cut off the victuals, they found the population hostile. While they were away the King's pardon and the Act of Parliament was read to the ships' companies, and half a dozen men tried to haul down the red flag. There were deck brawls, and aboard *Sandwich* Parker demanded to know whether the men wanted to continue with the mutiny or give it up. He was answered with shouts of: 'Give it up.' His impulsive appeal made the more committed men feel that he had entered a private bargain with the Admiralty. By his arrogant behaviour he had lost their sympathy, and from then on he was elected president of the fleet only by the day. With Sheerness preparing for a siege, only two of Duncan's ships of the line now stood between Britain and invasion, but, with the wind perfect for the invasion fleet, he remained rigidly in position across their path.

By this time, though, ships led by more moderate men were managing to slip away from the mutineers' net. Foolishly, the delegates made further demands, among them that courts martial for seamen should be made up of seamen and Marines. They still held power largely by intimidation and flogging, and men were threatened with ducking if they did not wear red cockades. Merchant captains crossing the Channel told of the vast Dutch fleet but it was believed in Holland that Duncan had more ships than he actually had, because he was constantly hoisting signals to an imaginary fleet over the horizon. Yet in the frigate *Circe*, the captain and his first officer had to sit back to back with loaded weapons defending the helm, while a minority of the crew and officers sailed the ship, the rest barricaded below in a state of mutiny.

Buckner had been removed from command and the delegates sent a letter to the Admiralty in which for the first time they used words like 'republic', 'revolution' and 'civil war'. By now newspapers were shouting for vengeance as loudly as they had been shouting for reason, and in reply the delegates started a blockade to stop food ships reaching London. Counter-operations were conducted by Vice-Admiral Lord Keith, who used deposed officers to command newly placed shore batteries.

Fortunately for the country, the wind that forced Duncan to cling on off the Dutch coast changed against the invasion fleet and he was able to claw off the coast and allow his worn-out men some sleep. Though London was not starving, she was beginning to feel the pinch and Bligh was sent to assist the anti-mutiny command. Unbelievably, however, on the King's official birthday the mutinous sailors turned out in their best rig and lined the shrouds and yards and a twenty-one-gun salute was fired and three cheers given.

By this time the mutiny was one month old. A few officers like Captain Lord Northesk, instead of whining about what had happened, tried to find out why it had happened and came to the conclusion that the mutineers were not traitors but men in a dilemma. But, though they claimed to be loyal, the men threatened to take the ships abroad if their demands were not met. All too often, however, a ship's company was held in sway by a dozen strong-willed men or the threat of the guns of companion ships.

But there was no longer contact with the shore and the average Briton was becoming convinced that the mutineers were Jacobins, French agents or traitors. Meanwhile, Trinity House men had scuttled buoys in the shipping lane and there was not a navigational aid left in the estuary. Resolution cracked and the delegates became desperate enough to start asking what ships' companies wished to do. Five choices were offered: surrender; a move to Texel to win over Duncan's ships and then proceed to Cherbourg to join the French; to sail to Scotland to decide what further to do; to head for Ireland and then join the French or vanish inland; or to sail for the 'New Colony', by which they meant North America or a new country to be founded in the Caribbean.

But as stores were redistributed ready for sailing, on Saturday, 10 June, scuffles broke out and, when the signal gun was fired, not a ship moved. Some did not have enough manpower. Others simply held back. Immediately officers with initiative started regaining their ships, and finally *Sandwich* hauled down her red flag. In *Leopard* there was a fight and men were shot, but the red flag was struck and she began to slip away. *Standard* fired on her, but the gunners obeyed the order of an officer to desist. Before long the counter-mutiny had run through the fleet, and by Monday there were only two red flags at the Nore. The government demanded unconditional surrender, and immediately a dozen ships ran up the red flag again. But there was no mention of a royal pardon and by Tuesday the red flags had vanished once more.

Delegate leaders were arrested and, when he could control *Sandwich* no longer, Parker released two junior officers who demanded that the white flag be raised. Warned that they would be fired on by bitter-enders, they replied: 'Fire and be damned!' The mutiny subsided in cheers, arguments, songs and tears. The reactions of the captains differed. When asked for names, one named only a handful. Another sent fifty men off to imprisonment. The last ships gave in and ex-'President' Parker, his hands tied, was taken ashore to Gravesend. The very last stand was in Bligh's *Director* and, when she submitted, Lord Keith telegraphed the Admiralty that the mutiny was 'quite extinguished'. Bligh was consistent to the end. When he returned to his ship he found thirty-one of his men accused of mutiny but, a strict man with his inferiors, he was equally strict with his superiors, and he protested so hotly that in the end only ten men and two deserters were charged.

A few delegates from *Inflexible* slipped into small boats and made their way to France, where they joined French privateers. Parker's court martial was held at Long Reach. Acting as his own counsel, he put up a spirited defence, but the government needed an example and he did not stand much chance. He was found guilty, condemned to death and hanged at Sheerness before ships which had been brought down for the occasion. The execution took place aboard Parker's own ship, *Sandwich*, and in full view of his wife, who by pure coincidence happened to be approaching in a boat.

A total of 560 delegates were imprisoned, and 412 of them appeared for trial. At least fifty-nine were sentenced to death and thirty-six were hanged; twenty-nine were transported, others were flogged or given hard labour. Nelson's comment was, 'I would rather see fifty shot by the enemy than one hanged by us,' and it is noticeable that not a single man from Bligh's *Director* received the death sentence.

It clearly wasn't quite over, however, and in September 1797 the crew of the frigate *Hermione*, of the West Indies Station, mutinied against their captain, one of the most brutal officers in the Navy, and he and six of his officers were murdered, the ringleaders escaping into South America. Their behaviour made Parker's transgressions seem mild, and the Admiralty pursued them without mercy.

At home, Duncan finally met the Dutch fleet at Camperdown in the usual butcher's shop of a naval fight. Seven battleships, two fifty-gun ships and two frigates were captured in a battle that was won by men who had been in a state of mutiny only a few months before. Bligh was there too. Howe commented that it would eradicate the seeds of discontent and Duncan, newly a viscount, used the opportunity to petition for a pardon for 180 repentant Nore mutineers imprisoned at Chatham. Pardon was granted.

If the mutineers did nothing else, they gave protesters the world over a new symbol. When, after Waterloo, the French found themselves dissatisfied with the returned Bourbons and revolution broke out once more in 1830, the revolutionaries adopted the simple red flag the British had snatched from its locker as a symbol of defiance. It was carried again in 1871 by the Paris Communards in their defiance of the government after the Franco-Prussian War and again by the Russians in their revolution of 1917. At British Labour Party meetings to this day the assembled delegates finish their debates by singing their official anthem: 'The People's flag is deepest red.'

The Black Sea

Despite everything, the mutinies in the British fleets were considered to have remained 'respectable'. Russian mutinies were different, and the mutiny in the battleship *Potemkin*, in 1905, indicated just how different.

The Imperial Russian Navy was divided into three, the Baltic Fleet, the Far East Fleet and the Black Sea Fleet. In numbers, it ranked third in the world, but the division of forces and the fact that her fleets could never be used together because of the distance between them meant that Russia was actually a second- rather than a first-class naval power. In addition, as a result of corruption and the incompetence of its officers, it had never had a seagoing tradition and its sailors were largely conscripted peasants, simple, childish and lacking in intelligence. F. T. Jane, the naval commentator, summed them up succinctly. 'Ivan,' he said, 'realises that he exists to be shot at, Jack that he exists to shoot at others.' Nepotism was rife, and no junior officer could hope for promotion if he did not possess influence. With morale low, there were never enough officers in ships and it was not uncommon for a midshipman to be in charge of as many as 350 men.

In the Russo-Turkish War of 1877 the Russian Navy had not done very well, its lack of daring exemplified by the small armed steamer *Vesta*, which, finding itself face to face with a Turkish ironclad, not unnaturally bolted. However, the captain compounded his failure by reporting that he had sunk the Turkish ship, and fame and decorations followed. Only when the war was over was the secret revealed by a letter from a Turkish admiral to the newspaper *Novoe Vremya*.

With the turn of the century Russia found herself at war again, this time with Japan. The Boxer rebellion, a war against foreigners in China, was ruthlessly suppressed in a way that left China open to all those powers involved in setting up colonial empires. Among them was Japan, just emerging into modernity and determined to find a place in the sun. Russia found herself in dispute with her over conflicting interests on the mainland of China, and war became inevitable.

The war started with an attack by Japan on the Russian Far East Fleet in Port Arthur, a Russian possession in South Manchuria. As in 1941 at Pearl Harbor, the attack came without a declaration of war. Three Russian ships were damaged, none of them seriously, but the effect on morale was tremendous. The following day the Russians put to sea but, after only a brief exchange of fire, broke off the action and returned to harbour, where they were virtually blockaded.

When the energetic and inspiriting Admiral Makharov arrived, he got rid of incompetent officers, sank blockships and raised morale, but when on 13 April he led his squadron out to meet the Japanese, his flagship struck a mine and blew up, killing him. Once again morale slumped. The Japanese surrounded Port Arthur and were able to shell the harbour from the hills, and eventually in August, under the threat of court martial, Admiral Witgeft took the Russian ships to sea. He was killed in the battleship *Tezarevitch*, and five more warships ended up interned in neutral ports. With the Battle of the Yellow Sea, the power of the Russian fleet was destroyed and the remaining ships returned to Port Arthur, where many of their guns and crews were removed for the defences of the port.

The Russian Navy was not finished, however. After the first battles, the Tsar's advisers remembered the ships of the Baltic Fleet and, under pressure from the war party, Admiral Rozhestvensky was ordered to prepare it for a voyage to relieve Port Arthur. The decision was taken in June and Rozhestvensky intended to sail in July, but such was the hopelessness of Russian naval affairs that he was unable to move until three months later.

It was a ceaseless struggle against the incompetence, perfidy and intrigues of his subordinates and the corruption of his superiors. In its organisation and administration the Russian Admiralty, presided over by a decaying nobleman, was ponderous, bureaucratic and inefficient, a rusting affair rotten with bribery and favouritism. Ships built in Russian yards were put together in such a leisurely fashion that they sometimes took as long as six years and joined the fleet with guns and armour that were already out of date. The sailors, limited to six months' sea training a year because of ice in the Baltic, had none of the aptitude of the sailors of other maritime nations, and no amount of discipline could make up for their lack of skill. One half, it was said, 'had to be taught everything because they know nothing, the other half because they have forgotten everything and when they remembered it was obsolete'.

Rozhestvensky had to use his knowledge of the graft-ridden stores and purchasing departments of the Navy and slash through webs of red tape, while gangs of resentful civilian employees had to be brought aboard the ships at pistol point to finish jobs which had been signed for as completed by foremen who hadn't inspected them.

The battleships looked formidable enough on paper, but their designers had been persuaded to add more and more comforts for the benefit of the officers, while they had none of the electrical firing mechanism of the Royal Navy and still relied on the non-instantaneous lanyard system. Coal was a problem. Rozhestvensky's fleet would consume 3000 tons daily and Russia had no coaling stations along the route to the Far East. By international law, neutral ports were closed to them and St Petersburg had to enter into a contract with the German Hamburg–Amerika Line to supply the armada from sixty colliers, all the way from the Baltic to the Yellow Sea.

The fleet finally left in October, the occasion a junket for the officers in the lavishly decorated wardroom of the flagship *Suvarov*. The squadron coaled at Libau, but by this time the ships were so overloaded that lower decks were almost awash and one of them, *Oryol*, promptly ran aground.

Russian intelligence had warned that Japanese spies, agents and torpedo boats were everywhere across their path – in fact there wasn't one within thousands of miles – and when their course took them near the Hull fishing fleet in the dark, the Russian officers were so certain they had run into Japanese raiders that they opened fire. Fishermen were killed and several Russian ships were holed by the shells of their companions. It brought Britain and Russia to the brink of war.

Rozhestvensky struggled on, beating his way with his ships round the coast of Africa. By this time, at Port Arthur the rest of the Russian Far East Fleet had been destroyed by gunfire from the hills, torpedoes or scuttling by their own crews, and the garrison surrendered in January 1905. Rozhestvensky was at Madagascar when he heard the news. Now that Port Arthur had gone there was really no point in continuing, but to him and his officers it had become a point of honour to do what they had sworn to do. But the 18,000-mile voyage had become a nightmare, and when they finally arrived they were intercepted by the Japanese Admiral Togo in the Strait of Tsu-Shima. Thanks to out-of-date equipment, lack of experience and panic, within an hour Russian sea power had been blasted off the surface of the water. Of the eight Russian battleships four were sunk and four captured; seven cruisers and five destroyers were sunk and one destroyer captured. A single cruiser and one destroyer reached Vladivostok, while the remnants of the fleet found their way into internment in neutral ports. Of the support vessels three were sunk, two reached Shanghai and one reached Diego Suarez. The Japanese lost three torpedo boats. Rozhestvensky was wounded and captured, and all that remained of the Russian Imperial Navy, the Black Sea Fleet, was locked up behind the Dardanelles.

There had always been revolutionary elements among the naval conscripts in the Black Sea Fleet, and the cause had gained strength when the Commander-in-Chief, Vice-Admiral Chukhnin, trying to effect economies at Sevastopol and Nicolaiev, sacked labourers in the dockyards and replaced them with blue-jackets who were immediately indoctrinated by their workmates. The disasters in the Far East made things worse, and the Black Sea squadron became a hotbed of revolutionary talk.

The commander of the battleship *Potemkin*, Captain E. N. Golikov, was well satisfied with the morale of his ship, however. She had just completed a refit and had been detached to Tendra for practice firing, dropping anchor on 26 June, accompanied by the 100-ton torpedo boat *N267*. Meat for *Potemkin*'s crew was brought aboard and hung on the spar deck from hooks, and the following morning, 27 June, a sailor swabbing the deck noticed that it was riddled with maggots. Within minutes other seamen had gathered round, protesting, but the ship's doctor, Surgeon Smirnov, insisted that the meat was fit to eat.

The protest seemed a minor flare-up, but Commander Ippolit

Giliarovsky, the second-in-command, was aware that there were troublemakers in the ship and that revolutionary pamphlets were being passed around. At the midday meal, when the men refused the bortsch made from the contaminated meat, he checked with the surgeon, who again pronounced the meat edible, and he demanded that the men eat their meal. When they still refused, he called them on deck and insisted, and when they still refused he threatened to have the ringleaders shot.

It was at this point that the ship's company, already well primed, broke into open mutiny. Shooting started and Giliarovsky was brought down, together with a midshipman alongside him. During the scuffle, an able seaman, Gregori Vakulinchuk, was fatally wounded and it sent the men in search of the officers. Several were murdered, while others leapt overboard. More were hunted down and finally the captain was found in his cabin. He had planned to blow up the ship and was dressed only in his underclothes, ready for the swim that would follow. He, too, was murdered and thrown overboard. The torpedo boat *N267* tried to escape but, threatened by *Potemkin*'s guns, was forced to return to her side. By the middle of the afternoon the mutiny was over, but the killing was by no means ended.

The great city and port of Odessa nearby was the fourth city of the Russian Empire, with a population close to half a million. Ships of all nations left the harbour every year with some £20,000,000 worth of grain and other products of Bessarabia, the Ukraine and the rich Dnieper Valley. It was one of the most beautiful cities of the Empire, but it was a hotbed of dissension – exacerbated by the disasters in the Far East. Though it had remained largely unaffected by the unrest elsewhere in Russia, by April strikes had started, and on 26 June a demonstration was broken up by Cossacks with some loss of life, and the already tense situation was made worse as *Potemkin*, seeking a refuge after the mutiny, steamed into the harbour on the evening of the 27th.

She was flying the red flag, that symbol of mutiny and rebellion that had been flown by the British sailors at Spithead and the Nore. Though influenced by the climate of the period and the effect of Tsu-Shima on morale, the ratings in *Potemkin* had risen against their officers not in revolution but in protest against bad meat. There was clearly more to it than this, of course, because troublemakers aboard had spurred them on, but the ship's routine had not changed and efforts were being made to run the ship in the old way, because at least a third of the ship's company had not gone along with the outbreak. When *Potemkin* arrived in Odessa, the ringleaders, all of whom claimed to be Social Democrats, got into contact with party members ashore. The ship was seen by the revolutionaries in the city as their saviour, and agitators swarmed aboard at once.

The sailors were a great disappointment to them. The chief skill of the ship's ringleaders was in oratory and proclamations, and their main concern was to obtain supplies and coal and to give a decent burial to their only casualty, Able Seaman Vakulinchuk. The strikers wanted them to start the revolution by bombarding the city with their huge guns, and as far away as St Petersburg the influence the ship had brought to bear was reflected in the belief that total revolution was a possibility. The Tsar reacted by declaring a state of war.

As Vakulinchuk's corpse was placed on a bier on the quayside it became a rallying point for strikers and dissidents. As the people of Odessa came to view it they were harangued by the agitators until reverence and sorrow gave way to demands for revenge and the crowd made its way up the Richelieu Steps, built to commemorate the Duc de Richelieu, the French émigré who had become Governor of Odessa and had been largely responsible for the city's development. But the telegraphed ukase from the Tsar had arrived by now and the crowd was met by Cossacks. What followed has been immortalised in Eisenstein's film, *The Battleship Potemkin*. Believing the ship to be backing them with its great guns, the working people did not flee when the Cossacks appeared, and when the Cossacks charged they were driven back down the steps. The steps were twenty-five yards wide, 240 of them in all, and the massacre took place down their entire length. The dead included women, children and innocent bystanders, and the terrified crowd were met at the bottom by more Cossacks who had been sent to the quayside to meet them. The slaughter continued along the quay until the place was covered with corpses and half the city was on fire. Only Vakulinchuk's unguarded bier was left intact.

An appeal to the ship to send men ashore to deal with the Cossacks was turned down, as was the plea for bombardment, and the plans for concerted action between the mutineers and the men ashore came to nothing. That night the street fighting reached a new pitch, and there were some 2000 dead as the police and the Army tried to drive the revolutionaries out of those parts of the city they had occupied.

The men from the ship did nothing, but when a party sent ashore to bury Vakulinchuk the following day was ambushed on its way back to the ship, they at last agreed to bombard the city. Knowing of a meeting of senior officers in the city theatre, it was decided that this would make a good target. A single six-inch gun was used, and only two shells were fired. One took the roof off a house and the other damaged the façade of a lodging house. No one was hurt. It confirmed everybody's opinion of Russian naval gunnery and showed why Admiral Togo had sunk or captured almost the entire Far East squadron at Tsu-Shima a month before.

The Black Sea Fleet was in turmoil by now, and the *Potemkin* affair only made things worse. Vice-Admiral Krieger, deputising for Admiral Chukhnin, who was in Moscow, decided to take the fleet to sea and capture *Potemkin* before the chaos could spread any further.

There had been several alarms at Odessa that the Black Sea Fleet was on its way, and the business there bumbled along in a hopelessly inept way. So far the seamen had achieved nothing. Their arrival had sparked off an uprising which had been crushed with the loss of thousands of lives, and the bombardment had been a ludicrous affair. For two days and three nights, bathos and anti-climax had followed one another in turn and now, on 30 June, learning that three great ships were approaching and terrified of being trapped, they made preparations to put to sea.

When Krieger's squadron and *Potemkin* met, and the loyal ships began to manoeuvre, such was the incompetence of their officers and the uncertain support of their crews that nothing was done and they merely moved round each other before parting. Reinforced by two more ships, the loyal vessels returned and approached *Potemkin* in two columns. *Potemkin* merely sailed straight down the middle and, to the admiral's dismay, as she passed *George the Conqueror* the *George*'s crew began to cheer, as the men at Spithead had cheered. The ships reversed course and once more *Potemkin* sailed through the avenging fleet, the officers watching helplessly. To complete the admiral's humiliation, *George the Conqueror* joined *Potemkin* and sailed with her towards Odessa.

Shipping in the Black Sea had come to a complete standstill and Chukhnin had now lost two of his seven first-class ironclads, while another was so riddled with agitators that she could not be trusted even in harbour. The Black Sea Fleet had virtually ceased to exist, and Chukhnin took the unprecedented step of sending the entire personnel home on indefinite leave. Only a few officers refused to go and, with the admiral's consent, took over the destroyer *Stremitelny*, and set out to find and torpedo *Potemkin* before any more damage could be done.

It seemed like total victory for the mutineers, but in fact it was the beginning of the end. Most of the *George*'s crew were far from won over. Like the mutiny in *Potemkin*, like the mutinies at Spithead and the Nore – for that matter like most mutinies, strikes or revolutions – it was a case of a largely passive majority manipulated by an active and determined minority, and despite the agitators who swarmed aboard, the *George* finally broke away on 1 July and, threatened by *Potemkin*'s guns, ran herself aground on the mud.

For the mutinous leaders in *Potemkin*, the joining of the *George* had seemed a triumph, but now fear, despair and indecision took over and it was decided to surrender. The sailors were sick of oratory and, exhausted and depressed, they weighed anchor and headed across the Black Sea, the air around the ship full of the sound of argument and recrimination.

Their reception at Constanza in Rumania was cool. They were offered sanctuary but were refused coal and supplies, so they turned away and steamed into the little port of Theodosia, dressed overall to give the impression that *Potemkin* was what she certainly was not – a happy ship. When the mayor refused them coal, they threatened to bombard the town and, in a panic, the place was evacuated. But the sailors found a number of coal barges and were on the point of taking them over when they were caught by a company of soldiers who opened fire, killing and wounding many of them.

It severed the last strands of determination, and the mutineers decided to return to Constanza. They were hungry and tired and no longer had coal to move their ship. When they anchored the leaders opened the sea cocks and, as the men went ashore in boats, the great ship settled on the bottom. She had barely sunk when the little *Stremitelny*, unaware of what had happened, arrived, determined to destroy her. She had chased *Potemkin* back and forth across the Black Sea but, as her commanding officer prepared once more to take up the chase, her boilers finally succumbed to the twelve days of extreme overwork and blew up.

Potemkin was refloated and rechristened *Pantelymon* (or *Low Peasant*) as a mark of disgrace, but she never again fired a shot in anger. As for the mutineers, some surrendered or were captured, and on 9 September sentences of death were passed on seven of them. Nineteen more were sent to Siberia and another twenty-five were sentenced to long prison terms. One or two made their way to England and a few remained in Rumania. But they were always blamed for every domestic crisis that arose, and found conditions even worse than they were in Russia.

They had achieved nothing. They had not raised the revolution and, by their insistence on a martyr's funeral for Vakulinchuk, had brought about the deaths in Odessa of up to 6000 people, many of them totally innocent.

Apart from stirring up more mutinies, not only in the Black Sea but also in the Baltic, the *Potemkin* affair had been a complete fiasco. But the Odessa Steps became as sacred a site to the people of Soviet Russia as Runnymede to the English and Yorktown to the Americans, and *Potemkin* became a symbol of the struggle of the people to throw off the yoke of autocracy.

*

With the stigma of the Japanese defeat receding, Russia seemed to have returned to domestic peace when the heir to the Austrian throne was assassinated at Sarajevo in June 1914 and, drawn in by treaties arranged years before, the Tsar found himself going to war against his cousin, the eccentric and often ridiculous Kaiser Wilhelm of Germany. At first there was great enthusiasm, but by the third winter of the war subversive pamphlets were being smuggled into Russia from Switzerland. The problems were still those of corruption and inept organisation and, in March 1917, the shortage of bread led to rioting in St Petersburg, or Petrograd as it had been renamed to make it sound more Russian. Tens of thousands of workers came out on strike, and for once the Cossacks did nothing.

Exhausted and disillusioned soldiers began to desert in hundreds, and in Kronstadt, the naval base across the bay, the sailors mutinied and slaughtered their officers, throwing them overboard with weights lashed to their feet, sometimes shooting one and burying a second alive with the corpse; while Marines were led by the Grand Duke Cyril, the Tsar's cousin, to make a humiliating obeisance to the new liberal government of the people.

The Tsar was forced to abdicate, but the people were still dissatisfied and the Bolsheviks were active and aiming for power. By October, while women queued, shivering, for bread and milk, and pointless ferocious political arguments went on in committee rooms and in the streets, the crowds thickened, waiting for something to happen.

Everybody knew that something was about to happen. Word had been spread by armed sailors with the name on their hat bands of the cruiser *Aurora*, anchored in the river Neva. 'Kronstadt is coming,' they said. Kronstadt had always been a baleful influence on the city because it was a constant hotbed of disaffection (in 1921 they even revolted against Communist dictatorship), and by this time the Baltic Fleet had been won over almost entirely to the Bolsheviks. Now, organised by Tsentroflot (the central fleet committee), which had taken over the running of the ships, the red-rosetted sailors poured into Petrograd and spread along the Nevsky Prospekt, the wide two-mile-long street that connected the city to the harbour, and began to gather near the Palace Square, the vast open space between the Imperial Residence, the Winter Palace, and the enormous half-circle of buildings opposite that housed army headquarters.

Since the fall of the Tsar, the palace had been occupied by members of Alexander Kerensky's Provisional Government, but they were considered too mild in their reforms and plans had been made to get rid of them. The Fortress of Peter and Paul had already been won over and, with barricades about the city, young officers who might have resisted were trapped in the Military Hotel by armed sailors who refused to let them leave. Flying the same red flag that had been flown at Spithead and the Nore and during the Paris Commune, *Aurora* fired a single blank shell that gave the signal to take over the palace, which was guarded only by a women's battalion and a troop of fifteen-year-old cadets.

As firing started, people fell flat on their faces or began to run. The thud of cannon intensified, though most of the shells were blank and meant only to intimidate. Sailors, soldiers and workers swept across the square, and the women's battalion surrendered immediately. A few cadets were bayonetted but there was virtually no fighting, though, in the mythology of Communist propaganda, the affair was magnified to an epic of struggle and heroism. In fact, life in the city was virtually undisturbed and the only damage was to the cornice of the palace, which had been struck by two shells from *Aurora*. But it was enough. Kerensky had to flee the country and Lenin was in control.

The calm didn't last. Officers were ordered to surrender their weapons and if they did not, they received bone-smashing blows from rifles held by sailors. By nightfall, the streets were littered with swords thrown away by prudent officers. Among them were the mutilated bodies of those who had refused.

The Black Sea base of Sevastopol far to the south away from the outbreaks remained unaffected by the revolution until delegates from what was called the 'Heroic Kronstadt Sailors' Soviet' arrived, and an orator wearing the badges of a leading stoker worked the sailors there into a frenzy. Lenin, he said, had described the Kronstadt sailors as the Saviours of the Revolution. 'What would he call you?' he demanded.

As the officers argued over what to do about the threat, work in the dockyard stopped. The pot in Sevastopol had been simmering for months, but by this time the men were wearing what they pleased, relieving themselves against the turrets of the flagship, spitting sunflower seeds on the holy quarterdeck, hoisting boats awry and flying the red flag.

The orgy of bloodshed began with attacks on all the places, such as clubs, hotels and messes, where officers might be found, and by 3 p.m. all resistance had ended. But sailors had been killed and the lower deck thirsted for more blood. It was a prelude to indiscriminate slaughter. Houses were broken into and officers, from post captains to midshipmen, were butchered in front of their families. By the end it was estimated that over three-quarters of the officers in the base had been killed. There was a rigorous hunt for the remainder, and it was agreed that they should be properly executed. One party operated alongside the sea at the landing stage, and officers were arranged in batches of about ten along the edge of a wooden pontoon, facing inboard, firebars lashed to their feet. Watched by an immense crowd, with observers clinging to lamp posts, they were pushed into the sea. More died in the same way dropped from a boat. In the naval club, others were despatched by smashing a grand piano's heavy lid down on heads held in place on the upper edge of the piano's side.

British naval officers arriving at the base in 1919 to help the White Russians in the civil war that had started called it 'cracking nuts'. They were often regaled by stories of the mutinies, and the shore by this time was littered with wrecks, among them a three-funnelled destroyer whose captain was said to have been stuffed into the ship's furnace.

The revolution in Russia had been a long time coming but when it came it came with a vengeance, and the mutinous Russian sailors were among the more prominent of those who ganged up to destroy their oppressors.

Kiel

Only three years separated the Battle of Jutland, which the Germans considered they had won, from the scuttling of the German High Seas Fleet at Scapa Flow. Though Jellicoe was denied victory at Jutland, there is no doubt that the Germans preferred not to risk another encounter, and from the monotony of harbour routine sprang the discontent which was the parent of the High Seas Fleet mutiny. And this in its turn led to the revolution in Germany which hastened the allied victory on land and the collapse of the German Empire.

What caused the mutiny? At first sight, the reason seemed to lie in the influence of the Russian mutinies and the hopeless state of Germany after the heavy reverses of 1918, but, according to Friedrich Ruge, who was an officer in the German light naval forces, it went far deeper than that – as far back even as the construction of the fleet.

The German fleet, he claimed, was more an object of emotion than sober understanding. In German history, only the Hanseatic League had possessed sea power and known how to use it, and the Imperial Navy originated with the establishment of the German Empire in 1871 after the defeat of France in the Franco-Prussian War. The naval rivalry between Britain and Germany worsened the political climate between the two countries, and Germany still remained substantially behind Britain as a naval power.

In 1914, without enough bases abroad, the High Seas Fleet was unable to operate against British sea communications from the Heligoland Bight, and no vital British line of communication ran through the North Sea. When war started the Germans expected another Copenhagen – the battle where Nelson destroyed the Danish fleet under the muzzles of shore batteries – but it did not come, and it was only when the land war bogged down after the Battle of the Marne that the offensive operations of the High Seas Fleet began.

On 31 May 1916, the two fleets met off Jutland, and in the first phase of the battle the German battle cruisers met with great success. When the main fleets joined, the Germans got into difficulties from which they extricated themselves by their excellent training, and on the whole the battle represented a tactical success for them because, with fewer ships, they inflicted considerable losses on the British. But the relative strengths remained unaltered and so did the strategic situation. Germany was still cut off from the rest of the world.

After Jutland, in the main the action was restricted to submarines and light forces, and the crews of the big ships saw little of it, being for the most part restricted to Wilhelmshaven, which, though technically well provided for, offered no relaxation or amusement for the crews. Wilhelmshaven dated only from 1869, and though there was a large hotel for officers and canteens for the barracks-based troops, there was nothing for the ships' crews. Hostels should have been provided because the ships, carrying bigger crews than in peacetime, were cramped.

By 1918, because of the British blockade, rations were meagre and everybody was living on the eternal swede, which even the best recipe failed to make appetising. Coffee and tobacco were short, beer was thin and, though there was wine, on the whole this benefited only the officers.

There were also tensions that were scarcely recognised. The technical personnel of the ships came from industrial backgrounds, and many of them before the war had belonged to trade unions. Engineer officers occupied a lower social status than deck officers, and, with a desperate shortage of soap, handling the coal by which many of the larger ships were still fired was an arduous job which the stokers felt was not sufficiently recognised.

Though Wilhelmshaven had little to offer the crews, neither had the bare landscape of Scapa Flow for the British. But Scapa was a long way from the influences of industrialised towns and all these shortages in the course of the long war had an increasing effect on German morale. In the summer of 1917 trouble started in several ships of the German fleet.

At the beginning of June part of the crew of the battleship *Prinzregent Luitpold*, known to the fleet as 'The Convict Ship', refused to collect their midday meal. This was repeated on the 19th. A week earlier, part of the crew of her sister ship *Friedrich der Grosse* – failed to appear for duty, and on 20 July 140 ratings of the light cruiser *Pillau* walked off the ship. They were punished with three hours' drill. On 1 August some fifty ratings in the *Prinzregent* refused duty and went ashore. When they were punished 600 ratings absented themselves the following day to listen to a mutinous speech made by a stoker named Köbis. The leading troublemakers were arrested, but on 16 August part of the crew of the battleship *Westfalen* went on strike while coaling, made written demands and threatened to use force. There was also trouble in *Rheinland* and *Posen*.

An enquiry established that, while the hunger strike was probably spontaneous, plans had been well prepared and a small number of revolutionaries had been able to persuade several thousand men to give passive support to a mutiny disguised as a peace movement. Several of the spokesmen were in touch with leaders of the Social Democrat Party and one of them, a rating by the name of Reichpietsch, from *Friedrich der Grosse*, who was only twenty-three and politically inexperienced, had probably been flattered by the way in which SDP members of the Reichstag had received him.

German ships were constructed on a small-compartment system. This design had resulted from the sinking in the 1870s of *Grosser Kurfürst*, an ironclad of the Prussian Navy which had been rammed accidentally by a companion ship. Because she disappeared within a few minutes, an attempt to make ships safer led to the small compartment design. This was largely the reason for the German ships' greater resistance to gun and torpedo damage at Jutland but now, in 1918, it proved a disadvantage. The narrow and irksome subdivisions which had saved the ships two years before were only bearable because the German crews lived ashore, and they made supervision of the men very difficult because the smaller compartments made excellent places to hold secret meetings.

The Social Democrats' aim was peace and, though the influence of the Russian revolution was not as great as was supposed, certainly the revolutionary character of the movement had been clear among the crews. The government's intervention broke all this up and several ringleaders, including Köbis and Reichpietsch, were executed while others were imprisoned.

The fleet command recognised the cause of the trouble – often merely food and leave – and their counter measures were in the right direction. But little was done about recreation. British sailors at Scapa had far fewer amenities and almost no distractions, but the men were kept busy. An eighteen-hole golf course was laid out, each capital ship being responsible for one hole. Boggy stretches of ground were levelled to serve as football pitches and there were also two amenity ships attached to the fleet. *Gourka* was a naval store vessel which could be used as a theatre ship for concert parties and amateur performances by officers and men. *Borodino* was a floating general shop purveying groceries and luxuries not included in naval rations, as well as cigarettes, tobacco, books and magazines.

In their free time, German officers, petty officers and ratings lived in almost complete isolation from each other. British officers played football and cricket with their men. In Germany, as more importance began to be laid on submarine warfare, the best and younger officers and men disappeared to the undersea boats and into flying and minesweeping, where they might expect to see some action. And while the Army promoted suitable NCOs into the gaps left by casualties, the Navy rejected this means of making officers.

The Russian revolution should have provided food for thought, especially as the troublemakers constantly referred to it and were clearly impressed by the fact that it was a way to bring about peace quickly in a war that grew daily more burdensome. With the entry of the Americans into the war, defeat became inevitable. When it became clear that the allied offensive in France could not be halted, officers saw in the High Seas Fleet a still intact fighting instrument of great power, and began to talk of a last great operation – a vigorous action that would be of value in the political efforts to secure an armistice.

The sortie that was planned was not, as has been said, an admirals' rebellion, and the supposed 'sacrificing' of the fleet was utterly incorrect, though it made good propaganda and a trigger for the mutiny which the agitators exploited to the full. The fleet had actually been assembled on 29 October, when the order for sailing was postponed and it became known that the battleships *Thuringen* and *Helgoland* had mutinied. With every man at action stations, submarines – always loyal because they contained the pick of the men of the fleet – were brought up, their guns loaded and their torpedoes primed, while the mutineers manned their own guns and trained them on the submarines. It was deadlock.

Negotiations achieved nothing, but an ultimatum undermined the mutineers' courage and they surrendered. The ringleaders were arrested and a steamer appeared with a company of marine reservists to take the mutineers to prison at Wilhelmshaven. Ashore, they were put aboard a train, but someone was foolish enough to give them a naval guard; during the journey the train was stopped and both guards and prisoners vanished into the countryside. The great sortie had to be abandoned and ships were ordered to Kiel. On the way the squadron commander had a number of troublemakers arrested, and when they were brought to prison in Kiel it was the signal for the rising to start there.

History provides plenty of examples of mutineers and their causes, but no one thought it could happen to the splendid High Seas Fleet. But neither the Russian revolution nor the incidents of 1917 had prompted German naval officers to look more closely at developments. The new factors were the agitation and rumour-mongering by the Social Democrats and enemy agents. As is always the case, the bulk of the crews were decent and reliable but were confused by stories that the proposed sortie was merely to save the honour of the officers, that the fleet was to be uselessly sacrificed, even that revolution had broken out in England.

Sailors' councils were formed and when, on 3 November, an attempt was made to impose discipline with a General Defence Alarm, instead of bringing the seamen to their duties it brought them into the streets, and a great tidal movement of sailors, dockyard workers and others headed for the Waldewiese, a large recreation park outside the town. It moved on foot, in street cars, in lorries, but it was sinister because it was quiet and orderly.

Inflammatory speeches set the mob moving again and, faced with an armed patrol, the agitators claimed that the rifles were loaded only with blanks. The confrontation resulted in eight dead and twenty-one wounded.

It set the sailors breaking into armouries for machine guns, pistols and rifles, and pieces of red cloth began to appear on uniforms. Previously a piece of red cotton threaded into a sailor's blouse had been enough to indicate his sympathies, but now shops were raided for bolts of red material and signal flags were torn up to provide red armbands. When the port admiral tried to negotiate, he was faced with a group of unkempt sailors and was forced to capitulate to their demands. A gigantic parade followed, with every man armed. Rifle shots occurred and officers were dragged from offices and cars and flung into cells, and a search began for loot in the shape of officers' dirks, swords and badges.

On 5 November, the same red flags that had been hoisted at Spithead, the Nore and in Russia appeared in Brunsbuttel and Lubeck, and on the 6th in Wilhelmshaven, Cuxhaven and Hamburg. Decrees were issued denying that the fleet was to be sacrificed, but it was far too late. Service authority was virtually non-existent and the sailors' councils were behaving with an amazing mixture of pomposity, impudence, naïvety and boundless utopianism. A stoker called Kuhnt elected himself president of the province of Oldenburg, which he claimed was an independent republic. Officers had to flee in carts, on bicycles and on foot to escape arrest. Epaulettes and badges of rank were torn off, resistance resulting in a beating.

Paralysed by the news and by the imminent ending of the war, the government in Berlin promised that troops would not be sent against the sailors; this turned the mutinies into a revolution. A great exodus from Kiel began as sailors on foot, in lorries, and in trains they put together and ran themselves, scattered in all directions. The fleet on which the Kaiser had lavished money and affection was no longer loyal to him. The titular head of the Navy, Grand Admiral Prince Henry, the Kaiser's brother, fled from Kiel wearing a red armband and flying a red flag on his car as he drove with his wife and son through picket lines of hostile sailors. There was no guarantee that the Kaiser would be as lucky.

On the 9th, with red flags everywhere in Wilhelmshaven – on ships, public buildings and private houses – Berlin, also beginning to descend into chaos, threw in its lot with the mutineers. The Kaiser abdicated on 10 November, and the war ended the following day. Under the terms of the armistice the German ships were to be interned in a neutral port, starting their journey on 18 November.

Considering that the fleet was now under the direction of a Workers' and Sailors' Council and a number of other equally pompous-sounding committees, this left little time. The vessels were disarmed and Admiral Sir David Beatty, determined to have no truck with mutineers and revolutionaries, insisted that a German flag officer should command. When it became apparent that internment was to be at Scapa the Germans were indignant, but there was little they could do about it. The sailors' council tried to insist that every ship should fly a red flag, but they were informed that such a flag was regarded as a pirate flag and could be fired on. A three-man sailors' council was elected and its leader, a signal rating who had done all his service on shore, with his cap on and a cigarette in his mouth, informed Admiral Ludwig von Reuter's Chief of Staff that he had taken over and that the Chief of Staff was merely his technical adviser. However, in the end he lost his nerve and ordered the hauling down of the 'red flag of freedom'.

When the Germans appeared, no one knew how to receive them because there had been rumours that they might come out for a final battle. In an atmosphere of excitement and tension, the British light forces led the way, flotilla by flotilla, to meet them. In a tumult of churned water and the hum of boiler-room blowers, 150 destroyers steamed east in a tremendous show of might, still prepared to do battle if the Germans decided on a Wagnerian gesture of self-immolation. Beatty was determined to make a show of it, and every ship in the Royal Navy that could be spared was there – from Dover, Harwich, Scapa and the Channel – 370 of them with 90,000 men, every ship flying a large number of white ensigns as if they were going into action. Each column consisted of over thirty battleships, battle cruisers and cruisers, a destroyer abreast of each flagship. Beatty led in *Queen Elizabeth*, flying the flag he had flown at Jutland.

They were expecting sixty-nine German ships, one missing because of engine trouble, one because she had struck a mine – humiliated ships run by committees of sailors who claimed that they were the brothers of sailors everywhere.

The German ships, still menacing in appearance, were led by *Friedrich der Grosse*, behind her *Seydlitz*, *Moltke*, *Derrflinger*, *Hindenburg* and *Von der Tann*, all famous ships blessed with the names of German heroes. Like grey ghosts in the mists, the two fleets met. The crews of the allied vessels, which included French and American ships, wore asbestos flame helmets, gauntlets and breast shields and waited at action stations. But the Germans were arriving without heroics, and as they approached the British sailors crowded the spaces round the funnels and gun platforms of their ships, pushing among the torpedo tubes and clinging to boats for a better view. Every British ship was stationed on a pre-selected German vessel, her guns trained across the narrow stretch of water.

As the destroyers hurried by, the sea was filled with movement. There seemed no end to the ships, the air vibrating to the sound of their washes and the shudder and hum of machinery. Reaching the end of the German column, the British vessels wheeled and brought up abreast of the German destroyers. Three light cruisers took up a position ahead of the Germans and over another a balloon hung, a man in the basket staring through binoculars at the German ships.

The Germans were in single line ahead – nine battleships, five battle cruisers, seven light cruisers and forty-nine destroyers, their turrets picking up the thin sunshine. There was no sign of triumph from the British ships. They found it hard, in fact, to believe that the German ships which had posed a threat for so long were now meekly surrendering. The British moved with precision, every man doing his job expertly to show that the German claim to victory at Jutland was nonsense, and the sea seemed full of enormous ships.

The Germans had been stripped of powder and shell, breech mechanisms, sighting instruments and range-finders, and they looked dingy and unkempt, their hulls streaked with rust as they cut through the water in what seemed the funeral tread of a defeated nation. When they reached the Firth of Forth the three parallel lines pressed closer together. As the Germans approached their prison anchorage, soldiers from the shore batteries lined the water's edge to watch, and boats of every description – steamers, yachts and rowing boats – all packed with civilians, milled about, savouring the triumph. The British sailors watched grimly as the manoeuvre of anchoring was executed in silence. But as each German ship reached its position and dropped anchor, its bulwarks became crowded with hungry men fishing.

'What a way to celebrate Der Tag,' someone said. 'Chucking out a fishing line to catch a herring.'

A senior officer going aboard the *Grösser Kürfurst* to check that there were no forbidden armaments was met by the sour smell of unwashed hammocks, blankets and clothing. The ship's flats were filled with litter, and pamphlets were everywhere. Every man seemed to wear a red ribbon on his blouse and the officers wore no epaulettes or badges. A sailor stepped forward, saying that he was chairman of the supreme sailors' soviet aboard the ship and that he was in command. When the British officer ignored him and demanded to see the captain, the sailor bristled with indignation. 'The captain has no power,' he announced. 'Everything has been changed by the revolution.' The British officer still ignored him and eventually, dumb with shame, a German officer led him to the captain.

There was a brief attempt by the German sailors to make contact with their British counterparts, but the British blue-jackets refused to acknowledge them with a cold aloofness that rocked them back on their heels. To the Germans who had spent most of the war in barracks within reach of Kiel's lights, bars and women, when the ships moved to Scapa, they found it desolation itself. They were not allowed ashore or on board other ships in case the subversive tendencies they had brought with them should inflame a growing discontent that had begun to manifest itself in the Royal Navy.

At Scapa, the crews were cut – no more than 200 men to a battle cruiser, 175 for battleships, and so on down the scale, just enough to move the ship if necessary. Those personnel due to return home left, and the remainder settled down to wait. It was a miserable winter as they fought boredom, cold, cockroaches, rats and, not least, the contempt of the British. The sailors' councils had expected their opposite numbers to greet them as comrades, but the censure in the eyes of the British lower ranks was as cold as it was in the eyes of their officers.

The Germans learned of the peace conditions on 11 May 1919, and immediately asked what was to become of their ships. Admiral von Reuter, however, managed to get rid of troublemakers so that, left only with loyal crews, he stated to his senior officers his intention to scuttle the ships rather than allow them to be handed over meekly without the consent of the German government, who were still negotiating peace terms.

After two days of storm and wind, on 21 June the British fleet at Scapa left to undertake exercises. The day was fine and at 11 a.m. – as a steamer, the *Flying Kestrel*, carrying hundreds of schoolchildren on an outing to see the surrendered ships, approached – the pennant Z, a forked red flag, was hoisted at the yard-arm of the light cruiser *Emden*, and all the German ships acknowledged it. Since nothing untoward happened, the few British still in the Flow were not suspicious, but in fact the most monumental shipwreck of all time was about to occur. The Germans had opened all sea cocks, watertight doors, scuttles, portholes, hatchways and ventilators, and had bent, disconnected or broken every connecting rod associated with bilge and pumping valves.

The smaller vessels were the first to go, then finally the big ships and, though the few British still in the anchorage tried to stop the Germans leaving their ships and there was some wild shooting, by evening fifteen out of sixteen capital ships were sunk in deep water. Of eight light cruisers five were sunk, and of fifty torpedo boats thirty-two had disappeared, only fourteen in shallow water. When the British started to raise the sunken ships, those in shallow water presented no great problem, but others did and the last was not raised until after the Second World War had started. By that time, of course, they were of no value to anyone except as scrap steel and for that by 1940 there was plenty of use.

Invergordon

At the time of the great fleet review at Spithead in 1911, when the waters of the Solent were covered with the huge ships of the Royal Navy in tremendous steel lines that were symbolic of the might of the British Empire, a letter appeared in the *Portsmouth Evening News*. It attacked the social conditions in the fleet and suggested what seemed at the time the ultimate horror of a trade union to improve the sailors' wages, leave and food.

It provoked angry comments and, doubtless, demands in letters to the editor for the writer's head. But there was some truth in what it said. There *were* vast differences between officers and men. With the end of the Great War these became more noticeable, and, encouraged by propaganda and by what they had seen with their own eyes, the men of the lower decks began to talk.

Disaffection unfortunately breeds more disaffection, but it is hard to believe that the triumphant British Navy which had seen the humiliation of the Germans in 1918 could have been involved in mutiny within thirteen years of the end of the war, and within eight years of the commencement of another one. But it was so. Those mutinies of the Russian and German fleets led to a mutiny in the Royal Navy of which few people these days are aware. Men cannot watch the disintegration of a vast naval organisation without asking questions and becoming infected themselves.

The British naval mutiny of 1931 was a direct result of the German mutiny of 1919 which, in its turn, sprang from the Russian mutinies of 1917, which could be traced back through the Communard-led rising of 1870 and the French uprising of 1830 right back to the mutinies at Spithead and the Nore in 1797. Mutiny had come full circle, right back to where it had started.

Conditions in the Navy had been sadly neglected during the war. Pay and allowances were so small that a man with three

good-conduct badges, representing thirteen years of faithful service, could have a daughter of sixteen working in a factory who was
earning more than he was. The situation had not much improved by
1931, with unfair discrepancies not only between ship and shore but
also between the various grades of the seamen themselves. The
officers were equally dissatisfied. The high social and ceremonial
factors of naval life had gone with the brilliantly uniformed eti-
quette, spit and polish, but nothing had taken their place, and Sir
Eric Geddes, deputy director of munitions during the war, had
been appointed by Lloyd George to save £200,000,000 a year by
economies in the Forces and the social services. His name became
a dirty word to officers who saw their service careers cut short
through no fault of their own.

The Geddes Axe, as it was known, uprooted more than 1200
naval lieutenants and lieutenant commanders from their chosen
profession with only gratuities and small pensions. There was a
growing sense of insecurity and both officers and men felt they had
been betrayed, particularly as the shortage of personnel so reduced
a man's time ashore that the old naval prayer about returning to
enjoy the blessings of the land had become only a mockery.

Big ships were still in favour with senior officers, monuments
to the creed of the big gun and the great capital ship which even
Fisher, its creator, had repudiated before his death. They remained
expensive symbols of an idea that had vanished with the war, and,
despite the cuts and the economic distress ashore, some officers still
seemed to live like lords. Roger Keyes, the Commander-in-Chief,
Mediterranean, somehow managed at Malta to create a staff whose
names sounded like a court circular, and officers were said to be
reporting for duty with a pair of polo mallets and a copy of *Debrett's*
under their arm. To those not so well endowed, the place seemed
to smell of privilege.

It came to an end with the farcical *Royal Oak* affair, which
arose from the proximity in the same ship of a choleric admiral, a
dogmatic flag captain and a neurotic commander. The Navy made
a fool of itself with an elaborate and well publicised court martial
over an incident which should have been dealt with quickly and
quietly by the Commander-in-Chief. As one French newspaper

commented, the Navy set out to wash its dirty linen in public, but it turned out to be only 'a slightly soiled pocket handkerchief'. It ruined Keyes's chances of becoming First Lord.

By 1931 the world was in the middle of a slump. Enormous reparations had been placed on defeated Germany and, determined she should never again be able to pose a threat, France had insisted on the utmost advantage being wrung from the victory. The immediate effect was that it impoverished Germany and, impatient of receiving their reparations, the French marched into the Ruhr in 1923 to run German industries themselves. But when the Germans refused to co-operate the whole industrial system came to a halt and in the ensuing months the German currency was wrecked. Meanwhile, in the United States the stock market crash had occurred and, between them, the two events affected the whole of Europe. In Britain the Labour Government resigned and a National Government took office, but the pound remained weak, and there was still a huge deficit and an unemployment figure of nearly 3,000,000, most of them adult males.

With the international economic situation still deteriorating, a new and unexpected pressure built up on sterling and, to save funds, a Committee of National Expenditure, under the chairmanship of Sir George May, was set up. It forecast an enormous deficit and recommended economies, among them a reduction in unemployment payments and a cut in the pay of teachers, police and the services.

It was a bad time to introduce cuts. Many British sailors had seen the revolution in Russia at first hand, even the refusal of allied troops to become involved in the civil war which had followed. French troops landing at Odessa had had to be withdrawn because of it, and in the Navy a protest meeting had been held aboard *Coryphée* concerning the same feeling, while on the river Dvina the crew of the gunboat *Cicala* had refused to sail. The mutiny had been dealt with ruthlessly, but the discontent remained and a battalion of Marines had refused duty at Murmansk. Others had been infected by strong Communist cells in German ports they had visited in the Twenties and, with the advent of the Labour Government in England, instead of going to their officers with their complaints as they previously had, men now went to their dockyard MP. They had to be handled very carefully.

In addition, after several years of peace, the old loyal wartime crews had disappeared and new men had joined up, many bitter because they had been forced into uniform by the absence of work ashore. They had none of the spirit of the earlier recruits and, having belonged to trade unions, did not hesitate to air their grievances. They even included a number of professed Communist agitators, who took full advantage of the frustration that had become so prevalent. Nevertheless, the decision to cut pay might still have passed off without trouble in the Navy, as it did in the other services, but for bad luck and some bad judgement.

The Atlantic Fleet was due to start its summer cruise, but the ships that began to sail northwards from their home ports on 7 September contained a number of agitators determined to make the maximum capital out of the cuts. Not long before there had been a minor mutiny in the submarine depot ship *Lucia*. She had been converted from a captured German freighter, and humorists liked to suggest that some of the ghosts of the High Seas Fleet were still hanging around her holds. She had been an unhappy ship with a long record of trouble and, because of the dirty state of her decks after coaling, weekend leave had been cancelled by a choleric first lieutenant. Nothing had been said about the crew not being allowed ashore for the normal Sunday afternoon leave, however, and when the duty watch were ordered to fall in they had remained sullenly on the mess deck until marched off under close arrest. Nobody was really surprised. The first lieutenant had a reputation for being tactless in the extreme, and it was obvious that the story had run through the fleet. The name *Lucia* could be heard everywhere, and intelligent commanders found themselves on the look-out for any of their officers who might be inclined the same way as *Lucia*'s first lieutenant.

The Navy no longer has the system of three manning ports, where ships were given their complements of men, but in 1931 these still existed and every one of them had a different character. Chatham was a Londoners' port, and the men mustered there were known for their Cockney wit and fearlessness, but were easily influenced by bad characters. Devonport was largely a port for placid and loyal West Countrymen, but they always included a few bitter unemployed Welsh miners. Portsmouth men came from all over the United Kingdom and it was necessary to be cautious with them also, because many came from the far north where there was no manning port and, since they always suffered at leave time by the length of their journey, they, too, were inclined to be bloody-minded. The differences between the men from the three manning ports were well known and on the whole, even on the lower deck, the men did not mix, but before the ships left Portsmouth there had been a meeting run by agitators which men from the cruisers *Norfolk* and *Dorset* had attended. Since *Norfolk* was a Devonport ship, it was wondered how they came to be there.

Both *Norfolk* and *Dorset* had visited Kiel after the war, and doubtless the first thing the men aboard saw was the war memorial painted red. The Communists had been active there ever since the German mutiny and they had doubtless found listeners among the British blue-jackets, some of whom visited the International Seamen's Club, which was known to be a headquarters of subversive influences. In fact, when the Chilean fleet had mutinied earlier in the year, it was claimed by the Chilean government that the deep-rooted cause of it was that their ships been refitted at Devonport, where the crews had acquired attitudes prevalent in British dockyards.

The May Committee's report, of course, made excellent propaganda and in view of the general unrest it was essential that officers in command should have full knowledge of the proposed measures of economy. The Admiralty therefore arranged for a signal to be sent to commanders-in-chief all over the world, explaining the position and the sacrifices demanded. The signal was received by every commander-in-chief except the Commander-in-Chief, Atlantic Fleet. It reached his flagship, HMS *Nelson*, quite safely but Admiral Sir Michael Hodges was not on board and when he returned from leave he was not shown the signal at once. The tragedy was compounded by the fact that almost immediately he became seriously ill and was rushed to hospital. The fleet's sailing was not cancelled, but Hodges' illness led to confusion because Rear Admiral Wilfred Tomkinson, who took over, sailed in a different ship, HMS *Hood*.

Taking over a ship is a long and complex business. Taking over a fleet has unlimited possibilities for things to go wrong, and it was Tomkinson's first command. The Admiralty should have postponed sailing, and Tomkinson should have had more guidance about the cuts. But Admiralty Boards come in various degrees – strong, medium and weak – and the one in 1931 was called simply 'a bad Board'. It had made no protest to the government about the cuts and failed to make sure that Tomkinson knew what was going on.

As the ships sailed he still had no inkling of what was to happen because *Nelson* was left behind with Hodges' staff and, of course, the all-important signal. This was not the end of the muddle. The Admiralty had sent a letter explaining the reductions, but this did not reach Tomkinson until four days later, 14 September, three days after the details had been released to the press.

The cuts that were proposed were deeply resented and *The Fleet*, a magazine read throughout the Navy, commented: 'God knows how any Royal Commission came to the conclusion that the poor misused matloe's pay can be reduced. They might be expert economists but never, surely, humanists. Did any of the commissioners ever visit a sailor's home to see how his money is spent? Did they ever live with sailors in small ships to see how it's earned?'

The name *Lucia* continued to be heard. When the men of *Lucia* had been found guilty and sentenced, it was noticed that the political masters of the Navy had reduced the sentences and put the captain and first lieutenant on half pay so that it smacked of politics rather than discipline. Another thing which bothered the Navy was the problem of what were called the 1919 men. Men who joined the Navy before 1925 earned more pay than those who joined up later, and it seemed that the government wanted not only to cut their pay but also to reduce it to the level of the other men's first, so that in effect it would be cut twice over. Most of the post-1925 men were unmarried with no commitments. The

1919 men were older men with homes and families. But, about to cut unemployment benefits affecting three million voters, the men at Westminster felt that service cuts affecting less than a third of a million, not all of them, because they were under voting age, on the electoral roll, would cause no political problems.

As the battle fleet – *Rodney*, *Warspite*, *Malaya*, *Hood* and *Repulse*, accompanied by four cruisers, including *Norfolk* and *Dorset*, submarine depot ships and destroyers – began to move north, first lieutenants found the flats outside their cabins filled with men wishing to see them. They were always decent older men who felt that they were victims of a breach of contract. Many had served through the war and it was difficult to help them, because there had been no lead either from the Admiralty or Parliament and the only comment on the affair came from a bored politician who said that the two scales of pay were 'an inconvenience'. Men with children found that there wasn't much between making ends meet and getting into debt; others had entered into hire-purchase agreements on the understanding that they would be paid the 1919 rates. Rents were hard enough at naval bases – even for poor accommodation – and there were plenty of people glad to make a living out of sailors, who were *not* conforming to the cuts.

The only way to avoid trouble was to encourage the men to bring their difficulties to their officers, but nobody made requests through the proper channels any more because they always seemed to go astray in the welter of paperwork presided over by admirals and civil servants in no danger of suffering themselves.

A few alert officers, on the look-out for trouble, enquired if any signals that might indicate concerted action against the cuts were being tagged on to the end of normal signals between ships, but wireless officers had seen nothing and the petty officers who might have spotted something were careful to maintain an attitude of neutrality. There was still sullenness and it seemed to be increasing. The men were listening to the BBC for information but the BBC confined itself to speculation about an emergency Budget.

First lieutenants doing the rounds were aware of ominous silences in their ships, but little was done as officers were all too often watching their own yard-arms. They were usually in total agreement with the men, but were well aware that what the seamen might be thinking of as a strike was still mutiny in the eyes of the Navy.

Warnings were passed to the petty officers to try to stop the resentment turning into public meetings and to watch out for the big talkers. Speculation about the Budget indicated increases in beer and tobacco which would leave remarkably little for the lower deck to live for, and it was still firmly believed that the government would not dare impose cuts of the magnitude proposed.

When the ships dropped anchor in Cromarty Firth the resentment seemed to have increased. The boats that went ashore brought back worried letters from wives, and newspapers with further speculation about the Budget. Puzzled senior officers, knowing of the impending pay cuts, felt sure there would be an official explanation from the Admiralty in the mail reaching the fleet. But there was no word, just the explosive accounts of the proposed cuts in the newspapers which were immediately seized on by the lower deck. The politicians' calls for sacrifice provoked only bitter laughter, which was made worse by the misleading way in which the cuts were set out in the less responsible journals. They seemed to affect only the lower ranks, and the agitators were quick to claim – though not without some justification – that the reductions in some cases would force men's wives to the point of starvation and even to prostitution. Coming unannounced as they did, they left the seamen with a feeling that the Admiralty couldn't care less.

It seemed, in fact, that officers drawing £2000 a year and upwards were to receive cuts of 10 per cent and other officers from 10 per cent to 3 per cent, while an able seaman's pay was to be reduced from four shillings a day to three shillings, a figure of 25 per cent. This took no account of allowances, but without the benefit of official explanations, the interpretation was inevitable. Other sections of the public affected by the cuts, such as teachers, were already protesting loudly and representatives of the Communist Party hurried north to take full advantage of the unrest in the fleet.

That evening *Nelson* arrived without her sick admiral and the men began to go ashore. There was a lot of shouting that was not the usual good-natured catcalling, and 'Good old *Rodney*,' was heard. 'We won't let them down.' A meeting was held in the canteen. There was some disorder, the troublemakers chiefly from *Warspite*, a lot of discordant singing about the town, impromptu speeches on the pier and alarm among the civilians at the ill-feeling that existed. As the men returned to their ships there was singing and arguing in the boats, but they came alongside quietly, though the words 'Down tools' were heard.

The midshipmen who had handled the boats considered that it was just Saturday-night rowdiness, but they had heard 'The Red Flag' being sung, and officers of the watch reported observing men talking in undertones and a general shifty demeanour. The situation as reported to Tomkinson was that the rowdyism was due only to drink. The truth was that there were men aboard the ships who had read of the mutinies at Spithead and the Nore and knew the methods used. Plans had already been laid for collective strike action and the men had returned to their ships to select leaders.

The following morning *The Times* gave the first genuine details of the cuts, its parliamentary correspondent pointing out coldly that, however things might seem to Parliament and despite allowances, an admiral's pay was being cut by 7 per cent and a 1919 man's by 25 per cent. The Admiralty letter outlining the pay cuts, when it was finally produced, made nonsense of the more lurid newspaper reports, but it none the less contained several blunders, and it seemed to have been drafted by people who were completely out of touch with the men's problems. What was worse, it arrived when feeling had already hardened and the men were in no mood to listen. It had probably been written without much thought, but to the fleet the subject matter was dynamite and should have been considered as important as any diplomatic mission. The letter even had the gall to suggest that senior officers weren't paid too much, and that middle-ranking officers' pay wasn't excessive, but that the pay of junior officers was more than necessary, and that of the men too high.

Word went round that there was to be a mass meeting in the

naval canteen ashore and that civilian agitators were to be there. The complaints, as in 1797, were not against the officers but against the government and certainly the government seemed to comprise the same old gang who had always seemed to be in power, yet had never understood the problems of the poor. The men had lost faith in the Board of Admiralty and were in no mood to listen, and jobs were done lackadaisically. The officers on the whole were wise enough not to chivvy the men because they felt that something was certainly brewing, and it was worrying that the petty officers were reporting nothing.

That night a crowd of blue-clad men streamed to the dockyard canteen from a football match and the officer in command of the shore patrol, a Lieutenant Elkins, finding that there was a meeting in progress and that the doors had been secured, managed to persuade someone inside to unlock them. As he entered there were immediate shouts of 'Get out' and the sound of breaking glass, and Elkins was forced out. No one had touched him; the men had just linked arms and walked towards him.

He managed to get in again, and received an apology and the information that what was being done was for the officers as well as for the men. As a patrol from *Hood* arrived the men began to hold a meeting on a nearby football field, and as the drifters took the men back to their ships 'The Red Flag' was heard and shouts of 'Six o'clock tomorrow.'

On Monday *Warspite* led out *Malaya* for exercises in the Firth. The remaining ships carried out their general drill, but with little willingness, and when *Warspite* and *Malaya* returned they were greeted with shouts of 'Scabs' and 'Blacklegs'. The men had learned their history. That night there was cheering from *Rodney*, answered by *Valiant* – the same sort of cheering that had marked the mutinies of 1797.

The next morning, *Repulse* was due to sail first, then *Valiant*, *Nelson*, *Hood* and *Rodney*. There was no sign of trouble but, though *Repulse* got under way, *Valiant*'s crew refused duty. With the help of junior officers, she was reported ready for sea, but then the Engineer Commander announced that he could not keep the stokers below. *Nelson*'s men stood or sat on the anchor cable to prevent it being hoisted in. In *Rodney*, the situation was so bad that no serious attempt was made to sail, and *Hood* followed suit. The light cruisers, which seemed to be watching each other for a lead, also did nothing.

In one ship fittings were smashed, and an officer had to lock himself in his cabin. Revolver racks were stripped and ready-use lockers emptied, and one of the heads of departments was pushed overboard. The evening papers were full of accusations and wild statements, and the rumour circulated that one of the Highland regiments was on its way to arrest the mutinous crews. A few black eyes were noticed, but it was hard to decide whether they belonged to men who favoured defiance or loyalty.

Tomkinson made it clear by signal to the Admiralty that nothing would be resolved without a decision about pay. The Admiralty's signal in return expressed its disapproval of what had happened, and the wiser captains didn't bother to read it to their men. That night shore leave was cancelled, but the whole length of the shore was lined with the cars of spectators and journalists.

It looked like deadlock. Two officers were hastily sent south to convince the Board of Admiralty of the need to investigate the grievances. Their pleas produced no result, but they did convince the Admiralty of the danger of the situation and the Board ordered the ships to sail south. It promised an investigation and the alleviation of hardship, but it also dropped a strong hint that further disobedience would be heavily punished, though there would be an amnesty for those who had transgressed only up to that point.

The departure south was far from a foregone conclusion. When the pipe to clear lower deck went, the men moved unwillingly, dressed in a variety of rigs, some even unshaven. There was a cheer from *Rodney*, but it was by no means as defiant as it had been, as if the ringleaders were beginning to fear that they were acting alone.

Owing to the good sense of certain commanding officers, and in spite of the continued efforts of the agitators aboard, the ships weighed anchor. It had been only a localised affair and did not affect the rest of the Navy, where the Admiralty letter had arrived on time, but it *was* a mutiny and for a while it had seemed that an unwise decision at Invergordon could affect the whole British Empire. The description of events in the press, and the Admiralty admission that the fleet – that most hallowed of service institutions which to most people still symbolised the strength of Britain – had refused duty caused a tremendous shock throughout the world.

Its consequence was a further financial panic. Over £30,000,000 of gold was lost within three days, four times as much per day as during the disastrous days that had followed the May Committee's report, and forty times as much as during the critical recession of 1929, and on 21 September the Bank of England was compelled to ask for authority to suspend the gold standard.

A new admiral, Sir John (Joe) Kelly, a full admiral with the amount of prestige to make his decisions stick, was appointed, and he didn't pull his punches. He said that the men were right and the Admiralty abysmal, and the three senior admirals involved in the enquiry agreed that the cuts, like the cuts in the dole, had been cold-blooded and inhuman.

The return of the ships to their home ports was far from joyful. In the pre-dawn darkness they crept in, their arrival timed so that there would be no one to see them. But the journalists were there, and by the time the last ship moved to her position daylight had arrived and people were watching. There was none of the usual cheering, however, and a few of the men were beginning to realise that they were going to catch the sharp end of their wives' tongues. Neighbours were aware that the country had lost £30,000,000 in gold as a result of their action.

The mutineers were subdued by the chilly welcome. They were chastened, far from proud of themselves, and anxious to explain. Though they knew that the Admiralty would have to climb down over pay, they knew also, despite the promises of no punishments, that there would be scapegoats. Names were asked for but, sympathising with the men, the officers gave very few. The enquiry was held in the office of the Commander-in-Chief, Portsmouth, and the gold lace was dazzling. It sat for two days and by the end the anger had dispersed. The condemnation of the Admiralty was clear and the government climbed down so that all cuts were limited to 10 per cent, which, though it was bad enough, was at least fairer.

The country was shocked. The government, like all governments in peacetime, had ignored the fighting services that had saved them in wartime. But it was a bit too close to the outcry that had followed Jutland, and faith in the Navy was shaken. The Admiralty had the last word, of course, and set about clearing its own yard-arm. The captain of *Hood* was relieved at once, and the captains of *Rodney* and two of the cruisers were informed that they would not be given another command. Admiral Tomkinson, after being praised for the way in which he had handled the situation, was informed that his career was at an end. Men were drafted out of ships or dispersed, while others were discharged from the Navy. One other curious thing resulted. Various means of sending surreptitious signals had been used between ships, between watches, even between individuals, and to this day whistling is discouraged in the Navy because it was used during the days of dissatisfaction to pass messages. Cooks are excepted, because, it is said, whistling indicates that their mouths are not full of other men's rations as they work, but this is probably apocryphal.

The Admiralty were firmly on top again, but the men had their own little triumph. When the Portsmouth ships arrived home, shore leave was granted and the first watches headed as usual for the pubs. The Home Office arranged for detectives to follow them in the hope of picking up information about agitators, but all they got for their trouble was a string of red herrings. Murmurings from the men, who were well aware that they were being watched, about 'Ginger's going to wreck the engines' set the detectives searching the town for non-existent red-haired stokers. The lower deck had got its sense of humour back.

CHAPTER 6

Men on stilts

HMS *Captain*

The Victorian era has very rightly been called an era of men on stilts – small men who appeared to be big because of what they produced. Elevated on a skill that was often incomplete, they appeared in large numbers during a period when ambition and ideas ran ahead of technical and scientific know-how – and nowhere was this shown so much as in the building of ships.

Ships had always been built of wood because, since it floated, it was clearly a good material to use to build something that was also expected to float. Their power came from the wind. But early in the nineteenth century the ironmasters entered the scene. With them came the steam-engine builders and the makers of paddlewheels, and after them the men who said that paddlewheels were all very well but the real answer was a screw at the stern which, when it revolved, drove the ship forward. It was obvious, these men claimed, that iron ships would be stronger. And, with their steam engines and screws, they were not dependent on the unpredictable winds that could leave a sailing ship motionless for days. This was important to the men who ran the growing international businesses of the nineteenth century. Having set out on a voyage, they felt that in steamships they would arrive at the other end roughly when they expected.

Unfortunately, some of the men who built the ships and the steam engines that drove them had ideas beyond their capabilities. Their ships and their engines were sometimes flawed and, though those who had opposed iron ships eventually had to eat their words, sometimes the iron ships failed, too. This false assumption of knowledge was not confined to the merchant navy alone; it also existed in the Royal Navy.

The wooden walls that had served seafarers so well in the early part of the nineteenth century were terribly vulnerable to accidental destruction, and the fire risk was acute, while gun ports close to the water were custom-built for disaster. The change from wood to iron brought new problems, however, and if the eighteenth-century Navy had been blighted by venery, politics and self-interest, the nineteenth-century Navy was blighted by self-satisfaction and the feeling that Nelson's greatness had made everything right for ever. It very nearly did for Britain. A few more years of it and the Germans might have wiped the floor with her at sea.

Nelson had made the Navy great. Following a period when naval battles had been a sort of formal dance with ships drawn up in two lines to hammer at each other, his daring tactics had resulted in the destruction of enemy fleets in a way never seen before. It was Rodney, experimenting at the risk of professional extinction when manoeuvring his fleet against the French in 1782, who changed the pattern. Finding the enemy on an opposite bearing, instead of laying his ships alongside in the usual manner, he sailed through the French line and, encircling their ships in groups, hammered them to extinction. To this new idea Nelson added his own brand of intellect and daring to produce the tactical plan for Trafalgar.

But after Nelson, initiative seemed to die. Stifled by Victorian bureaucracy and the belief among British naval men that they were so superior in ability to all other seafaring nations that only their presence was needed to secure victory, the Navy became stultified. There was a saying that the naval men had an arrogance and a certainty in themselves that showed from the highest admiral down to the lowest pink-cheeked midshipman. Yet after Trafalgar the Navy saw action only in bombarding forts and single-ship affairs where they were sent to show the flag in some minor native insurrection. To add to this came the confusion and controversy caused by the change from Nelson's wooden walls to the new iron ships, and from sail to steam. It was almost as if, together, they were too much for senior naval men brought up in the old traditions.

The early days of ironclads marked more than one piece of gross folly, but perhaps the greatest folly of the Admiralty Board was in allowing a man untrained in naval architecture to be responsible for the design of a new first-class iron battleship. The fleet had hitherto consisted of ships designed for fighting at close range with a huge armament of up to 130 guns arranged on three decks, and in the 1860s a long controversy had been running about whether guns mounted in turntable turrets should displace the time-honoured method of batteries along the ship's side, even whether they should be grouped together in a central armoured citadel, each gun firing to one side only.

Because no one was certain which way ship design, affected by armour-plating and the increasing power of the gun, would go it was a period of ugliness. Ship design had altered little since Nelson's day, and ship constructors were loath to depart from the successful types they knew. An immense amount of experience went into the building of them, but little theoretical naval architecture as it is now known. As a consequence, naval officers considered themselves fully capable of designing warships, and until 1842 this was accepted. For solid shot the thick wooden sides were an adequate defence. Shells that burst inside the ship were something very different and the first explosive shells rendered fleets as out of date as the dodo.

In 1846 experiments were begun to determine the resistance of iron plating to gunfire, but small lightly built vessels were used as targets and the shells went straight through them. Captain Chads of HMS *Excellent*, the naval gunnery school, was of the opinion that iron could not be employed as a material for the construction of vessels of war, and this led to the condemnation of seventeen iron vessels in the course of building, one of which was *Birkenhead*, a paddle frigate built in 1846 which was converted to a troopship. In accordance with her original role as a frigate she had been divided by watertight bulkheads, but the trooping authorities cut huge openings in them. On 17 January 1852 she sailed from Queenstown with 680 people on board, of whom fifty-six were women and children. Near the Cape of Good Hope she struck a reef and the openings cut in the bulkhead allowed water to flood the troop accommodation so that the fore part of the ship became immensely heavy compared with the relatively buoyant after part. The men were drawn up on deck and the women and children were ordered into the boats. The boats were barely clear of the ship when the ship broke in two. The captain ordered everybody to jump overboard and make for the boats. The officer commanding the troops, however, realising that they would swamp the boats, ordered the soldiers to stand fast and the ship sank under the men still standing in their ranks. All the women and children were saved.

The break-up of *Birkenhead* caused grave doubts about the iron ships, but as the French had successfully covered wooden ships with iron plate Britain felt she must follow suit, though not without the feeling among some naval officers that she had been forced to and that somehow the French were not playing the game. However, in 1859 HMS *Warrior* – to be built of iron with a midships section backed by teak – was ordered, and only after the trials of *Warrior* and her sister ship did the traditionalists in the Navy admit the victory of iron.

However, naval officers who still considered themselves capable of designing warships did not realise that without theoretical training they were quite incompetent to work with the new material, and the story of *Captain* is the story of two men: Captain Cowper Phipps Coles – brilliant, inventive, impatient, persistent and arrogant; and Edward James Reed, Chief Constructor of the Navy – scientific, assertive, cautious, expert in his field, a civil servant trying to find the road naval science should take at a time when navies were being rebuilt with new materials, new ideas and new armaments. Reed was often criticised by his detractors for not showing more enterprise, but he had always to remember in a period of enormous change that the Royal Navy had to remain an effective fighting force anywhere in the world. Coles had airy ideas about design and an inflated confidence in his own ability, yet no one put him in his place and he had many supporters among those naval officers who felt that no one who wasn't a Navy man had the experience to refute him.

He was the son of a Hampshire clergyman, born in 1819, who went to sea straight from school. In 1853 he was flag lieutenant to Admiral Sir Edmund Lyons in HMS *Agamemnon*, in which he served during the Crimean War. When the unprotected wooden ships failed to make any impression in their attacks on the forts of Sevastopol, the Russian Black Sea naval base, he had the idea of placing a gun on a raft which could be taken close inshore at a point where Russian guns could not be trained. His raft was used to attack Taganrog, at the head of the Sea of Asov, where he destroyed a quantity of Russian stores. It was the sort of exploit that delighted the British newspaper-reading public and Coles, already showing a flair for publicity, had made sure that he had a newspaperman along with him.

Admiral Lyons was very impressed and Coles was sent to England to supervise the building of a fleet of the rafts, but the war came to an end before they could be completed. With the coming of peace, he was placed on half-pay, but he was ambitious and in 1859 filed his first patent for a revolving turret. He felt that a gun should provide all-round fire and yet offer as small a target as possible, and his view was that Reed was only tinkering with the problem. The answer, he felt quite rightly, was to turn the gun rather than the ship and that, to give a clear field of fire, the ship had to have low sides instead of the high ones common at the time.

The monitor design, as it was called, was sound enough for coast and port defence, but it was Coles's idea to build a ship which could go anywhere in the world, and for this, since steam engines were still in their infancy and ships needed to carry enormous amounts of coal to feed them, they still had to have sails. Reed would not consider putting sails on such ships as Coles proposed, so Coles enlisted the support of the press, which knew less about it than he did, and gained the full backing of the prestigious *Times*, even of the Prince Consort, the Queen's husband. In 1862 the Board of Admiralty finally ordered a turret ship based on a system devised by Coles. She proved very satisfactory and, as she was intended only as a coastal defence ship, she was able to have a low freeboard and only steadying sails.

Soon after the ordering of this ship, the *Prince Albert*, Coles's case for low-freeboard turret ships was strengthened by the homeric battle between the little *Monitor* against the more powerful *Merrimac* during the American Civil War, and he used pamphlets, letters to newspapers, articles, models and lectures to prove that he was right. He was backed more and more by the press and public and by naval officers who did not realise the technical impossibility of some of his ideas.

In April 1862 Coles threw down a public challenge in a letter to *The Times*, undertaking to build a ship better and cheaper than *Warrior*, and attention was drawn to the differences of opinion between him and Reed, the Chief Constructor of the Navy, who had to be consulted over Coles's proposals. Partisanship ran high and Coles's supporters accused Reed of being jealous of the gifted non-professional Coles. Members of Parliament were not less restrained and virtually demanded that Coles should be given his head. In the end the Board of Admiralty agreed to the construction of a low-freeboard turret ship to Coles's design.

Captain was laid down at Laird Brothers' yard at Birkenhead in 1867, and Captain Hugh Talbot Burgoyne, VC, only son of Field-Marshal Sir John Burgoyne, was appointed to command her. Having already commanded a turret ship for two years, he was considered to be an expert on the type. Reed was not happy with the design of the new ship and warned of the use of too much iron in the structure but, on the whole, he did not belittle the plan, though he always remained concerned that the deck would be only eight feet from the water and wondered if this was enough for a sea-going ship.

Captain floated out of dry dock in March 1869, and the Admiralty was represented by Hugh Childers, the First Lord, who was so impressed by the ship that he arranged for his midshipman son, Leonard, to be transferred to her. Despite the enthusiasm, F. K. Barnes, Reed's assistant, noted that the ship floated much deeper than her designed draught and that she weighed 427 tons more than intended, which reduced the freeboard of eight feet by thirteen inches. She also had a narrow beam for her length but was intended to carry the highest masts in the Navy. What was more, Barnes's calculations were for a crew of 400 men, and the

Admiralty had decided that *Captain* should carry a complement of 500, adding a weight that would reduce the height of the deck above water to six feet nine inches.

The ship was completed in January 1870 and went to Portsmouth for fitting out. The question of stability seemed satisfactory, but the overweight had now risen to 857 tons and the freeboard reduced to six and a half feet. After trials she joined the fleet off Finisterre, where, with Coles on board, she stood up well to a gale. She had sailed with *Monarch*, also a new ship, and Vice-Admiral Sir Thomas Symonds, in command of the Channel Fleet, commented favourably on the ability of both ships to fire their guns in heavy weather, though he considered that under sail alone they could not keep up with the fleet.

Captain made a second cruise, alone this time and again with Coles on board, and seemed to be able and successful despite her strange appearance with her low freeboard and two decks, the lower one carrying the turrets, the upper one for the working of the sails. Coles and his supporters were jubilant and *The Times* preened itself on its foresight in backing him.

Captain sailed a third time in August 1870, with Coles on board once more, and the news of her foundering in the Bay of Biscay came as a tremendous shock to the nation. It seemed inconceivable that she could have succumbed to what was no more than a summer storm. Only a few scientifically minded men had had their doubts about her, but even they had not expected to have them confirmed so quickly. The press could not believe that the ship had been lost through any fault of their idol, and *The Times*'s paean of praise for the dead Coles sounded more like a condemnation of those who had doubted his ship.

Captain had simply disappeared some time during the night of 6-7 September. Admiral Symonds had visited her on the 6th and, as the wind rose, he noticed as he returned to his own ship, *Lord Warden*, that the sea was washing over the lee side of *Captain*'s decks and that the lee gunwale was level with the water.

There was no indication of heavy weather, but by 1 a.m. a gale had set in. It was not a violent one and was of short duration; *Captain* was last seen astern the flagship, apparently closing under steam. She was heeling a good deal to starboard, the Admiral noticed, and he was worried enough to watch for her light. Some time after 1.30 a.m. he noticed that she was no longer visible through the mist and rain, and when the gale abated at about 2.15 a.m. on the 7th and the clouds cleared and the moon came out, it was noticed that there were only ten ships instead of the eleven there should have been, and that *Captain* was missing.

At the time, there was much confusion about the meaning of stability. Even experienced seamen felt that a stiff ship – a ship that did not roll – was a safe ship and that a ship which rolled was inherently dangerous. In fact, the opposite was true. A ship that rolls is a little like a kelly doll which can be knocked over and promptly returns to the upright. It was very confusing to Victorian laymen, but that did not prevent them advancing their inexpert theories in the press and in Parliament. *Captain* was a stiff ship and, with her low freeboard, had a very limited safety margin if she tilted. As she rose after dipping her gunwale, she lifted an immense amount of water which poured off in a cascade dubbed by the junior officers 'the young falls of Niagara'.

On the night of the foundering, Gunner James May took a last look around before going to his cabin, but as the weather worsened he wakened at midnight and decided to take another prowl round the turrets which were his charge. He lit a lantern and walked to the after turret, which he entered from the port side against the slope of the deck. James Ellis, a twenty-nine-year-old gunner's mate, was called to the bridge by Captain Burgoyne and told to put the steel covers on the sighting holes in the tops of the turrets. As he set off to perform the task, he heard Burgoyne ask how much the ship was heeling, and heard him told eighteen degrees. Burgoyne ordered the foretopsail halliards released, then the maintopsail halliards and the topsail sheets. This would have stripped the sails from the masts and freed the dangerous wind pressure that was steadily bearing the ship over.

But it was too late. In the after turret May felt the ship tilt at an angle he had never known before – and she went on tilting until it was obvious that she could never right herself. He dropped his lamp and scrambled through the twenty-two-inch sighting hole to find the water level with his head. The ship was already on her side. The weight of her masts and guns carried her farther and the movement was steady and irresistible. Leading Seaman Charles Tregenna had leapt for the foretopsail halliards at Burgoyne's command but, with his sailor's instinct, as the ship heeled he made for the high side, then walked on to the now horizontal ship's hull.

The two great turrets ripped themselves out of the ship as she turned turtle, leaving two huge holes for the sea to pour through. Everything broke loose and there was an explosion that was probably a boiler bursting, then May found himself in the sea close to Captain Burgoyne and another seaman. They managed to reach the steam pinnace which had floated off upside down, and eventually he found himself in one of the ship's launches which should have been lashed down but had been missed by the retiring watch. The launch picked up a few more men, but not Burgoyne, who refused to move from the upturned pinnace – it was thought until the rest of the men in the sea were saved – and they lost sight of him. As they tried to manoeuvre to see if there were more men in the water, a huge sea washed one of the survivors out of the launch and he was lost.

With Tregenna handling an oar over the stern as a rudder, with daylight and with the gale dying rapidly, they managed to reach the shore north of Vigo. Late the following day they contacted the British Consul at Corunna with the news.

Symonds's squadron had scattered to search for the missing ship, but nothing was seen. Then *Monarch* picked up one of her topgallant yards and *Lord Warden* another, while *Psyche* reported passing two cutters bottom-up with a large amount of wreckage, among which was the body of a sailor. It had to be assumed that *Captain* had been lost with all hands. Out of the total complement of 500, only Gunner May and seventeen men from the starboard watch had managed to escape.

The inevitable court martial began at Portsmouth on 27 September. Nominally it was to try May and the surviving men but, as so often happens, it was the reputations of much more highly placed officers that were at stake. The few survivors made it clear that when the disaster occurred the ship was carrying her fore and main topsails, both double-reefed, and her fore topmast staysail. The yards were braced sharp up and the ship had little way on her. As the new watch was being mustered, Burgoyne was on deck and was heard to shout his orders and demand plenty of men to handle the downhaul for the sails.

It soon became clear that the survivors had thought themselves in a fine ship. Though Burgoyne had perhaps been slow to let go the sails, they all expected that the topmasts would have carried away before the ship capsized. The narrow upper deck had been far too crowded for working in an emergency, however, and it seemed also that someone had allowed the first watch to go below before the second watch were all mustered on deck.

One witness who had watched the ship from the fleet considered that *Captain* had had the look of an overloaded ship, and it was felt that Burgoyne had allowed too much sail, as his night order book had indicated that it redounded to the credit of everybody if the ship could keep station with the fleet, as much as possible under sail alone. This emphasis on sail had been imposed by higher authority, partly because of economy but as much as anything else because it was still felt that, in spite of the advance of steam, the measure of a seaman's ability was always his skill with sail. *Captain* had carried more sail than other ships in the fleet, and it was felt that pride in the new vessel had impelled the officers to dare the wind in order to keep up. Burgoyne had been warned to be cautious in handling his ship, but it was clear from remarks by both Burgoyne and Coles that they felt they had a sound ship and were eager to prove it.

Mr W. B. Robinson, Master Shipwright and Engineer of the Royal Dockyard, gave it as his opinion that the ship was overmasted. Nathaniel Barnaby, President of the Council of Construction, felt that the experiment of *Captain* had been a dangerous one, and claimed that not enough care had been taken to secure the draught of water that had been planned. He felt that the ignorant clamour by people such as journalists and Members of Parliament had led the Admiralty to do something its experts had advised it not to do.

Reed was the most important witness, and he soon made it clear that he laid the blame for the disaster entirely on Lairds, the builders, and Coles, the designer, and that the opinions of the Admiralty experts had been disregarded. He had had misgivings but had not expected them to be proved right quite so quickly – rather that the ship would be carefully nursed through her early career and, as her faults were discovered, that she would be withdrawn from service.

The court's findings were that the ship capsized 'by pressure of sail assisted by the heave of the sea', and 'that the sail carried at the time . . . was insufficient to endanger a ship endued with the proper amount of stability'. The court also recorded their conviction that *Captain* had been built in deference to public opinion and in opposition to the views of the Constructor and his department. They also pointed out that the gross departures from her original design, which made her stability dangerously small, had not, if they were known, been communicated to Burgoyne.

Certainly the gale had not worried the other ships in the squadron, and it was now Coles's turn to be condemned. He had really understood little about stability and very little about wind pressure, and it was pointed out that the angle of heel under a steady pressure was very different from a sudden squall; in other words a 'live load' was heavier than a 'dead load', something that can be understood by anyone suddenly imposing his weight on a bathroom scale, which will momentarily show twice the weight as when the load is steady.

Reed had been more right than he had realised or he would have protested at the ship ever going to sea. His reputation was untarnished, and he went on to design a number of unrigged turret ships, though one of them, *Devastation*, was considered to be unsafe. It was felt that her low freeboard made her too much like *Captain*, and when commissioning at Portsmouth a notice was found fixed to her gangway. It read: 'Letters for *Captain* can be posted aboard.'

HMS *Victoria*

Designs continued to change and ships began to be built with a new weapon, the ram, a jutting peak of steel projecting from the stem which could be driven at an enemy to sink him. It was a weapon which had been used as long ago as ancient Rome and it suddenly found new supporters, while the collision between *Vanguard* and *Iron Duke* off the coast of Ireland in July 1875 certainly showed that it could sink a ship.

The two ships were sisters and shortly after being formed into the port division of a squadron of four ships under Vice-Admiral Sir Walter Tarleton, were sailing in line astern when a sudden and unexpected fog came down. They were at eight knots, *Vanguard* leading, and her captain, Richard Dawkins, felt justified in reducing speed to six and then to five knots, giving signals by steam whistle to indicate to the following ship what he was doing. Soon afterwards a small sailing ship which had been seen just before the fog closed in appeared ahead of him, and the helm was ordered hard-a-port. Having heard no answering signals from *Iron Duke* astern, Dawkins assumed that she was far enough behind to be of no danger to him. Unfortunately the captain of *Iron Duke* was equally nervous in the fog and played for safety by altering slightly to port at just about the time that *Vanguard* altered to avoid the sailing ship. She rammed *Vanguard* just abaft the transverse bulkhead separating the engine room from the boiler room. The ships were in contact for a minute and a half, then *Iron Duke* backed away and vanished in the fog.

Dawkins ordered the whistle to be blown constantly to indicate where he was, and *Iron Duke* managed to locate her and send boats. Watertight doors were closed, but the boiler-room fires were already out and, as it was soon clear that the ship was sinking, Dawkins concentrated on saving his men. The only casualty was Dawkins's dog, though the ship disappeared in just over an hour.

The court martial at Devonport began on 10 September. The president was a rear admiral, and of the nine officers who comprised the court all but three were from wooden ships, which probably explains the futility of many of the questions asked. It was soon evident that they didn't appreciate the changes that had taken place, and there was a fixed idea that Dawkins could have saved his ship if he had not concentrated on saving lives. There is a tendency in enquiries to feel that, having been convened, their work must be shown not to be for nothing, and this one found every possible fault with *Vanguard*'s personnel, even down to the carpenter, and when questions were asked about why the steam pumps were not used, it was clear that the officers comprising the court were unable to understand that steam pumps could not be used without steam. When this was explained, the court wanted to know why the hand pumps had not been rigged in time. Since the engine-room flat immediately became full of water it had been impossible, and in any case the pumps could have removed only 30 tons an hour when the ship was taking in between 800 and 900 tons an hour. The court blamed Dawkins for the collision, and produced a damning list of indictments which were plainly ridiculous. The elderly officers of the court were well up in copybook maxims about the carpenter's duty to plug holes in wooden ships, but knew little about ironclad steamships. Admiral Tarleton was blamed for what was considered a too-high rate of knots as the fog appeared but was exonerated, and the affair produced a jingle, doubtless written by a naval man, which went:

> We can't punish admirals because they're like us,
> And, of course, all our duties we know.
> But a lieutenant's diff'rent, he can't answer back,
> So into the jug he must go.

The accident certainly proved the power of the ram, but it raised doubts about the vulnerability of ironclads. It also showed the undesirability of having all the boilers in one compartment since its flooding deprived the ship of all steam for the pumps. Watertight doors were proved to take too long to close, and in addition it was shown that two ventilation holes which could not be closed had been cut in the vital engine-room bulkhead, a hangover from the days of wooden ships when the carpenter had to have free passage about the vessel to plug shot-holes with wood and oakum. The officers of the court martial probably had this obsolete practice in mind when they berated the unfortunate carpenter for not doing the same in an iron ship.

That the court's decision was a farrago of nonsense was indicated only three years later in an accident which, as described already, led indirectly to the German success in battle at Jutland in 1916 and to the success of the mutiny in the German fleet in 1918. It occurred in May 1878, when three ironclads of the Prussian Navy, all new, were passing Dover and Folkestone so close together that to watchers on shore they looked like one ship. Then, off Sandgate, they were seen to stop and the leading vessel, *Grosser Kurfürst*, was seen to be sinking. In a few minutes there were only two ships, and in place of the missing vessel there was only a mat of heads belonging to struggling men. The ships had been bunched too closely and the men at the wheels were inexperienced.

Once again the blame lay with two small ships crossing the squadron's course. *Grosser Kurfürst* had attempted to avoid them, and was rammed by *König Wilhelm*. *Grosser Kurfürst* disappeared in seven minutes, taking nearly 300 of her crew with her. Only the presence of fishing boats enabled many of the rest to be saved. Dawkins's decision to concentrate on saving his men seemed to be justified.

The Navy didn't change, however. It still remained happily arrogant about its skills and ability, then in 1893 came news of a disaster which shook it to the core and made it wonder not only if its ships were well designed but also if its admirals knew what they were about.

It seemed from the report in *The Times* that two of Her Majesty's great ships had collided on the afternoon of 23 June near Tripoli. HMS *Camperdown* had run down HMS *Victoria*, the flagship of Sir George Tryon, Commander-in-Chief, Mediterranean, and about 370 officers and men, including Tryon himself, had been lost. The disaster was debated in all the great houses and in naval circles in London even before the facts were known. Where the responsibility lay was soon established, but the reason for it has been the cause of speculation ever since.

The chief clue lies in the character of Tryon himself. He was born in 1832 into a wealthy, influential family and joined the Navy before the Crimean War at the age of sixteen. He was a man of great character and forcefulness, and rose more quickly than his contemporaries. He was ambitious, popular, tall and handsome and believed in putting on a show, but he was without doubt extremely competent and knowledgeable in his profession; he was a post-captain at the age of thirty-four, and the last naval officer to hold the plum job of the Civil Service – Secretary to the Admiralty. But there is no doubt that his success had led him to be intolerant of lesser minds. In an era when most played for safety, he was dashing, flamboyant and had made many enemies, not least because he was the leader of a small group opposed to the traditional attitudes at the Admiralty.

The Navy had not been engaged in any major action since Nelson. Although involved in the Crimean War, its duties then had largely consisted of escorting the troops to Russia, providing a flank guard to the troops marching on Sevastopol, and bombarding Russian ports. But, though there were undoubtedly highly intelligent men available, the stagnation remained. The replacement of wooden ships by the ironclads of the 1850s had brought great opposition from the men who had served in the wars of Napoleon, and this obstinacy and reserve remained in the reluctance to sacrifice sail for steam, while the coal needed for the steam engines was loathed. Battleships, in fact, came to be regarded less as men-o'-war than as showpieces kept spotless for ceremonial occasions. Coal fouled decks, canvas and brasswork, and it is significant that until the present century engineer officers were considered inferior to deck officers.

With the peace the British Empire had brought to out-of-the-way places, the so-called Pax Britannica, there was little for the ships of the greatest navy in the world to do save hold grand reviews and elaborate manoeuvres. But the manoeuvres weren't even war manoeuvres and, as time went on, they became more and more complicated so that the signalling that was needed to carry them out grew more and more complex. Keen for the ships under his command to perform the complicated manoeuvres in vogue in an efficient manner, Tryon's alert intelligence told him that they depended for success on the swift passage of messages, and that the naval signalling system needed simplification. Like Kempenfeldt before him, he was determined to make signalling easier, and it was one of the first things he considered when he was appointed to the command of the Mediterranean Fleet in 1891.

Signalling, he felt, had become an obsession, with signal books huge volumes and signals multiple hoists of coloured flags. Nelson's famous signal at Trafalgar, 'England expects that every man will do his duty,' had required eight hoists of three flags each for the first eight words and four of seven for the word 'duty'. Signalmen, in fact, had become so numerous that they got in the way of senior officers, and anyway, Tryon considered, at the first burst of accurate enemy fire both signals and signallers would be swept away. What was needed was something a great deal easier, and one of his first memoranda to his captains was about the simplification of manoeuvring signals. To the consternation of older officers his new system virtually eliminated the signaller. He called it the TA system because he felt that all that would be necessary would be for the flagship to hoist the two code flags, TA, after which ships would need only to follow the movements of the leaders of the divisions. He made it clear, however, that the TA system was only a supplementary, not a substituted, form of signalling, that orthodox signals could still be made where necessary and that under it absolute precision was not to be expected in manoeuvres. A few alert senior officers saw the advantages of the system, but others, equally experienced, were hostile, considering it dangerous in application.

Because no one had the courage to express their doubts openly, Tryon's authority and enthusiasm swept the doubters along. Though mistakes were made, the summer manoeuvres of 1892 were considered to be successful. By the following summer, Tryon's grip on his fleet was secure and he decided to instil more confidence into his captains by introducing sudden and unusual orders to make them think. His method was to alter formation in unorthodox fashion in order to create conditions which might occur in wartime, and he began to work out a programme for the manoeuvres of the fleet. His idea was to transform a tradition-bound fleet into 'a fighting force full of imagination, daring and initiative'. Despite his successes, or perhaps because of them, Tryon was not popular with many officers, who had seen him promoted over their heads and had suffered from his scathing comments on their performance.

On 27 May 1893 Tryon, in his flagship *Victoria*, led the First Division to sea from Valetta harbour, Malta. Following them came the Second Division's flagship, *Camperdown*, under Rear Admiral Albert Hastings Markham, who was to join the Second Division which was already at sea off the coast of Turkey under the command of Captain Gerard Noel in *Nile*, and was to join the fleet for combined exercises in the eastern Mediterranean.

Markham was very different from his commanding officer. He was a serious-minded, unimaginative man, nearly ten years younger than Tryon, and he had had his broad stripe only a year. It was his first appointment as rear admiral, and, still new to the methods and enthusiasm of his commanding officer, he found problems in adapting to the new TA system.

He had been humiliated by Tryon during manoeuvres off the south-west coast of Ireland in 1888. There had always been a tendency for war games to be treated indifferently by older officers used to ceremony, spit and polish. Tryon regarded them as full-dress rehearsals for war, and by the use of guile he had slipped easily past Markham, who was supposed to be blockading him at Berehaven in Bantry Bay. Though his success made him the darling of the English people, older officers felt he had not played fair.

Markham was no weakling, however. His cousin was Sir Clements Markham, the Arctic explorer, whom he tried to emulate and whose example he followed by leading an Arctic expedition of his own in 1875-6. Handicapped by scurvy, he had reached what in those days was the 'farthest north', eighty-three degrees twenty minutes. But he was a sensitive, courteous man and was never a dedicated career officer in the way Tryon was. His interest lay chiefly in archaeology and exploration, and he had no time for wardroom parties or dinners. By the time he became deputy to Tryon he had become a quiet, unsociable man who preferred writing to managing his ships, and he got into the habit of following his chief without question. The two men met for the first time as Commander-in-Chief and deputy in March 1892, and even to the humblest blue-jacket the difference between them was obvious at once.

Markham took over from Noel when the Second Division joined the fleet off the coast of Egypt and the ships sailed up the Syrian coast to Beirut, with stops at Acre and Haifa to show the flag, practise gunnery and carry out evolutions. The ships spent five days in Beirut with shore leave for everyone, weighing anchor on the morning of 22 June. By modern standards the ships were small, none exceeding 12,000 tons, and, because the advantage of having squadrons composed of sister ships was not yet understood, they were of widely different types with different turning circles. Of these, *Victoria*, completed in 1890, was the latest. With her twin side-by-side funnels, she was reputed to be the most powerful ironclad afloat, as well as the largest and most strongly protected. Her main armament consisted of twin 16.25-inch guns, the largest in the Navy, even in the world. Four hundred yards astern was *Camperdown* and, as they left Beirut, Tryon decided to try a daring movement.

He never believed in making a straightforward passage from one anchorage to another and, after five easy days ashore in Beirut, he felt that his ships needed something to bring them back to fighting pitch. Around 2 p.m. when everyone off watch was trying to take it easy in the humid air, he called his flag captain and *Victoria*'s staff commander to his cabin and told them that to bring the ships into their anchorage in Tripoli Roads he intended to form the fleet into two columns, six cables apart, and reverse the course by turning inwards. The conditions were good and Tripoli Bay was wide enough for the evolution to be performed with safety. The only snag was that the flagships of the two divisions could not turn with safety towards one another at a distance apart of six cables or 1200 yards, because the combined turning circles of *Victoria* and *Camperdown* were not less than eight cables or 1600 yards.

The staff commander, Thomas Hawkins-Smith, was a grizzled officer of the old school and he had the courage to query the distance. 'It will require at least eight cables, sir,' he pointed out.

Tryon hesitated a moment. 'Yes,' he said. 'It shall be eight cables.'

But when Lord Gillford, his flag lieutenant, came later for orders, Tryon told him the signal the yeoman was to make was 'Form columns of divisions line ahead, columns disposed abeam to port and six cables apart.' To make certain the flag lieutenant could not mistake the order, he wrote the figure 6 on a piece of paper which he handed to Gillford.

The TA flags were already bent on the halliards. They had been hoisted some days before and, since so much was being left to the judgement of ships' captains, had not been rescinded. Captains were expected to be guided by the movements and helm signals of the flagship. As the signal to form columns was hoisted it was acknowledged by the other ships, but aboard *Victoria* Hawkins-Smith was disturbed. 'Haven't you made a mistake?' he asked Gillford. 'The admiral intended the distance to be eight cables.'

'I think not,' Gillford said, showing him the paper with the figure 6 written plainly on it.

Hawkins-Smith wasn't satisfied. 'Please go to his cabin and make certain,' he said.

Gillford found the admiral still in his cabin, conferring with the ship's captain, Maurice Bourke, a tall handsome man unusual in those days for being clean-shaven. 'The staff commander,' Gillford said, 'has asked me to remind you that you had agreed to eight cables, sir.'

Bourke joined in. 'You certainly said it was to be more than six, sir,' he agreed.

Tryon was obviously displeased that his orders had been questioned. 'Leave it at six cables,' he said.

As the flagship lowered its signal to indicate that the order should be carried out, the other ships did the same and all except the two leading ships reduced speed so that the others could slip in behind them. *Victoria* and *Camperdown* then drew closer until only six cables separated them. By this time the anchorage at Tripoli was only eight miles away and the captains and deck officers in every ship were wondering what method the admiral had decided on to bring the two columns into Tripoli Roads on their correct anchorage bearings. But only in *Victoria* was there any real anxiety, and even there only Bourke, Hawkins-Smith and Lord Gillford were aware of Tryon's risky intentions.

The overweight and bulky Tryon appeared on deck, puffing his way up as the ships entered the bay at a speed of just below nine knots. From the narrow fore-and-aft bridge of *Victoria* he could see *Camperdown* 1200 yards to port, with the ships of the Second Division in line behind her. Astern of his own ship were *Nile* and four other battleships, *Dreadnought*, *Inflexible*, *Collingwood* and *Phaeton*. At this point Tryon turned to his flag lieutenant and told him to make the signal to reverse the direction of the two columns, one altering to port and the other to starboard, but preserving the order of the Division. The Second Division's signal was at the masthead, the First Division's at the yard-arm.

The acknowledgement of a signal is to repeat it 'at the dip', or not fully hoisted. When the signal is completely understood, it is hauled fully up. All the ships indicated that the signal had been understood – with one exception, *Camperdown*, Markham's flagship, which kept her signal at the dip. Markham did not understand *Victoria*'s signal. Neither did the officers on the bridge of *Victoria* but, having already drawn Tryon's attention to the discrepancy inherent in the signal, there was no more they could do, though the flag lieutenant tried by indirect means to draw the admiral's attention to the suicidally short distance between the two flagships by ordering a midshipman to take the distance to *Camperdown*.

The youngster's reply was quite clear. 'Six cables, sir,' he reported.

The men behind Tryon glanced at each other but Tryon appeared not to have heard. Aboard *Camperdown*, Markham was just about to query the signal when Tryon impatiently told the yeoman to semaphore him with: 'What are you waiting for?' *Camperdown*'s repeat was finally hauled up to indicate that Markham had understood the order. But if he had, he understood it in a different way from what Tryon had intended.

As the signal came down, Hawkins-Smith on his own initiative ordered: 'Extreme starboard helm.'

As *Victoria*'s helm was put over, the ships behind followed her round. As *Camperdown* began her turn the two flagships approached each other at a combined speed of eighteen knots. Tryon was looking astern at the other ships in his column. As he had once said to Bourke, a captain's job was to look forward, an admiral's to look aft. Having given his orders, he wasn't concerned with the manoeuvring of his flagship but with the behaviour of the other ships of the fleet.

Bourke, however, was becoming concerned and ordered a midshipman to take the distance between the two converging ships once more. The midshipman's answer was that it was three and a quarter cables. The next seconds would be critical. Only if one of the closing flagships reversed its helm and one of its screws could a collision be avoided. He appealed to Tryon. 'We had better do something, sir,' he said. 'We shall be very close to *Camperdown*.'

Tryon appeared not to have heard and Bourke made another appeal. 'We are getting too close, sir,' he said. 'We must do something. May I go astern with the port screws?'

Still there was no reply and twice more Bourke asked for permission. At last Tryon turned and for the first time saw the horrifying nearness of *Camperdown*. 'Yes,' he said at once. 'Go astern.'

'Full speed astern port screw,' Bourke ordered, then, without requesting Tryon's permission, he added, 'Full speed astern both.'

But nothing could now prevent a collision. With *Camperdown*'s turning circle wider than the *Victoria*'s, she was now virtually at right angles to her, and on the bridges of both ships, the officers were rigid with paralysis, unable to do anything. Only below did anyone show any initiative. Lieutenant Herbert Heath, acting executive officer in the absence of Commander John Jellicoe, who was sick in his bunk with Malta fever, ordered: 'Pipe "Close the watertight doors and out the collision mat."'

By this time barely two hundred yards separated the two great ships, and it was clear that the blow would not be a glancing one. Only Tryon made any movement and, when *Camperdown* came within hailing distance, every man on her bridge recognisable, he cupped his hands and shouted in an anguished voice 'Go astern! Go astern!'

It was too late, and *Camperdown*'s steel ram, with all the weight of the ship's 10,000 tons behind it, drove its way through the plating below *Victoria*'s waterline forward of the bridge. A stoker petty officer in his mess had his leg broken and was showered with coal as it burst through the bulkhead from one of the bunkers. With everybody ducking from the flying fragments of wood and steel, *Victoria* was driven seventy feet to port, *Camperdown*'s bows locked into her side, and it was at this moment that Tryon was handed a delayed semaphore signal from *Camperdown* in answer to his demand to know what Markham was waiting for. 'Because I didn't quite understand your signal,' it read.

Victoria immediately began to settle and heel to starboard. Then, with the damage control party struggling to get a collision mat in place over the gaping hole, instead of going ahead to try to block the hole *Camperdown* began to go astern and, with a fearful screeching of steel on steel, heaved her way out of the cavity. As water rushed in at a rate of around 3000 tons a minute, the list increased. Bourke requested permission to check the water-tight doors and, as he vanished, Tryon turned to Hawkins-Smith. Though the ship was badly damaged, she did not appear in danger of sinking.

'Do you think she'll continue to float?' he asked.

'I think she ought to keep afloat,' Hawkins-Smith reassured him. 'Shall we steer for the land to try to beach her?'

There was a short discussion about the depth of the water, then Tryon ordered Hawkins-Smith to go astern with the port engine, and ahead with the starboard.

'What speed, sir?' Hawkins-Smith asked. 'Full?'

'No. Go seven knots.'

But before the ship could gather steerage way the hydraulic steering failed, as also did the boat hoist with which the sick Jellicoe was trying to hoist out the boom boats. Gillford, who had been watching the other ships, pointed out that boats were being lowered.

'Annul sending boats,' Tryon ordered. Clearly he didn't think that *Victoria* was in any danger. She was the newest, finest and most heavily protected ironclad in the Navy and was honeycombed with watertight compartments which even then were being closed. Besides, as Hawkins-Smith pointed out, the blow had been struck well clear of the ship's vitals. The men with the collision mat knew differently. As the ship heeled, water began to pour more quickly into hatches and through gun ports, vents and scuttles which had been left open to catch the slightest breath of air in the hot afternoon, and as the bows dipped below the sea and the muzzles of the two tremendous guns she carried touched the water, the list increased and Tryon realised that the end was near.

'I think she's going,' he said.

'Yes, sir,' Hawkins-Smith agreed. 'I think she is.'

'Make a signal to send boats immediately,' Tryon ordered Gillford and, turning to a sixteen-year-old midshipman, he told him to see to his own safety.

But before the boy could move, and a little more than nine minutes since *Camperdown* had struck her, *Victoria* gave a sickening lurch to starboard. Below deck, the collision party, the water sweeping round them, gave up their hopeless task and reported on deck. Around 600 men fell in four deep under the captain's orders, their backs to the sea as if on parade. On the order 'Right about turn' they swung as one man to face the water; then, as the ship gave a heavy lurch, an officer gave the order to save themselves and the men broke ranks, leaping over the side or scrambling round on the ship's bottom as she rotated.

The engines were still working, driving her bows further below the surface; then, as she turned over and disappeared, the screws began to carve into the men crowding in the sea so that the water became red with blood. Fifteen minutes after the collision, *Victoria* vanished in a swirl of foam, and what had been a stately formation of ships approaching its anchorage had become a scene of wild disorder. Suspecting trouble from the enigmatic order, Noel, of *Nile*, had expressed his intention of keeping well clear of anything that might happen, and he now carried out that intention. But, though there were no other collisions, the ships ended up facing in all directions, with one flagship down by the bows and in danger of sinking, the other vanished, leaving only debris and hundreds of bobbing heads in an area where the calm sea had been churned to frenzy.

Since no order had been given to evacuate boiler rooms and engine rooms, not one of the men below was saved. A huge wave spread out from where the ship had gone down and as it expended itself it took down many more men, while others were killed or injured as spars or timber broke loose and shot to the surface to smash into the swimming men.

A few bodies were recovered, to be buried later at Tripoli. Tryon's was not among them. He was last seen with his hands on the bridge rail and, like Hawkins-Smith, was probably caught up in the network of stays and guys on top of the charthouse. Hawkins-Smith fought his way clear, but he considered that Tryon's bulk had prevented him escaping. With him went twenty-one other officers and 336 ratings.

Among the 300 survivors was Commander Jellicoe, later to be C.-in-C. of the Grand Fleet in the First World War and the commander at Jutland. Also saved were the three men who could describe best what had happened, Captain Bourke, Hawkins-Smith and Lord Gillford.

The return to Malta was very different from the departure. The ships straggled in, in ones and twos, the last of them *Camperdown*, her bows patched up. The legends started almost at once, among them the story that the capsizing of the ship had been caused by the tearing away of her huge guns and turrets. Men swore that as the ship heeled, the guns had swung and broken from the mountings, taking the ship down with them. Not one officer confirmed the story, however, and it was even said to be a technical impossibility, yet the story was in circulation even as the survivors were hauled into the lifeboats.

Another story was that the shore had been lined by Syrians waiting for the accident because it had been prophesied by a local fakir, and that huge crowds had gathered at the gates of Malta dockyard because word had been heard of some great disaster.

Admiral Sir Reginald Bacon told a story later of naval officers lunching at the Whitehead torpedo works at Weymouth when the stem of a wine glass broke of its own accord. 'That should mean a big naval disaster,' one of the officers remarked, and it was later recalled that the glass broke at the precise moment when *Victoria* had disappeared. Finally, there was an odd little footnote. On the night of the disaster, with the London season at its height, Lady Tryon had given a reception to around two hundred people at her house in Eaton Square. Several guests claimed to have seen Sir George descending the staircase and one or two even claimed to have spoken to him.

Meanwhile blame had to be apportioned. The disaster was a stunning blow to naval pride. Ironclads had been lost before, but never in such incredible circumstances. That two flagships of the crack fleet of the world's greatest navy should collide in daylight, with ample searoom and in perfect weather, as a result of an impossible order given by a past-master of manoeuvre – these things lay outside normal experience. Suggestions were made that Tryon had been suffering from the effects of Malta fever, even that he had been drunk, which was nonsense.

Rear Admiral Philip Colomb believed that Tryon 'thought he had a much greater . . . control over his ships than was really possible'. Of Markham, Admiral Sir John Fisher said, 'If I were Markham . . . I could never hold up my head again.' Yet Admiral Lord Charles Beresford considered Markham would be 'crucified alive for another man's blunder'. Admiral Sir Charles Dundas summed it up: 'It is very clear that the Rear Admiral did not understand the signal . . . and went blindly into the danger zone.' He had, he said, 'no earthly excuse for mastheading his answering pendant', and thought it nonsense that he felt he was obliged to obey the signal.

The German comment was significant, and indicated what they had begun to think about their British opposites. Grand Admiral Tirpitz, father of the German Navy, thought that the collision showed a lack of ability. 'The English,' he observed, 'seemed to be very behind in tactics.'

Whatever the views, someone had to pay, and a court martial

started on 17 July at Malta aboard *Hibernia*, an old wooden three-decker which was used as a floating hulk to house transient ships' companies. The president was Vice-Admiral Sir Michael Culme-Seymour, Bart, who had been appointed Tryon's successor. The charge covered Bourke, Tryon's flag captain, and the surviving officers and men from *Victoria*. Bourke's sword lay on the table as a symbol of the swords of every officer who had been in the ship. There were 219 lower deck survivors and twenty-six Royal Marines – others were still in hospital or excused absence – and the men were herded together in clean bell-bottoms, freshly washed jerseys and wide-brimmed straw hats. Of the surviving officers, only the members of Tryon's personal staff, who bore no responsibility for the handling of the ship, were not charged.

With the temperature in the nineties, the court, consisting of Culme-Seymour, Vice-Admiral R. E. Tracey, superintendent of Malta dockyard, and seven captains, listened to a statement written by Markham. It was clear and concise but gave no explanation for what had happened. Statements were also offered by Bourke, two officers from *Victoria*, and Lord Gillford. A letter was also submitted by Captain Charles Johnstone, Markham's flag captain. It produced a surprise. He had apparently discovered that when orders had been given to go full astern on both engines, only three-quarter speed astern was rung to the engine room.

When Bourke was interrogated, he was reluctant to produce anything that might incriminate his admiral and said as little as he could. But he indicated that he had more than once reminded Tryon of the turning circle of the ship and that Tryon had still insisted on six cables. Without doubt, Bourke's reluctance to talk about his chief's refusal to listen was what gave rise to the whispering campaign that Tryon had been drinking.

But it was Lord Gillford who produced the evidence which destroyed Tryon's reputation. Like Bourke, he tried not to condemn Tryon, but he was obliged in the end to admit that he had heard Tryon say, 'It was all my fault.' Hawkins-Smith confirmed this. 'There was no conversation,' he said of the last moments on the bridge. 'But he . . . said, "It is entirely my doing, entirely my fault." '

Though Bourke was the man on the charge, no one doubted that Markham was on trial, too. He was received on board *Hibernia* with a salute of thirteen guns but, from his evidence and that of Captain Johnstone and Markham's flag lieutenant, it soon became very clear that *Camperdown* was not a tightly run ship and that there was carelessness and a lack of energy and initiative on the bridge. Though the fleet was manoeuvring, there had been no one at her starboard telegraph, which had had to be worked by a midshipman who didn't understand it, and it was he who put it to three-quarter astern instead of full astern. In addition, insufficient helm had been applied and it also seemed very clear that Markham, chivvied by being asked to explain his delay, had actually ordered the signal to be hoisted and the helm put over before he had understood it. Even after the manoeuvre had begun, the men on *Camperdown*'s bridge were still arguing about what the signal meant.

For ten days the court thrashed the matter out. Markham said his first reaction to Tryon's order was that it was not possible, then it had occurred to him that *Victoria* intended to circle round his Division which, he said, 'would have been a manoeuvre of perfect safety'. It was, he said, the only safe interpretation of the signal. Anything else was 'an absolute impossibility'. He added, 'Therefore I expected that the captains understood the signal the same way that I did.'

Feeling that the captains would support him over what he had done, Markham asked that they be called, but it seemed that the signal had not been completely understood by any of them. Captain Custance, of *Phaeton*, said he had noticed nothing wrong with the signal, but then immediately realised as he did his mental arithmetic that he had mistaken the radius of the turning circle for its diameter, and he felt Tryon had done the same. Captain Wilson, of *Sans Pareil*, *Victoria*'s sister ship, noticing the two flagships exchanging signals, had assumed that they were arranging which should pass outside the other. Van der Meulen, of *Inflexible*, thought *Victoria* would circle outside *Camperdown*. Others thought the same, but all seemed to think that the manoeuvre as ordered was impossible. Markham admitted that it was Tryon's irritable signal which had led him to carry out the manoeuvre without further delay. Bourke, the man on trial, spoke of his absolute faith in the Commander-in-Chief. He had not been clear in his mind what was to happen but was confident in the C.-in-C.

There seem to have been an awful lot of officers taking Tryon on trust. The order had been questioned by at least two men and Tryon had not altered it, but only the experienced Noel, of *Nile*, had questioned the distance and requested a repeat as he felt that the signal had been taken wrongly. When the signal was repeated, no matter how he tried to interpret it, he could not make out what was intended, and his hope all along, he said, was that Markham would object and would not turn. Finally he made up his mind to use his screws to turn inside *Victoria*, whatever she did.

The court found that the disaster had been caused by Tryon's order and that everything possible had been done to save *Victoria* and the men in her, and finally that no blame attached to Bourke. The court, however, expressed regret that Markham had not protested more strongly, but felt nevertheless that it was not in the best interests of the Service to censure him for obeying the orders of his superior officer.

Despite the result, there were still doubts, and the old hands in the Navy felt the verdict showed that the TA system was not sound. Markham came in for another reprimand, this time from the Admiralty in a minute in which they pointed out that his belief that the Commander-in-Chief would circle round him was not justified by the proper interpretation of the signal.

But what *was* the proper interpretation of the signal? The Admiralty was careful not to say. Tryon had wanted the order of the Divisions preserved. *Camperdown* was to port of *Victoria*, and if the ships could have turned inwards successfully *Camperdown* would have ended up to starboard of *Victoria*, with her attendant ships following her, so that the order of the Divisions would *not* have been preserved.

As Markham had recognised, the order which Tryon's signal seemed to demand could only have been achieved by one Division circling round the other. Markham had thought *Victoria* was going to circle round him, but Tryon had failed to make this clear and it might easily have been that he intended *Camperdown* to circle round *Victoria*. It wouldn't have mattered which he had intended, because the distance in that case wouldn't have mattered and the evolution could have been carried out, but no signal was given to indicate either what Tryon intended or which ship was to be outside the other.

All these possibilities were considered by Lt.-Commander R. T. Gould, who studied the disaster. He suggested that it had nothing to do with the TA system, and that it had occurred simply because Tryon had made a natural slip in working out the distance. Evidence had been given that it was possible to confuse the radius of a ship's turning circle with the diameter. Custance, of *Phaeton*, had made the same mistake, and Vice-Admiral Tracey, one of the members of the court, mentioned in private that three years earlier, flying his flag in *Anson*, he had been second-in-command to Tryon in the naval manoeuvres of 1890 when Tryon had signalled precisely the same fatal manoeuvre. Tracey's flag captain, Bouverie-Clark, had maintained so stoutly that the manoeuvre was impossible that Tracey flew his repeat hoist at the dip *and kept it there*. Tryon cancelled the manoeuvre. The admiral, Gould felt, could make mistakes like anybody else and his subordinates ought to have borne this in mind and acted accordingly.

Yet even this explanation does not entirely stand up. The order and the distance had been queried more than once and Tryon had had plenty of time to think about it, in which case, with his undoubted intelligence, why had he not realised his error? Just before the accident, he had issued a memorandum, which was read in court. It made the point that, though an order should be implicitly obeyed, and while guided by what their superior officer intended, officers should act on their own responsibility. It also pointed out that, though orders should be followed, ships should not be endangered and that risks which were justifiable in wartime were not justifiable in peace. Was it that Tryon had deliberately hazarded his ships to see which of his captains would have the initiative to question his orders?

Markham admitted that he had not thought of the provisos in the memorandum, nor was he aware of a recent amendment to the General Signal Book which stated clearly that while it was the duty of every ship to preserve as correctly as possible the station assigned to her, this did not free her captain from the responsibility of avoiding danger.

The tragedy lay in the exaggerated conception of discipline which was revealed – the feeling that duty must be done at all costs and that obedience was paramount. Confronted with the fact that the leader they trusted had made an error, Tryon's captains took refuge in the assumption that he had something up his sleeve, while the few who anticipated trouble, instead of protesting, merely contented themselves with making arrangements to keep their yard-arms clear.

Though the question of who was to blame had been established, there was still another question to be resolved. Why, after being rammed well forward at a speed of no more than six knots – and with watertight doors – had *Victoria* sunk so quickly? The *Illustrated London News* asked 'whether . . . our tremendous first-class ironclads are more dangerous to each other and to their own crews and officers than . . . to a foreign enemy'.

It was a good point. *Victoria* was a new ship, the latest in design, and the fact that she had capsized in a matter of fifteen minutes seemed to demand an investigation into the Admiralty's design policy. After all, it was only twenty-three years since *Captain* had disappeared.

It was certainly a period of bizarre naval architecture, when the great ironclads used by the world's navies resembled yachts rather than fighting ships and presented gunnery experts with insoluble problems regarding how to mount the enormous guns which had become the fashion. The US ship *Maine*, which blew up in Havana harbour, Cuba, five years later and started the Spanish-American war, had a great gun turret on either side, one aft, one forward, and gaps in her superstructure to allow the guns to fire across the deck. *Victoria* was slightly more orthodox, but because of the shoe-like outline that came from the low freeboard forward and high freeboard aft, and the fact that in any sort of sea her long, low forecastle seemed to slip beneath the waves, she became known as 'The Slipper'. She and her sister ship were 'The Pair of Slippers'.

Her great guns were each 111 tons in weight and, in the opinion of many, were the final mistake in years of mismanagement in ordnance that had followed the disappearance of muzzle-loaders. HMS *Thunderer*'s 12.5 rifles had exploded, killing most of the men in their turret, and *Victoria*'s main armament was considered to be equally dangerous. They were so heavy and so long that when first fitted the muzzles had drooped. It was blithely suggested by the manufacturers that a simple remedy would be to give the guns a little more elevation so that the shell arrived at its destination just the same.

Though the Admiralty managed to prove that these guns were not the cause of *Victoria*'s end, their colossal weight must have had some effect on it. They looked a tremendous threat, but they were clumsy to train and slow to fire, and firing them, it had been felt, would damage the ship's structure. The lavish praise that had been given at *Victoria*'s launching was now forgotten and the press, with its usual pragmatism, began to discover the ship's faults. As the *London Standard* pointed out, there was a painful suspicion that the principles of shipbuilding which had prevailed for so many years in the Navy might turn out to be unsound. Capsizing, it continued, was an ignoble form of destruction. 'To be capsized . . . is almost to be made ridiculous.'

Though the Admiralty managed to dodge an enquiry into their general policy, they had to make public the technical reasons for the disaster. The efficacy of the ram was certainly proved, but nobody seemed to notice that it had been as dangerous to the ship which had used it as to her victim. *Camperdown* had a hole ten feet by six torn in her stem, and her fighting power had been reduced to nothing. Had it not been for the quick improvisation of a wooden barricade, a calm sea and skilful handling, she would have followed *Victoria* to the bottom.

Nevertheless, those favouring the ram were pleased that their theories had been proved. As a weapon, the ram had already been discarded by the French, but the attitude among the pundits at the Admiralty was that it was still the most fatal weapon in the naval armoury – more fatal than the torpedo. The influential *Brassey's Naval Annual* even suggested that the accident was likely to make officers in naval actions more disposed to use it, and the press took the same line. 'A blow with the ram,' the *Sphere* stated, '. . . even when delivered at half speed requires only to get home to smash the stoutest ironclad ever built.' Even in America, despite the vain attempts of *Monitor* and *Merrimac* in the Civil War to finish each other off with the ram, the weapon was held in high esteem, and the New York *Tribune* described the sinking as a 'portentous reminder of the weakness of the vaunted modern navy . . . under the impact of the ram'. It set up a strange avenue of thinking. Why on earth, if ships were fitted with such great guns as *Victoria* carried, aimed with precision instruments and capable of hitting and destroying an enemy at a distance of miles, would they be expected to fight at sufficiently close quarters to use the ram? Were they expected to go alongside each other like Nelson's ships? Surely any ship attempting to do so would be blown out of the water at once.

The argument obscured the main theme – why had *Victoria* capsized? If it was due to a fundamental weakness in design that ran through all the ships of the Navy, then it could be said that Britannia no longer ruled the waves, and that the accident laid her wide open to an attack by any of the great powers jealous of her overseas possessions.

The blow she had been dealt was worked out as being roughly equivalent to the striking force of a twelve-inch shell and, if the armour belt was no protection against the ram, it would have been no protection against such a shell, which was something that could be expected if she were involved in an action. The suggestion that she would not have capsized if her turret ports and upper-deck battery ports had been closed was equally ludicrous, because she could not possibly have gone into action and fought with them closed. In other words, like other ships with large unarmoured ends, she deserved to be regarded less as a fighting ship than as a floating death trap.

The report of the Director of Naval Construction that was presented to Parliament in November was long, highly technical and very reassuring. The watertight doors had not all been closed, and water was able to find its way down a coal chute to cause the initial list. The more serious lurch came when water entered the battery in large quantities through the armoured doors and the broadside gun ports. Since it was a blazingly hot day and every port and door that could let in air was also open, this had added to the rapidity of the sinking.

The report argued that all that was required was sufficient time to close the watertight doors, but since disasters provide their own conditions and time is the last thing allowed, it seemed a poor sort of explanation, though it was true that the belief in watertight doors had caused too many to be around. Self-closing doors were nevertheless ruled out, but it was noticeable that it was not long before they began to be fitted. Finally, though the report claimed that the accident did not suggest insufficient stability in the design, *Victoria*'s sister ship, *Sans Pareil*, was quickly modified and always remained suspect and unpopular until she was sold for scrap in 1907.

The report seemed to answer nothing. Despite the denials, there was surely something radically wrong with Britain's ironclads, and it was noticeable that not one of those off the coast of Tripoli that fatal afternoon was thought fit to be kept even in the reserve by the time the Great War started. All were relegated to guardship duties within five years, only the *Camperdown* avoiding the demotion until 1900.

In some ways the accident was a blessing in disguise, and the Victorian ships and their officers were scrapped just in time. They would never have been a match for the Kaiser's upstart Navy with its eager officers and brand new ships.

The Ks

It took the Admiralty an incredibly long time to learn to live with technology at the turn of the century. With the triple expansion-reciprocating engine only twenty-five years old, the quadruple version less than five, the steam turbine only three, and battleships suddenly capable of an incredible sixteen to twenty knots, admirals and captains trained in sail were not capable of handling such powerful vessels.

Though the Navy had gained new prestige from the review in the year of Victoria's golden jubilee and could always claim the taxpayers' money at the expense of the Army, while Jack Tar became a sentimental figure symbolising the jingoism that surrounded the Empire, the mentality of the men at the top didn't change much. At this time there were men who had entered as cadets and retired as admirals without ever having fired a shot in anger, and men still afloat to whom naval history was nothing but posturing heroics in an empire of brass and new paint. Having so often shown the flag in ports across the world and acted as unofficial ambassadors, they considered that, if nothing else, they knew how to behave and their ships were the envy of the world. It was that very envy which led to the building of the German Navy, while the self-satisfied attitude of the British led to results no one ever expected.

Even as it had preened itself amid the centenary celebrations of Nelson's victory at Trafalgar, F. T. Jane, the founder of *Jane's Fighting Ships*, was saying, 'The cult of Nelson is pure unadulterated moonshine.' No sailor, he felt, would be more efficient because 'England Expects Every Man To Do His Duty' was inscribed on some part of his armoured battleship. Since Nelson's ships had sailed the seas, he complained, warfare had considerably altered, yet the belief persisted that the victories of the Napoleonic Wars had secured for England eternal domination of the waves.

The 'wooden walls' officers had all gone by 1911 but their attitudes remained. When the White Star *Olympic* – at 45,324 tons the largest liner in the world – collided with the cruiser *Hawke* on her maiden voyage in Southampton Waters she was put out of commission for six weeks. The ships had sighted each other in plenty of time and the Admiralty claimed that the collision was caused by *Olympic* passing too close to *Hawke*. White Star argued that the cruiser's rudder had been fitted the wrong way by mistake. This was also quite wrong, but the old naval arrogance might still have been at work. *Hawke* undoubtedly had the right of way, but good seamanship should have recognised that a large deep-draught ship like *Olympic* should have been accorded a right to the middle of the channel. But naval ships – of all countries – were apt to consider their dignities too closely and were very reluctant to alter course. Perhaps *Olympic* was as unlucky as her senior officers. Captain E. J. Smith, Chief Officer H. F. Wilde and First Officer W. M. Murdoch all lost their lives in *Olympic*'s sister ship, *Titanic*, within a year, while *Olympic* herself, converted to an armed merchantman in 1914, ran aground near Shetland within two weeks of her commissioning.

By this time the big-gun-big-ship men were in the ascendancy at the Admiralty. When he became First Sea Lord, Admiral Sir John (Jacky) Fisher was well aware of the Navy's deficiencies and the out-of-date ideas behind them. He considered the Navy 'drowzy, inefficient and moth-eaten', filled with splendid seamen but containing no men of vision, and he literally took it by the scruff of the neck and dragged it into the twentieth century. He was a strange man, asiatic in appearance, vicious, libellous, even at times seemingly unbalanced in his furies. Yet he loved dancing and young women enjoyed having him as a partner, and his ideas about ships were sound. In the words of his arch enemy, Admiral Lord Charles Beresford, with whom he conducted a running fight for years, he took a twelve-knot navy with breakdowns and made it into a fifteen-knot navy without breakdowns. To counter the German threat he produced brand new ships with high speeds and big guns and, to pay for them, sold dozens of older and smaller ships from foreign stations. While his sagacity was admired in Britain, it sent ripples of doubt through the outposts of the Empire, where a small old ship in the harbour was considered a far better defence against marauding raiders than a big ship based in England.

Britain had got its new Navy, but there was still a lot of dead wood about in the shape of Victorian senior officers. They were far from being Nelson's 'band of brothers'. The Fisher-Beresford feud split the Navy down the middle, and when the new naval staff was formed in 1912 its chief, Vice-Admiral Sir Frederick Charles Doveton Sturdee, was considered 'one of the curses of the Navy'. He was a pompous man 'who would not listen to anyone's opinion', while Admiral Sir Archibald Berkeley Milne, Arky Barky to the Service, Commander-in-Chief, Mediterranean, was known best as a 'sea courtier'. He had spent almost nine years in royal yachts and owed his rapid promotion to court influence. He was dapper to a degree and loathed by the shrewd Fisher, who considered him totally unfitted to be senior admiral afloat.

The Navy's role in the late nineteenth century had been small but it had lent active support in the Nile campaigns and the Boxer rebellions. The Boer War was conducted hundreds of miles from the sea, but again the Navy made sure that it was noticed by providing naval guns on carriages. During these campaigns a number of young officers who distinguished themselves were to come to the top during the First World War, or the Great War as it was called at the time for the reason that nothing greater had then been fought.

In 1914 the Navy entered a full-dress war after a hundred years of peace and a dynamic revolution in weapons. 'Only a superman could have handled these weapons without making mistakes,' Admiral Sir William James said. With its huge preponderance of ships, it was regarded as the summit of power and prestige, yet from 1815 its effective function had been simply to remain a fleet-in-being of overwhelming superiority. A century of inaction had bred a widespread indifference to gunnery and tactics, and wealthy captains even paid from their own pocket for 'lavish and purely ornamental fittings that would have been more appropriate to a millionaire's yacht'. Lord Charles Beresford admitted that at the age of fifty-six he had handled three ships together for only five hours in his life, and that was a great deal more than his brother admirals.

The failings became obvious at once. When the war began on 4 August 1914, *Goeben*, a German capital ship of 23,000 tons, escorted by the light cruiser *Breslau*, of 4500 tons, was in the Adriatic and it was imperative that they should be stopped from bolting home. Owing to obscure orders from the Chief of Naval Staff, Sturdee, the inertia of the C.-in-C., Mediterranean, Milne, and the vacillation of the commander of the First Cruiser Squadron, Rear Admiral Ernest Troubridge, instead they escaped to seek refuge with the Turks.

Who in the end was to blame has been argued ever since. Instead of behaving like Commodore Harwood, who forced the battleship *Graf Spee* to an ignominious end in the river Plate in 1939 by the skilful use of three small ships, Troubridge, a descendant of one of Nelson's most famous captains, with a squadron of four armoured cruisers and the two light cruisers *Gloucester* and *Dublin*, decided, largely on the advice of his flag captain, that *Goeben* was too powerful and turned away.

His behaviour contrasted strongly with that of John Kelly, the captain of *Gloucester*, who was that same forthright John Kelly who was later to be appointed to deal with the Invergordon mutiny. Outgunned and outpaced, he pursued the Germans to the very end but, in the event, they passed through the Dardanelles and presented the ships to the Turks by whom, it was announced by the Germans, they had been 'annexed'. Their presence brought about the Turkish declaration of war against the allies that resulted in the slaughter of the Dardanelles. Troubridge's court martial was notable chiefly for the way in which Milne, in protecting his own skin, added to Troubridge's difficulties. It was also ironic that the Sea Lords had to comment not only on Troubridge's failure but at the same time on the sinking by a submarine of three old armoured cruisers, *Aboukir*, *Hogue* and *Cressy*, off the Dutch coast on 22 September.

British admirals had tended to think nothing of the submarine, even to regard it as unfair, a 'damned un-English weapon', but it did for the three old cruisers in less than an hour, so that the Navy was court martialling two of its admirals for neglect of duty almost at the same time: Troubridge for not stopping *Goeben*, and Rear Admiral Arthur Christian for deserting his squadron on the Broad Fourteens. Blame for them being there rested with Sturdee, but it was Christian who had turned away in his ship, sister to the sunken vessels, claiming that she was short of fuel – though one of the lost ships had even less. Christian was a strange man, like his namesake in Bligh's *Bounty* a man who could not take criticism. As commandant of the training establishment *Osborne*, he had condemned without a hearing Cadet Charles Archer-Shee for the alleged theft of a postal order and had refused to listen to the boy's defence. Accused of leaving his squadron, he claimed that he was being persecuted.

The disasters made people wonder about the Navy. It even made the Navy wonder about the Navy. Certainly what happened to Troubridge influenced the decision of Sir Christopher Cradock when, again largely thanks to Sturdee, his squadron found itself faced with immensely superior German ships under Graf von Spee off the Coronel Islands on 1 November during the week of Troubridge's court martial. Troubridge's action – or inaction – caused Cradock to choose to fight and he went down with two of his ships and 1400 men.

Nevertheless, the Navy's contempt for its enemies remained. It was obvious even in the lowest ordinary seaman, who claimed that German sailors were not made at sea but in Kiel, and that, they said, was like the Serpentine. The expected great battle between the two fleets was known to them as the Big Smash, but the plan for it surmised that the Germans would wish to stand and fight when it was obvious that, with their inferior numbers, they might prefer to run away. The Commander-in-Chief, Admiral Sir John Jellicoe, he who had survived the sinking of the *Victoria*, known as Silent Jack to the fleet, was considered by some to be too cautious, too plodding, and an old woman with an obsession about submarines. Sir David Beatty, in command of the battle cruisers, with his aggressive attitude and his hat cocked over one eye, was considered the epitome of a fighting admiral; but there was a suspicion that while Jellicoe could do with a bit of Beatty's drive, Beatty could do with a bit of Jellicoe's technical knowledge.

As it was, the Battle of Jutland at the end of May 1916 ended up as a propaganda victory for the Germans. Though Tryon's vaunted system had died discredited and wireless telegraphy had appeared, the men in command failed to use it properly and the opportunity to destroy the German fleet was missed because, when sighted, its position was not passed to the main fleet. Lack of training, foolhardiness and bad ship design snatched outright victory from the British, and dockworkers jeered the returning ships. No one had noticed that you can't plan a battle from harbour or fight it swinging round a buoy at Scapa Flow.

Though senior officers thought only of big ships with big guns, thoughtful younger officers had already come to regard them as an uneconomic hazard. The loss of a big ship was a disaster, and it was necessary for them to be escorted by flotillas of smaller ships on the look-out for their hidden enemies, the mine and the U-boat. British losses started a fear of the U-boat that was out of all proportion to its capabilities. At sea British admirals were terrified of meeting a daring undersea commander, and they had so neglected the new weapons that they had not even arranged protection for Scapa Flow, where the Grand Fleet was sent for safety.

Britain was entirely dependent on imports, but once the submarines began to operate her position immediately became dangerous. With mines and submarines making it impossible for British ships to cruise off the German coast as in the days of Nelson, German and neutral ships were instead stopped on the high seas and brought into British ports, and, since the Germans had failed to stock up with raw materials, the noose immediately tightened round the German neck. There was a noose round the British neck too, however. The submarine menace was real and there were times, as in the Second World War, when shipping was being sunk faster than it could be built.

As early as October 1914, the Navy was in something of a panic and look-outs began to see submarines everywhere. Even at Scapa Flow alarms were raised, and on 1 September Jellicoe had taken the entire fleet to sea, dodging – and even firing on – a U-boat that wasn't there. The same thing happened again a month later. The result was that the Admiralty suddenly awakened to the fact that the submarine was a remarkably effective weapon.

Although Britain had sixty-four submarines in commission at the outbreak of the war, only seventeen were capable of operating beyond her coasts. Germany was reported to have forty-six long-range boats and to have built secretly 100 to 200 smaller ones. It was wildly untrue, but it showed the difference in preparedness. The British submarine service had been badly mismanaged before the war. Fisher blamed Commodore Roger Keyes, at that time Flag Officer (Submarines). Fisher had been First Sea Lord before, and on his return to office on the outbreak of war he was horrified to learn that Britain had fewer submarines than when he had retired.

Since the submarine was still in its infancy and was slow, it was considered only as a coastal defence weapon, and the admirals, who still thought in terms of great fleet battles, had no time for anything that couldn't operate with the great ships. Blame for the lack of submarines was flung in every direction. It was the fault of Churchill, of Fisher, of Keyes, of Asquith, the Prime Minister, even the builders, Vickers. The reaction was an attempt to make good the missing boats, and Fisher began placing orders, telling the Superintendent of Contracts that he would make his wife a widow and his house a dunghill if he brought paperwork into the business. 'I want submarines,' he said, 'not contracts.' Most of what were produced were modified versions of the well-proven E-class boats.

But then fleet senior officers heard that German submarines could travel as fast as a battleship, and the torpedoing of the battleship *Formidable* on New Year's Day 1915 aggravated the rumour. Even Fisher was taken in and he ordered the Director of Naval Construction, Sir Eustace Tennyson-d'Eyncourt, to design a submarine capable of at least twenty knots. The response was that only with steam could more than twenty knots be guaranteed. Instinct had long since told Fisher that boilers, funnels and submarines did not mix, and he decided to stay with the E-class type of boat with extra power.

The counter-measures appeased senior officers, but they believed that battle fleets should have their own undersea boats capable of working at a speed of twenty-one knots. Submariners, who did not relish manoeuvring beneath the keels of fast-moving battleships, did not share the enthusiasm. Jutland had not been fought at this time, and the waking hours of the big-ship men were dedicated to planning and rehearsing it. If submarines could be built to accompany the fleet, they felt, they could hit the enemy ships as they deployed or retreated.

Keyes shared this dream. Even Fisher believed that fast submarines should be used with the fleet, and the belief that the

Germans were equipping their own fleet with fast underwater weapons finally cracked his resistance to steam power. He gave in and the K-class submarine was born.

The new boats, submersible destroyers as they were called, were laid down in 1915. They were to be the largest, fastest and heaviest submarines to be built anywhere in the world at the time. An earlier design of d'Eyncourt's for a boat 338 feet long and displacing some 1700 tons, bigger than some destroyers, was brought out. The proposed steam engines would give it a surface speed of twenty-four knots, nine faster than the E-class boats, and its armament consisted of four twenty-one-inch bow torpedo tubes, four similar beam tubes and two guns, and she would have a range of 3000 miles. This general design, with a few modifications, was accepted, though Fisher insisted on an auxiliary diesel engine as a safety measure.

When the boats appeared they were certainly fast and between August 1916 and May 1918 the Navy commissioned seventeen of these revolutionary vessels.

They were a disaster. No class of modern warship has ever suffered so many calamities as the K boats. They were involved in sixteen major accidents and countless smaller mishaps. One sank on her trials. Three were lost after collisions. A fifth disappeared. Another sank in harbour. They achieved nothing against the enemy and out of twenty-seven built eight were lost from causes other than enemy action, four were scrapped within four years of commissioning, and another six within nine years. The loss of life in them was appalling and they became objects of hatred and superstition and the men in them were described as 'the suicide club'. Though there were men who regarded them with affection, most went to enormous lengths to avoid serving in them. Experts declared that they were obsolete before they were launched and were the products of bad strategy, and that their continued use in the face of so many accidents showed the bigotry of the naval minds of the period. Because of the war, most of the disasters escaped public notice, since the court martials and enquiries were held in secret, but even after the Armistice the Navy revealed little about them.

The first major disaster occurred in January 1917, to *K13*. Her captain, Lt.-Commander Godfrey Herbert, was not unfamiliar with steam submarines, having been aboard the French steam submarine *Archimède*, when with seven British submarines she had tried to trap the German fleet on its return from bombarding Scarborough and Hartlepool in December 1914. A heavy sea had so bent the funnel that it couldn't be lowered for diving, and as water poured down the crew, including Herbert, had bailed out the boiler room with buckets.

K13 was built by Fairfields at Govan. *K3*, built at Barrow, had been commissioned only fourteen months after the signing of the contract and, of the other twelve ordered in 1915, all but one were either nearing completion or undergoing trials. Yet the Admiralty had already ordered seven more so that, without tests on a prototype, they were committed to twenty-one warships of a revolutionary design. Yet *K3*'s diving trials had been far from successful and might well have been the end of the future King George VI, who was on board with the Commander-in-Chief, Portsmouth. Trimmed for diving, she suddenly put her bows down at a steep angle and dived, flinging the men inside, including the Prince, across the deck. With her bows buried in the mud 150 feet below the surface, the stern reared above the surface, the propellers spinning in the air, and it took twenty minutes to free her and bring her up. On her first patrol in the North Sea she took a sea down both funnels which extinguished both boiler fires and flooded the boiler room, and only the auxiliary diesel engine Fisher had insisted on enabled her to reach port.

The other completed boats, *K2*, *K4* and *K13*, had so far given no hint of serious trouble, and Herbert took *K13* to sea with a feeling of confidence. In addition to the crew of fifty-three, on board were fourteen directors and employees of Fairfields, five representatives of sub-contractors, five Admiralty officials, a Clyde pilot, and two extra passengers – the commanding and engineering officers of *K14*, which was being built at the same yard.

Things went wrong from the start. Someone accidentally switched off the starter motor on the steering gear, putting the helm out of action, so that *K13*'s bows grounded on a mudbank.

As the ebbing tide pulled the boat round she was lying athwart the stream when a Glasgow steamer, trying to squeeze past between her and a dredger at a quay on the opposite side of the river, jammed herself against her with a screeching of steel and a lot of bad language. *K13* was eventually able to proceed downriver, and off Greenock Herbert put her through the routine procedures of a surface trial, then at midday headed for Gareloch for the final diving trials. The day was fine and a small steamer, *Comet*, took on board those whose services were not needed for the dive. Running with only the conning tower above water, it was noticed that the submarine had steadily increased her weight. The engineer officer, Engineer-Lieutenant Arthur Lane, a careful, painstaking man and the son of an engineer rear admiral, announced that the boiler room had sprung a small leak, and it was decided they would submerge after lunch.

Before boarding *Comet* for lunch, Lane asked the Admiralty overseer, Frederick Searle, to look at one of the four ventilators between the funnels, which he said was sticking. Searle assured him that there was nothing to worry about, but Lane asked his chief ERA to examine them again. The chief ERA reported them fully open.

Before getting under way Herbert signalled his intention to another new submarine, *E50*, which was commanded by a friend of his, Lt.-Commander Kenneth Michell, which was also undergoing acceptance trials in the loch. Passing the order 'Diving Stations', Herbert walked along the hull to watch the funnels being lowered into wells in the superstructure. In the control room a red light appeared, illuminating the word 'shut', and Herbert ordered half speed ahead on both motors and the flooding of all but four of the main external ballast tanks, then clambered down the conning tower, closing the hatch behind him.

While he had been on the superstructure, one of the passengers from the sister ship *K14*, Engineer-Lieutenant Leslie Rideal, noticed that a light supposed to shine steadily to indicate that the mushroom hatches were closed was flickering. Lane did not consider it important, but as *K13* dived the boiler room was reported to be flooding, and Rideal saw water spouting from an exhaust pipe leading from the boiler room. The Admiralty's boiler-room overseer had also seen water streaming in and rushed to inform the captain. As he arrived, Lane was already shouting a warning and the Fairfield assistant manager was also on his way with the same information.

Herbert ordered 'Hard to rise! Blow two and three!' but still the submarine went down and Chief Petty Officer Oscar Moth, the coxswain, reported her out of control. The forward keel, weighing ten tons and able to be dropped in an emergency, was freed, watertight doors were closed and all forward tanks were blown. It made no difference. A mile away, from *E50*, Michell saw *K13* go under and immediately afterwards saw two specks on the water. It was assumed that they were the tips of the periscopes which had broken surface, but on the shore in front of the Shandon Hydropathic Hotel, opposite which the submarine had gone down, one of the maids realised that the objects were the heads of two men who cried out before vanishing. But when she reported what she had seen no one believed her.

Stern first, the submarine came to rest on the bottom. In the control room, as Herbert ordered the motors stopped, thick jets of water shot from the voice pipes from the after compartments, spraying the port switchboard and starting the fuses blowing. Electric cables crackled, smoked and burst into flame, using precious oxygen and polluting the air with dense white smoke.

The voice pipes were plugged and the fires put out, but when Herbert tried to telephone Lane he found the telephone dead. Taking stock of the situation, he found that there was still ample lighting but that reserves of compressed air were running low, and they could not shed the after ten-ton keel because it was controlled from the engine room. Of the eighty men who had been aboard, thirty-one had been lost. Among the forty-nine still alive was Professor Percy Hillhouse, Fairfield's naval architect who had given evidence at the enquiry into the loss of *Empress of Ireland*. Imperturbably, he began to calculate the quantity of air available and decided that if the survivors remained still it would last fifteen hours. If they had to work hard, its consumption would rise steeply. Petty Officer Moth, who had run the gauntlet of the Dardanelles in an E-class boat, thought it a poor way to die.

As the light began to fade, on the conning tower of *E50*, Lt.-Commander Michell began to be concerned. He moved his boat to the spot where *K13* had disapeared but, finc'ing no trace of battery acid in the water he was reassured. When darkness came, however, he became alarmed enough to send his first lieutenant ashore to ask for salvage plant of all kinds to be sent. One of the Fairfield directors, who had reached shore in *Comet*, also asked for help.

In *K13*, a jammed watertight door was opened, providing a possible escape route and additional air, and as water kept fusing circuits, two civilians were kept busy rewiring. There were a few sandwiches aboard but no one felt hungry, though shortage of air made everyone thirsty.

Rescue work had been delayed by confusion. The senior men at the Navy's Clyde HQ and at Fairfields had gone home, and it was well after 10 p.m. when the first rescue vessel, *Gossamer*, an old gun boat, arrived. She carried a diver but no diving suit, and Fairfields had to send to Glasgow to fetch their own diver. But his suit, which had not been used for years, burst and he was dragged half-drowned from the water while the Fairfields car raced off to find another suit. Two more rescue ships arrived, a trawler and *Thrush*, an old sloop fitted out for salvage work. But as she had come straight from towing a mined ship into harbour, she was short of gear and had neither a diver nor a diving suit on board. At daybreak, Fairfield's diver tried again.

During the early morning, it was decided that someone should try to leave the submarine via the conning tower to help the rescuers. Herbert felt that he should be the last to leave and Goodhart, the commander of *K14*, agreed to try. The attempt was timed for midday, Herbert accompanying Goodhart into the conning tower to control the rising water and the compressed air which would enable him to escape. As the hatch below them was clipped, Goodhart opened the sea valve and the icy water began to rise. Breathless and with their ears drumming, Herbert turned on the high-pressure air and Goodhart knocked the clips off the upper hatch. With the pressure inside and out equalised, he pushed the hatch open and shot out.

It had not been Herbert's intention to follow him, but he was swept off his feet and carried upwards and through the second hatch above clear of *K13*. On the surface, attempts were being made to raise the bows of the submarine when suddenly there was a tremendous surge of air that churned the water between the two lifting vessels and a man appeared in the middle of a huge bubble. It was Herbert.

'Where's Goodhart?' were his first words.

No one knew what he was talking about and he explained what had happened. But there was still no sign of Goodhart. By this time, Michell had taken *E50* alongside *Gossamer* and was running the rescue attempts. An attempt to attach a high-pressure air hose to the submarine failed when the divers could not find the external connection, though eventually they succeeded. It was thirty-five hours since she had dived, and the foul air coming up was said to be almost black.

The trapped men used the incoming air to recharge the empty air bottles and to attempt to blow the tanks. They had almost given up hope when they detected movement and, as the bows rose, *Thrush* and the trawler hove in on the wire which had been passed beneath the submarine until her nose was now only eight feet below the surface.

A four-inch armoured hose was now attached, and a bottle of brandy was lowered down the pipe followed by milk, chocolate and coffee. Another attempt was made to heave *K13*'s bows out of the water and, around midday, they slowly broke the surface. Michell called up two mud barges and used them to support the submarine.

By now, the men below were in darkness save for three torches and, with the submarine at a steep angle, were constantly slipping on the oil-covered deck. The tide was rising, but finally the rescuers managed to cut a hole in the pressure hull and the exodus began, the civilians first. The last man emerged shortly after 10 p.m. fifty-seven hours after *K13* had dived. With high tide, the hole was only three inches above water. At six the next evening the weight of the submarine tore the bollards out of the barges and she sank.

A court of enquiry was told that divers had found that the four thirty-seven-inch ventilators over the boiler room had been left open and that the indicators in the boiler room *showed* they were open, and that the engine-room hatch was also inexplicably open. The Admiralty overseer said that he had tested every valve not once but several times, and it was decided that Engineer-Lieutenant Lane had failed to close all the openings before signalling to the control room that the engine and boiler rooms were shut.

On 15 March *K13* was brought to the surface. Thirty-one coffins were prepared for the bodies that were expected, but only twenty-nine were found. Goodhart was found trapped under the roof of the wheelhouse, though Engineer-Lieutenant Lane and John Steele, a civilian, were missing. But the mystery of the open hatch over the engine room was solved, and at last the maid at the Shandon Hydropathic Hotel was believed. The two men she said she had seen were the missing two, and they had evidently opened the hatch when the air pressure inside had equalled the water pressure outside and had escaped, only to succumb to the sudden reduction of pressure in their lungs. Currents had carried them down the estuary and one body was found on a distant bank of the Clyde two months later.

None of the officers or civilians in *K13* ever went on board a submarine again. A few of the crew went back, among them Petty Officer Moth, who within a few weeks became completely bald. Though he didn't know it, he wasn't yet finished with *K13*.

Since human error appeared to have sunk *K13*, no one at the Admiralty worried, because new boats often developed idiosyncracies. But there was also an amazing amount of self-deception and excuses, and the Navy, the shipyards and the Treasury, to say nothing of reputations of men in Whitehall, were committed to the new submarines.

And the faults didn't go away. *K1*, built at Portsmouth, had so many problems that her trials lasted five months. *K2* suffered an electrical explosion and fire on her first diving trials. On her acceptance trials, boiler-room vents jammed open. On her first submerging at Devonport, *K6* refused to surface until a dockyard worker on board traced the fault to the compressed-air system. *K4*, leaving her Barrow yard, went aground during her trials. *K14*, sister ship to the ill-fated *K13*, sprang a leak while at anchor and had to return ignominiously to the yard under tow. All the faults so far had been small, but they could have been lethal and defects in the design soon began to be apparent as the Ks joined the Grand Fleet at Scapa Flow.

Perceptive submariners felt that the defects would never disappear because they were inbuilt. The bows of the boats lacked buoyancy and in bad weather K boats had to reduce speed, heave to or dive, and these faults made it impossible to keep station with the fleet. The forward gun could not be manned because most of the time it was half-submerged, while the deck torpedo tubes were useless and it was uncomfortable on the bridge and equally uncomfortable below. Water coming down the conning tower saturated the men below, earthed the switchboards and gave shocks to anyone touching the conning-tower ladder, while large waves still managed to shower water on the control platform of the engine room.

But it was the diving characteristics that worried submariners most. The K boats' great length tended to make them inert, and they were far more difficult to control than a submarine of normal length, while the flat areas of the upper deck and superstructure were found to act as extra hydroplanes. At some time in their careers, most of the class nose-dived out of control.

Yet a crash dive, that basic tactical defence, was virtually impossible because it took around five minutes to shut off boilers, retract funnels, close ventilators and hatches, evacuate the boiler room, fill the ballast tanks and submerge. It was sometimes even possible for a captain to walk along the superstructure during diving procedure to check that all the holes were closed, something that was important because the smallest piece of flotsam could prevent the funnels or the ventilators from being properly secured. Finally, because of their size, the K boats were classed as self-contained warships and did not have a depot ship where the crews could enjoy a change from their cramped quarters; irritation burst out in squabbles and fist fights.

By this time it was clear that the German High Seas Fleet had no intention of giving battle again. Jutland had been an enigma. Though the British had lost more ships and men, they had turned the key on the Germans' prison and had won a greater victory than anyone realised because, through denying the sea to the Germans, Germany was being slowly starved out of the war. But the Grand Fleet now had a class of ship it didn't know how to use, and the K boats hardly distinguished themselves. Though *K7* torpedoed an enemy U-boat, *U95*, the torpedo failed to explode.

They were used with the fleet in attempts to draw out the Germans, but working with the big ships was always hazardous and on 16 November 1917 *K4* ran down *K1*, which had to be sunk with gunfire. The accident confirmed submariners' belief that the submarine's true role was as a lone weapon.

By this time *K13*, raised, refitted and renumbered *K22*, had reappeared. She was regarded as a jinx boat and men drafted to her often developed mysterious illnesses which prevented them joining. In October 1917, she sailed from the Clyde to join a new flotilla of K boats at Rosyth. The flotilla was numbered thirteen and what was to become known as the Battle of May Island was about to begin.

Operation EC1 was devised early in 1918 by Vice-Admiral Sir David Beatty – now C.-in-C., Grand Fleet, in place of Sir John Jellicoe – to exercise his cruiser squadrons, practise deployment and keep his bored fleet in fighting trim.

With Beatty in his flagship, *Queen Elizabeth*, the force was to consist of twenty-six battleships, nine cruisers, four light cruisers and numerous destroyers. The Rosyth base would provide three battleships, four battle cruisers, two cruisers, fourteen light cruisers, the two K-class flotillas, each led by a light cruiser, and the usual attendant destroyers. The two forces were to meet in the North Sea and the exercise was to take place during the night of 1 February.

The Rosyth Force was to leave on the evening of 31 January,

and to navigate forty warships through the defences of the Forth estuary in darkness and in radio silence, each ship showing only one stern light, called for a high level of skill and nerve. A U-boat had been reported off May Island in the entrance to the Forth, and Sir Hugh Evan-Thomas, in command of the Rosyth Force, for safety ordered a speed of twenty-two knots for one hour after passing the island, later reducing it by one knot to twenty-one.

At 6.30 p.m., Commander E. W. Leir, in the light cruiser *Ithuriel*, began to lead his K boats downstream astern of Evan-Thomas's flagship *Courageous*. The 2nd Battle Cruiser Squadron moved off in line astern and destroyers were to join them downstream. Behind them would be the 12th Submarine Flotilla led by Captain C. J. C. Little in the cruiser *Fearless*. With the entire force in line astern, the order was *Courageous*, *Ithuriel*, *K11*, *K17*, *K14*, *K12* and *K22* (the old *K13*), *Australia*, *New Zealand*, *Indomitable*, *Inflexible*, *Fearless*, *K4*, *K3*, *K6* and *K7*, followed by the battleships. The submarines were to travel 400 yards apart, showing a blue stern light at half-brilliance. The cox'n of *K22* was CPO Moth. As the force moved downstream, twenty miles ahead, directly in their path, were eight minesweeping trawlers whose commander, incredibly, had not been informed about Operation EC1.

With a light low-lying mist beginning to show, *Ithuriel* soon lost sight of *Courageous*. Behind *Ithuriel* was the leading K flotilla and the whole force was in a line thirty miles long. Three-quarters of a mile behind *Ithuriel*, the commander of *K14*, Commander T. C. B. Harbottle, noticed that the leading boat of the group, *K11*, was reducing speed and turning to port. The next moment *K17*, which he was following, also turned to port, and seconds later the outlines of two minesweepers appeared. Ordering a turn, he saw his boat swing safely to port but, before the swing could be corrected, the helmsman shouted that the helm had jammed. Calling for the navigation lights to be switched on, Harbottle was relieved to see the following boat also switch on her lights and concerned himself with getting clear of the oncoming battle cruisers.

Just then the helmsman reported that the helm had freed itself, and Harbottle decided to return to his position in the line. But the watch officer on *K22* had lost sight of his next ahead, *K12*, the boat behind *K14*, and just as CPO Moth was reflecting that one year before to the day he had been rescued at Gareloch, *K22*, steaming at nineteen knots, slammed into *K14*. With both boats crippled, the captain of *K22*, Lt.-Commander Charles de Burgh, sent a coded wireless message to *Ithuriel* about the collision. *K22* was in a fit state to proceed to harbour, but Harbottle asked de Burgh to stand by because *K14* was liable to sink. *Ithuriel* and the other three submarines had continued eastward, unaware of the accident, and it was more than an hour before *Ithuriel*'s radio decoded and passed to Commander Leir the distress call from *K22*.

By this time the four ships of the 2nd Battle Cruiser Squadron were bearing down on the spot where the two submarines lay flashing and radioing for help. *Australia* had just increased to twenty-one knots when a red Very light was seen ahead, and almost immediately another light began to flash a message reporting the collision and demanding assistance. The men in *K14* and *K22* watched anxiously as the battle cruisers and their attendant destroyers thundered past on both sides in the dark.

The last of the battle cruisers, *Inflexible*, unaware of what had happened, saw lights ahead but was too late to take evasive action. Moth, on the bridge of *K22*, was horrified to see a destroyer sweep past only ten feet from *K22*'s bows, then out of the night he saw the towering bows of a big ship heading straight for them. *Inflexible* smashed into the already battered submarine, bent thirty feet of her bows at right angles then tore along her side, wrenching away the external ballast and fuel tanks and pushing her under the water until only the superstructure and the bridge showed, before rushing on into the darkness. Once again Moth thought it a rotten way to die.

K14 was still afloat and firing red Very lights at the rate of one a minute as the surface ships raced by. *Ithuriel* had at last picked up *K22*'s distress call and at that moment a message came from one of the following submarines that *K22* had not been seen for some time. When another message giving information about the collision arrived, Leir decided to turn back to give assistance.

A message was prepared for transmission to *Courageous* but for some reason it did not leave *Ithuriel* immediately.

Signalling problems had always plagued the British Fleet and now played their part in the disaster that was building up. A minute after *Ithuriel*, followed by her submarines, completed her turn into what Leir thought was a safe area south of the battle cruisers, he was astonished to see *Australia* and the battle cruisers coming straight towards him. He managed to keep clear but the three submarines, manoeuvring with the maddening sluggishness of their class, lay directly in the path of the oncoming ship. The battle cruiser passed *K12* with only two or three feet to spare, and *Ithuriel* and the other submarines passed a harrowing few minutes dodging the accompanying destroyers.

Five miles behind the battle cruisers came the second group of K boats, led by *Fearless*, under the command of Captain Little. *Fearless* had intercepted *K22*'s signal and warned her charges to keep a sharp look-out but, as they passed May Island, Little felt that they were safe. Unfortunately, the delayed signal from *Ithuriel* had still not gone out to indicate that *Ithuriel* and her submarines were now on an opposite course, and when it came it was too late.

Even as the signal was received, the officers on the bridge of *Fearless* saw lights ahead but, as the ship was put to full astern and hard-a-port, they realised that they were heading for *K17*, and the next second *Fearless* slammed into her, sinking her bows deep into the submarine forward of the conning tower. *K17* twisted herself free, and rolled along the side of *Fearless*. There was no panic, and the survivors gathered on deck, but eight minutes after she had been hit, *K17* slid below the surface.

To the boats astern of *Fearless*, the sounding of sirens came one on top of another until it was impossible to tell who was doing what. *Ithuriel* and *K11*, meanwhile, totally unaware of the increasing chaos behind them, continued on their errand of mercy. *K22* and *K14* had collided miles away, *Fearless* had sunk *K17*, and now *K12*, having dodged *Australia*, was now heading on a collision course towards *K6*, the third in line of the 12th Flotilla. In avoiding her, *K6* struck *K4* and almost cut her in half. As *K6* hauled herself clear, *K7*, coming up behind, found herself about to hit her. By quick reaction, she managed to avoid a collision, but almost immediately found herself faced with the sinking *K4*, which went down so fast, however, that *K7* barely touched her.

It was not finished yet, because behind the last K boat came the three battleships of the 5th Battle Squadron which, thanks to the delayed message from *Ithuriel*, had no knowledge of what lay ahead and at twenty-one knots the three great ships roared through the remnants of the K flotillas, cutting the swimming men to pieces, while survivors from *K17*, who had been dragged to the deck of *K7*, were knocked overboard again by their wash. From *K17* only nine men survived.

It was *K22*, the old *K13*, which had triggered the accident and CPO Moth was not at all surprised. The blame was placed by the court of enquiry on the submarine commanders; and the First Lord of the Admiralty, Sir Eric Geddes, who was a politician and had no knowledge of the sea, blamed the standard of efficiency. No one blamed the boats, and the idea of fleet submarines remained.

The submariners, however, well knew the K boats' lack of manoeuvrability. They claimed that they had the speed of a destroyer, the turning circle of a battleship and the bridge-control facilities of a picket boat. May Island had shown that they could not safely work with surface craft, nor even in flotillas.

A successful experiment with a revolutionary idea or a useless theme pushed to its limit to protect reputations? The submarine is essentially an aggressive weapon, to be used alone or, as in the Second World War, in loosely knitted packs. As an adjunct to the fleet, it proved valueless. Apart from *K7*'s hitting *U95* with a dud torpedo, the K boats had done nothing to prove their worth, though the Admiralty had gone so far as to order more. After May Island the K flotillas were used only to give warning of the movements of enemy vessels so that surface vessels could lie in wait for them. With no chance of action, it was a boring job and the erratic behaviour of the boats themselves provided the only excitement.

Because still they gave trouble. On her trials *K16* nose-dived into the seabed at the very spot where *K13* had disappeared, and it was a far from unusual sight to see a K boat with her stern sticking out of the water after she had nose-dived and stuck her nose in the mud. *K15* distinguished herself by doing her dive, not bows first but stern first. *K3* stuck to the normal routine and hit the seabed at a depth of 266 feet with damage along her entire length. Unmoved by the K boats' record, the Admiralty remained convinced that the large submarine had come to stay. Fisher even began to believe in a submarine dreadnought, a submersible with a twelve-inch gun. Using the keel of a K boat but reverting to diesels for power, the M class of monitor submarines was born.

Influenced by the poor behaviour of British torpedoes, Fisher's idea was that if a torpedo attack should fail, the big gun could be used, the gun appearing above the water just long enough to fire one great shell before disappearing again. The idea took hold and the keels of *K18*, *K19*, *K20* and *K21* were turned over for use as M boats – known to submariners as 'Mutton boats'.

M1, the original *K18*, went into commission in the spring of 1918 and behaved well, but a warship with the fire power of one shell was ridiculous, and instead of using her against the Germans *M1* was sent to the Mediterranean, where she had no contact with the enemy at all.

The boats continued to have a bad reputation, but naval thinking seemed determined to keep the class alive. Attempts to whitewash them appeared in documents published by the Admiralty, and a great deal was made of the fact that no other nation was building similar submarines. After the Armistice, the steam submarines lost none of their ability to get into trouble. Twice in a month *K15* dived out of control, *K8* caught fire, *K14* was almost lost as a result of a boiler explosion, and finally *K5* buried her nose in the bottom of Largs Bay.

The *Naval Review* still wrote enthusiastically about them, however, but during a big mock battle exercise *K9* had difficulty getting underwater while the jinx-ridden *K22* was seen to be having difficulty surfacing. Then, as the K flotilla finished its work, someone noticed that *K5* had vanished. She had gone with the loss of fifty-seven men. Five months later, *K15* sank at her moorings and it was found that the vents on the external ballast tanks had leaked. She was brought to the surface and taken by tug to the mud flats near Whale Island, where she lay for months.

The big-ship men still clung to the idea of fleet submarines, but whenever submarines operated with surface ships there were problems and submariners died. And still the accidents occurred. *K22*, the original *K13*, was very nearly lost when she dived with her funnels raised, then on 12 November 1925 *M1*, the old *K18*, was seen to dive off Start Point and failed to reappear. She had been struck by the Swedish ship *Vidar* while submerged.

The remaining boats were scrapped, and *M2* and *M3* – formerly *K19* and *K20* – were withdrawn to an experimental flotilla at Portsmouth. According to an old superstition among sailors, a change of name never changes the character of a ship. *M2* was converted into a submersible seaplane carrier with a hangar replacing the twelve-inch gun in front of the conning tower. *M3* was converted into a minelayer.

Then on 26 January 1932, off Portland, *M2* disappeared with sixty men on board. She had reported that she was about to dive, and in the afternoon the captain of the coastal steamer *Tynesider*, putting into Portland, said he had seen a large submarine west of Portland and wanted to know if submarines ever dived stern-first.

Divers found *M2* lying on the bottom with her stern embedded in sand and her bows clear of the sea floor. The watertight hangar door, the conning-tower hatch and the hatch between the hangar and the pressure hull were all open. It was suggested that the hangar door had been opened too soon on surfacing. Experienced submariners insisted that what had happened was that the hangar door had been opened when the submarine was safely on the surface, but that the boat had slid backwards below the water. Soon afterwards *M3*, originally *K20*, was scrapped. It was the end of an experiment expensive in money, material and lives.

Was it simply bad design or sheer bad luck? Some of the boats built up a large number of sea hours and there were men who had faith in them, and other maritime powers had also seen the advantage of large long-range submarines. Technically some submariners even considered them a success, but they were tremendously unlucky and they had neither been successful with the fleet nor fulfilled the true lone function of a submarine.

The Second World War finally killed the idea of the big surface ships, but after the record of the K boats, it is perhaps ironic that today the big submarine driven by steam is the most vital weapon in the armouries of the great powers. Modern submarines are similar in length and displacement to the K boats but, unlike the K boats, they have no oil furnaces, no funnels and no air intakes. They carry nuclear rockets, and the heat that raises the steam to drive their turbines comes from a nuclear reactor.

Yet the sea never changes. No matter what improvements are made to ships, the sea remains what it always was. Every ship or boat that casts off its contacts with the land is entering the unknown, and even now, on the brink of the twenty-first century, the sea appears no safer than it ever was.

Modern man, with his computors and electronics, cannot find the complete answer. Everyone who lives by the sea knows its dangers only too well, yet yachtsmen – many of them experienced – die every year, and the fatalities among deep-sea men and civilians continue to occur. The only certain thing that can be claimed for the sea is its uncertainty.

SELECT BIBLIOGRAPHY

Allfrey, Anthony, *Man of Arms* (Weidenfeld and Nicolson, 1989)

Barnaby, K. C., *Some Ship Disasters and Their Causes* (Hutchinson, 1966)

Bailey, M. and M., *117 Days Adrift* (Nautical, 1974)

Bond, Geoffrey, *Lakonia* (Oldbourne, 1966)

Coles, Alan, *Three Before Breakfast* (Mason, 1979)

Crankshaw, Edward, *Shadow of the Winter Palace* (Macmillan, 1976)

Christian, Glyn, *Fragile Paradise* (Hamish Hamilton, 1982)

Croall, James, *Fourteen Minutes* (Michael Joseph, 1978)

Divine, David, *Mutiny at Invergordon* (Macdonald, 1970)

Dobree, B. and Mainwaring, G. E., *The Floating Republic* (Bles, 1935)

Dugan, James, *The Great Mutiny* (André Deutsch, 1966)

Everitt, Don, *The K Boats* (Harrap, 1963)

Gallagher, Thomas, *Fire at Sea* (Muller, 1969)

Gould, Commander R. T., *Enigmas* (Bles, 1929)

Hoehling, A. A., *They Sailed Into Oblivion* (Yoseloff, 1959)

—— *The Great War At Sea* (Arthur Barker, 1965)

Hough, Richard, *The Fleet That Had to Die* (Hamish Hamilton, 1958)

—— *Admirals in Collision* (Hamish Hamilton, 1959)

—— *The Potemkin Mutiny* (Hamish Hamilton, 1960)

Hawkey, Arthur, *HMS Captain* (Bell, 1963)

Johnson, Brig. R. F., *Royal George* (Knight, 1971)

Kirby, P. R., *The True Story of the Grosvenor* (Oxford University Press, 1960)

Lansing, Alfred, *Endurance* (Hodder and Stoughton, 1959)

Larn, Richard, *Shipwrecks of Great Britain and Ireland* (David and Charles, 1981)

Logan, Marshall, *The Tragic Story of the Empress of Ireland* (1914)

McLeay, Alison, *The Tobermory Treasure* (Conway, 1986)

McCormick, Donald, *The Mystery of Lord Kitchener's Death* (Putnam, 1959)

—— *Pedlar of Death* (Macdonald, 1965)

Ortzen, Len, *Stories of Famous Shipwrecks* (Arthur Barker, 1974)

—— *Strange Mysteries of the Sea* (Arthur Barker, 1976)

Padfield, Peter, *An Agony of Collisions* (Hodder and Stoughton, 1966)

Ruge, Friedrich, *Scapa Flow* (W. H. Allen, 1969)

Ruhen, Olaf, *Minerva Reef* (Angus and Robertson, 1963)

Rushbrook, Frank, *Fire Aboard* (Brown, Son and F., 1980)

Schubert, P. and Gibson, L., *Death of a Fleet* (Hutchinson, 1933)

Thomas, G. and Morgan-Witts, Max, *The Strange Fate of the Morro Castle* (Collins, 1973)

Van der Molen, S. J., *The Lutine Treasure* (Adlard Coles, 1970)

Williams, Mark, *Sunken Treasure* (Cassell, 1980)

INDEX

Robinson, Master Shipwright,
  W. B., 188
Rodney, Adml Lord, 11, 180
Rodney, HMS, 172, 175–6, 178
Rogers, Snr Op., George W.,
  61–7, 71–3
Rose, Lt-Cdr Earl, 68
Rowe, Jacob, 111
Royal Adelaide, 76
Royal Anne, HMS, 9–10
Royal Charter, 21–2
Royal George, HMS (1782), 9–19,
  131
Royal George, HMS (1797), 133
Royal Oak, HMS, 167
Royal Sovereign, HMS, 131
Royal William, HMS, 135–6
Rozhestvensky, Adml, 145–7
Ruge, Friedrich, 156
Runyon, Damon, 71
Rushbrook, Fire Chief Frank, 72

Salta, 49
San Juan de Sicilia, 114–15
San Fiorenzo, HMS, 137
San Salvador, 108, 110
Sandwich, HMS, 137, 140, 142
Sandwich, Earl of, 133
Sans Pareil, HMS, 205, 211
Sarah Sands, 42
Saxe, Jakob, 35, 38
Schacht, Hjalmar, 121
Scott, Capt. R. F., 81
Searle, Frederick, 221
Searle, Richard, 12–13, 15
Seine, 24
Seydlitz, 163
Scheele, Dr Walter, 55–6
Shaw, 2nd Mate, 98
Shackleton, Sir Ernest, 81–90

Shillong, 24
Shovell, Rear Adml Sir C., 76, 94–5
Sixtus, Pope, 107, 111
Skagerrak, 26
Skynner, Capt. Lancelott, 102–3
Smart, John, 17–18
Smith, Capt. E. J., 213
Smollett, John, 110, 114
Solas Rules, 23
Spee, Graf von, 216
Spender, Arthur, 56–7
Spencer, Earl of, 128, 133, 134
Standard, HMS, 142
Steele, John, 225
Stockholm, 24–5
Storstad, 29–40
Stratheden, 51
Sturdee, Vice-Adml Sir F.C.D.,
  213–14
Stremitelny, 151–2
Suvarov, 146
Symonds, Vice-Adml Sir Thomas,
  146, 185–6

Talbot, Richard, 12
Tampa, 68–9
Tarleton, Vice-Adml Sir W.,
  190–1
Tennyson d'Eyncourt, Sir E.,
  218–19
Teutonic, 28
Tezarevitch, 145
Thrusbh, 223–4
Thunderer, HMS, 209
Thuringen, 160
The Times, 1, 174, 183–5, 192
Tirpitz, Grand Adml, 203
Titanic, 2, 3, 7, 23–4, 29, 35–7, 48,
  62, 213
Tobermory Galleon, 107–16